The Administration and Supervision of Special Programs in Education

Second Edition

Anita Pankake
University of Texas at Pan American

Mark Littleton
Tarleton State University

Gwen Schroth
Texas A&M University

KENDALL/HUNT PUBLISHING COMPANY
4050 Westmark Drive   Dubuque, Iowa 52002

Cover photos by Photos.com

Copyright © 2001, 2005 by Kendall/Hunt Publishing Company

ISBN 978-0-7575-1841-6

Printed in the United States of America
10 9 8 7 6

Contents

About the Authors and Contributors

Authors

Anita Pankake is Professor of Educational Leadership at The University of Texas Pan American, Edinburg, Texas. Her e-mail address is: apankake@utpa.edu.

Mark Littleton is Professor of Educational Administration at Tarleton State University, Stephenville, Texas. His e-mail address is: Mlittleton@tarleton.edu.

Gwen Schroth is Associate Professor (retired) from Texas A & M University-Commerce, Commerce, Texas. She is currently working with Walden University through their on-line administrators preparation program. Her e-mail address is: rschroth@leonardonline.net.

Contributors

Danna Beaty is an Assistant Professor of Educational Administration at Texas A & M University-Commerce, Commerce, Texas.

Reba J. Criswell is a doctoral candidate in the Department of Counseling at Texas A & M University-Commerce, Commerce, Texas.

Miguel de los Santos is Professor of Educational Leadership at The University of Texas Pan American, Edinburg, Texas.

Bob Dunbar is Assistant Principal at Austin Academy for Excellence in Garland Independent School District, Garland, Texas.

Diana Freeman is Principal of Sunnyvale School in Sunnyvale Independent School District, Sunnyvale, Texas.

Rick Geisel is Assistant Professor of Educational Leadership at Grand Valley State University in Grand Rapids, Michigan.

Leo Gomez is Professor of Curriculum and Instruction at The University of Texas Pan American, Edinburg, Texas.

Francisco Guajardo is Assistant Professor of Educational Leadership at The University of Texas Pan American, Edinburg, Texas.

Miguel Guajardo is Associate Professor of Educational Leadership at Texas State University, San Marcos, Texas.

Brenda Kallio is Assistant Professor in the Department of Educational Administration and Community Education at Central Michigan University, Mt. Pleasant, Michigan.

Richard Lampe is Professor in the Department of Counseling and Coordinator of the School Counseling Program at Texas A & M University-Commerce, Commerce, Texas.

Jerry Lowe is Professor of Educational Leadership at The University of Texas Pan American, Edinburg, Texas.

Velma Menchaca is Interim Dean and Professor of Educational Leadership at The University of Texas Pan American, Edinburg, Texas.

Gayle Moller is Associate Professor of Educational Leadership at Western Carolina University, Cullowhee, North Carolina.

Mary Alice Reyes is Executive Director of the Texas Migrant Council, Donna, Texas.

Jose A. Ruiz-Escalante is Professor of Curriculum and Instruction at The University of Texas Pan American, Edinburg, Texas.

Norma Salaiz is Career and Technology Education Coordinator for Edinburg Consolidated Independent School District, Edinburg, Texas.

Alejo Salinas, Jr. is Clinical Professor of Educational Leadership at The University of Texas Pan American, Edinburg, Texas.

Noe Sauceda is Assistant Professor of Educational Leadership at The University of Texas Pan American, Edinburg, Texas.

Jerry Trusty is Professor in the Department of Counselor Education, Counseling Psychology and Rehabilitation Services and Coordinator of the Secondary School Counseling Programs at Penn State University, University Park, Pennsylvania.

Karen Watt is Assistant Professor of Educational Leadership and Texas AVID State Director at The University of Texas Pan American, Edinburg, Texas.

Jody Westbrook-Youngblood is Director of Professional Learning, San Antonio Independent School District, San Antonio, Texas

Mary Kay Zabel is Professor of Special Education at Kansas State University, Manhattan, Kansas.

Introduction

Schools of today are more sophisticated and offer an increasing array of programs. No one person is likely to possess a complete understanding of every program delivered in the typical public school. Consequently, this second edition of *The Administration and Supervision of Special in Education* is designed to provide school personnel—particularly school administrators and teacher leaders—with the knowledge needed to successfully manage the various special instructional and support programs in schools. For some readers, this book will be their first contact with school programs such as Title I/NCLB, TRIO, and migrant. For others, this book will serve as an excellent resource to increase understanding of programs with which they interact daily.

Each chapter of the book begins with a list of objectives and ends with thoughtful questions that highlight some of the important points of the chapter. Most all chapters include a history of the program and appropriate legislative and legal backgrounds for the program. Following the material presentation in each chapter is a case study; this scenario is designed to demonstrate the application of the chapter concepts in a school/district setting.

As was the case in the first edition, the first chapter is focused on special education. In this edition, however, we have added a separate chapter for 504. Both present concise overviews of these programs, both of which affect all schools. While these chapters are not intended to replace a well-written text, treatise or basic introductory course on special education, they are designed to provide a concise, yet thorough understanding of special education and 504 issues and procedures. Prospective school administrators and teachers are well advised to carefully read the text regarding federal and state laws and regulations. Special education programs and 504 are very sophisticated and require a great deal of attention to detail. A section on school leaders' roles in special education/504 is included to provide guidance to novice and experienced administrators alike.

The advent of the sweeping legislation commonly referred to as No Child Left Behind (NCLB) required a complete rewrite of the previous Title I chapter. This new chapter offers readers an overview of this 2001 authorization of Title I and changes as they are currently known. The NCLB legislation is just now being implemented and interpreted; readers are encouraged to use this chapter as a place to begin their extensive study of these new federal requirements for schools.

In the first edition, a chapter detailing three federal efforts (Upward Bound, Talent Search and Student Support Services) to assist low income students pursue postsecondary education appeared. In this new edition, the TRIO programs are again overviewed, but this time along with information on other programs including GEAR UP and AVID. While sharing a similar purpose each of these programs is unique in design and delivery. Research regarding the success of these academic intervention and enhancement programs is presented for consideration.

Chapters focused on programs for migrant students, bilingual students, gifted and talented students and young children provide information to educators that include developmental stages and social and environmental perspectives influencing the children and families involved. The authors for each of these chapters have provided some practical instructional strategies and resources for immediate use. Information regarding the funding for each of these programs is crucial for school leaders to know. The complexity of funding for migrant and bilingual programs will need additional attention beyond what is shared in this book. Early childhood programs are funded differently depending on the population served, while most gifted and talented programs are dependent on local support. Knowing the source of funding and how the funds may be spent is crucial from an accounting point of view and from a program quality perspective.

Career and Technology education programs have a rich history and continue to be advocated throughout the country. This chapter may be of most interest to principals and teacher leaders in secondary schools; however, all educators can glean important information related to making schooling relevant to students and aligned with community needs. Career and Technology programs also have strong student activity program components. In addition to job skills, these student activity programs provide students with leadership and group processing skills.

The school counselor has become a necessary and vitally important member of the school community; consequently we include a revised chapter on what constitutes an effective counseling program. Few school administrators (and even fewer teachers) have a formal counseling background. Furthermore, the role of the counselor is not well-defined, generally with the job description varying from school to school.

The last few chapters in this second edition provide some information on important components of special programs, but components that are not limited to special programs. The chapters on staff development, teachers leaders, accessing central office resources, and parent involvement address issues involved in all educational programming. Still, an attempt has been made in each of these offerings to make specific connections to the influence they have on the special programs delivery, students, and staff.

We are deeply indebted to those who spent many hours preparing their contributions to the book. The names of the contributors are listed at the beginning of each chapter, yet it is apropos to mention them once again. Our very special thanks to:

Danna Beaty	Reba J. Criswell	Miguel de los Santos
Bob Dunbar	Diana Freeman	Rick Geisel
Leo Gomez	Francisco Guajardo	Miguel Guajardo
Brenda Kallio	Richard Lampe	Jerry Lowe
Velma Menchaca	Gayle Moller	Mary Alice Reyes
Jose A. Ruiz-Escalante	Norma Salaiz	Alejo Salinas, Jr.
Noe Sauceda	Jerry Trusty	Karen Watt
Jody Westbrook-Youngblood	Mary Kay Zabel	

Putting this book together has provided the three of us the opportunity to work together; for that we are grateful. Along the way we experienced some frustrations and challenges, yet still we are pleased and proud as we survey this finished product. We certainly hope you find it helpful.

Anita Pankake, Mark Littleton, & Gwen Schroth

Special Education 1

Brenda R. Kallio
Richard T. Geisel

While the passage of EHA was a significant step toward the provision of educational guarantees for disabled children, history would show us that it was the Civil Rights case, *Brown v. Board of Education* (1954), that would become the basis for many of the improvements in the educational rights of special needs students.

—Brenda R. Kallio & Richard T. Geisel

Objectives

1. Report the legislative history of special education
2. Discuss the social impetus behind the development of special education in public schools
3. Discuss the major educational components of the Individual with Disabilities Education Act
4. Discuss the referral and evaluation process for special education programs
5. Outline yearly progress as it relates to special education students

Introduction

Administrators play a critical role in securing a free and appropriate education for special needs students. Implementation of special education programs is not easy and may at times become a daunting task. To assist administrators in their quest to stay abreast of current special education practices, this chapter presents information on the history of special education legislation and discusses many of the principles fundamental to the Individuals with Disabilities Act (IDEA). (Note: This chapter is based on federal legislation and readers should be advised that individual state guidelines may differ slightly from federal law.)

History of Special Education

During this country's early years, disabled students were not entitled to public education. In fact, a Massachusetts court ruled that student misbehavior resulting from imbecility was grounds for expulsion (*Watson v. City of Cambridge, Massachusetts, 1893*). Likewise in 1919, a Wisconsin court ruled that a handicapped student could be excluded from regular public school classes because his handicap had "a depressing and nauseating effect on the teachers and school children" (*Beattie v. Board of Education, Wisconsin, 1919*). There were, however, areas of the country that recognized the educational needs of disabled students [Hartford, Connecticut (1817) established the American Asylum for the Education of the Deaf and Dumb, and New York (1818) established the Institution for the Education of the Deaf and Dumb] (Alexander & Alexander, 2001). However, educational opportunities such as those offered in Hartford and New York were the exception and for much of our country's history, a vast majority of disabled children were taught by parents in the privacy of their homes and/or lived out their lives secreted in basements and attics.

Although support for expanding the educational opportunities of special needs students was limited, The White House Conference on Children (1910) had as one of its primary goals the establishment of remedial programs for special needs children. Ultimately, the Conference hoped to move society away from the then prevalent philosophy of isolation (institutionalizing or ignoring disabled children) toward an attitude of segregation (separate classrooms within public schools). For several decades it appeared as though the Conference had been successful in altering society's views of education for disabled children and between 1910 and 1930 the number of classes and support services for disabled children increased. However, the number of programs and services began decreasing during the 1930s. Some contend the decline was due to the Great Depression and its incumbent financial constraints. Others believe the decline was due to large numbers of persons who professed that education, as a democratic ideal, required high educational standards . . . standards unattainable with the inclusion of disabled children (Yell, 1998).

So, despite conferences espousing goals recognizing the educational rights of disabled children, the passage of various state compulsory education laws, and relatively obscure special education court cases, the educational rights of disabled children did not significantly change during the first 70 years of the 20th Century and schools continued to exclude students who were "feeble minded," "mentally deficient," or deemed unable to reap the benefits of education (*Department of Public Welfare v. Haas, 1958*).

The plight of disabled children began to change when, in 1970, Congress passed legislation that recognized the educational entitlements of special needs children. This 1970 legislation, the Education of the Handicapped Act (EHA), required, among other things, that states provide free and appropriate education to special needs students, provide appropriate assessment, and notify parents of their children's educational rights.

While the passage of EHA was a significant step toward the provision of educational guarantees for disabled children, history would show us that it was the Civil Rights case *Brown v. Board of Education* (1954) that would become the basis for many of the improvements in educational rights of special needs students. While the U.S. Supreme Court's decision in *Brown* specifically addressed the issue of "separate but equal" as it pertained to racial minorities, parents and advocates for special needs children began asking the courts to apply *Brown*'s doctrine, separate is inherently unequal, to educational opportunities for disabled students. Thus, it was a racial anti-discrimination case that served as the guiding precedent for the 1972 benchmark special education decision in *Pennsylvania Association of Retarded Citizens v. Pennsylvania (PARC)*. In addition to requiring that a free education be provided to all mentally retarded children between the ages of 6 and 21, the ruling in *PARC* defined "education" as broader than pure academics. In addition, the Supreme Court ruled that mentally retarded children could benefit from schooling when "education" was defined in the proper context. The Court's *PARC* decision also included language promoting the education of mentally retarded children in the least restrictive environment.

In *Mills v. Board of Education* (1972) the Court's ruling extended the educational rights previously granted to mentally retarded students *(PARC)* to **all** disabled students. The *Mills* decision also outlined procedural safeguards for labeling, placement, and exclusion of students with disabilities. These safeguards included:

- the right to a hearing (with representation, a record, and an impartial hearing officer),
- the right to appeal,
- the right to access personal records,
- written notice at all stages of the process. (Yell, 1998, p. 60).

In addition to the rulings from *PARC* and *Mills,* federal legislation passed during the early to mid 1970s (i.e., the Americans with Disabilities Act and Sec. 504 of the Rehabilitation Act) prohibited discrimination against disabled persons and required employers to make reasonable accommodations if the person was "other-wise qualified." Initially, this legislation was designed to protect disabled veterans; however, the legislation was quickly applied to public education. In 1975, Congress passed legislation [Public Law (P.L.) 94–142] that mandated children with suspected disabilities must have access to non-discriminatory testing and placement in the least restrictive environment (LRE). Other features of P.L. 94–142 included a more clearly outlined procedure for parental due process; guidelines for free and appropriate education (FAPE); and procedures for identification, evaluation and placement. P.L. 94–142 also expanded the age parameters set forth in *PARC* (6–21 years of age) to include children ages 3–6, allowed parents who sued for violations of P.L. 94–142, and won, to recover attorney fees and other legal costs, and intimated that federal funds would be made available to reduce state and local costs for special education programs.

The rights of disabled children continued to grow and in 1986 Public Law (P.L.) 99–457 mandated that all states provide programs for disabled children beginning at birth. And, in 1990, Congress passed P.L. 101–476 which, in an attempt to make the terminology more politically correct, changed the name of the current disability legislation from Education for All Handicapped Children Act (EAHCA) to Individuals with Disabilities Education Act (IDEA). In addition to the name change, the 1990 version of IDEA required school districts to include transition plans in the Individualized Education Plans (IEPs) of all special needs children once the child became 16 years of age.

In 1997, Congress amended the special education legislation and the newly reauthorized special education legislation (P.L. 105–17) by emphatically stating that children with disabilities are to be full participants in school programming and that "special education" is a service and not a place (Council for Exceptional Children and National Association of Elementary School Principals, 2001, p. 5). Public Law 105–17 also mandated transition planning with interagency responsibility, placed greater emphasis on improving results, further delineated procedural safeguards, changed the composition of the IEP team and the content of the IEP document, established voluntary mediation and added language regarding the discipline of students (manifestation determination).

[Note: IDEA was due to be reauthorized in March of 2004. At the time this chapter was written, the House of Representatives and the Senate have both proposed changes, however the reauthorization has not passed the House of Representatives. For more information about the proposed reauthorization see Appendix A at the end of this chapter.]

Major Principles of IDEA

Over time, several components of the P.L. 94–142 reauthorizations have stood out as IDEA provisions that affect administrators on a regular basis. Therefore, the topics selected for discussion in the balance of this chapter have been chosen for their relevance to special education issues.

CHILD FIND

Under IDEA's child find requirements, states are required to locate, identify and evaluate disabled children from birth to age 21. The process for locating disabled children is not specified at the federal level and states are allowed to establish individual plans as long as the plan identifies the agency responsible for the child find, outlines the child find procedures, and details the resources available to sustain the child find program. In most cases, public schools are assigned the task of locating all disabled children within their jurisdiction. Techniques for finding children include contacting nursery schools, pediatricians, and nearby medical facilities. Additionally, districts frequently post notices in public places such as grocery stores, run public service announcements with radio and TV stations, and place ads in newspapers. Each district should adopt board policy regarding compliance with child find requirements. It should be noted that failure of a parent to identify their child as disabled does not relieve the district of its child find responsibilities [34 C.F.R. §300.125(a)(1)(i)].

CONFIDENTIALITY OF INFORMATION

Parents of special needs children are permitted to inspect their child's records and may seek to amend or remove documents they believe are inappropriate. If the parents request a change or removal from a document in the student's file and the district disagrees, the parents may write a letter stating why the document should be removed or amended and the district is obligated to include the letter in the student's file. Should the district and the parents agree on the removal or change in the contents of a special needs student's file, the district may destroy or adjust the documents accordingly.

Districts in the process of destroying old student records should consult state law for specifics on the manner of destruction, the length of time records must be retained (the length of retention may be longer for special needs children than for regular education students), and the specific rules for notifying specified persons that the records are to be destroyed.

DISABILITY CATEGORIES

Currently, there are 13 categories of disability protected by IDEA (see Table 1). Not all students with disabilities are protected under IDEA. The statute extends only to students whose disability falls within the scope of the specified list of disabilities and only to those whose disability has an adverse impact on their education. For example, a student who exhibits inappropriate social behaviors would not be eligible for special education services unless the behaviors hindered the student's ability to make reasonable academic progress.

The original list of IDEA disability categories did not include autism, attention-deficit/hyperactivity disorder (ADHD), or traumatic brain injury. The categories of autism and traumatic brain injury were added with the 1990 version of IDEA; however ADHD was not given a separate category. Instead, the Department of Education has stated that children with ADHD may be granted special education status under the categories of specific learning disability, serious emotional disturbance, or other health impaired.

DISCIPLINE

The U.S. General Accounting Office (GAO), at the request of Congress, conducted a study to determine whether the discipline sections of the 1997 IDEA affected the ability of schools to maintain a safe environment conducive to learning. As a part of their study, the GAO found more incidences of serious misconduct in non-special education student populations. However, the rate (percentage) of serious misconduct was greater in the special education population (Markowitz, 2001, p. 1).

When the investigators focused on "if and how" administrators met the IDEA discipline requirements, they found that 86% of the principals surveyed in the GAO study reported their school district policies provided special education protections in excess of IDEA requirements. Yet, only 64% of the administrators knew they were not allowed to suspend a special needs student for more than 10 cumulative school days during a school year for an incident related to the child's disability. (Note: For example, administrators may not suspend a special needs child for four days, then three days and then four days as the cumulative total of days of suspension total more than 10 days). Only 24% of the administrators knew they were required to determine whether the student's misconduct was a manifestation of his/her disability whenever discipline was being considered (Markowitz, 2001, p. 3). The numbers from the GAO study would indicate that not only were the administrators not *exceeding* the minimal discipline standards set forth in IDEA (as they had reported doing), but in fact, administrators were not *meeting* IDEA expectations with regard to disciplining special education students.

Table 1 **Disability Categories According to 20 U.S.C. 1401(a)(1)(A)(i)**

- mental retardation
- speech or language impairment
- deaf-blindness
- emotional disturbance
- specific learning disability
- autism
- deafness
- hearing impairment
- visual impairment
- multiple disabilities
- orthopedic impairment
- other health impaired
- traumatic brain injury (TBI)

Discipline, as a component of IDEA, has proven to be both complicated and controversial. Change of placement due to behavior, manifestation determination, the stay-put provision, and behavior intervention plans have proven to be some of the most controversial aspects of the statute and will be discussed in the sections that follow.

Change of Placement Due to Behavior

School personnel may suspend or otherwise change the placement of a special education student for 10 days providing the same change of placement would be applied to regular education children who break the same school rules. In addition, a disabled student may be placed in an interim alternative educational setting for a maximum of 45 days for weapon and/or drug offenses. A 45-day interim alternative placement must be determined by an IEP team and special education students assigned to an alternative setting must continue to receive the services and modifications set forth in their IEP. According to the IDEA, a change in placement does not alter the services the student is to receive. It only changes the place where the student receives the services.

Prior to implementing disciplinary measures that involve a change in educational placement, the IEP team must determine whether there is a relationship between the student's disability and the misbehavior, and whether an inappropriate placement resulted in the misbehavior.

Manifestation Determination

To determine whether a child's behavior is related to his/her disability, the district is required to conduct a manifestation determination hearing. If it is decided the misconduct is not related to the disability, the child may be disciplined the same as a regular education student. Should the team find the misconduct is directly related to the child's disability, the child must receive special accommodations and the discipline adjusted according to the severity of the child's disability. Courts have upheld the manifestation determination provision of IDEA and continue to prohibit the unilateral exclusions of special education students from educational settings for behavior that manifests from the child's disability (*Honig v. Doe,* 1988).

Should a manifestation determination be required, IEP teams will be in a better position to determine the relationship between the student's behavior and the disability if the team has laid an appropriate foundation at previous IEP meetings. IEP teams that have asked parents whether their child is able to follow the school rules as outlined in the school handbook, whether their child knows right from wrong, and whether their child exhibits discipline problems outside of the school environment have established baseline information that becomes invaluable should the team hold a manifestation determination hearing.

Stay-Put

Unless the school and the parent agree to a change of placement, a child involved in mediation or due process hearings must remain in his or her current educational placement. If school personnel contend there is danger the child will hurt himself or other children during the course of due process proceedings, the district may ask the court to sanction a temporary change of placement until a permanent change of placement is agreed upon [34 C.F.R. 330.526(c)(1)].

Behavior Intervention Plans

In the case of children whose behavior impedes their learning or that of others, districts are required to address the child's behavior with the creation of or the adaptation of an existing Behavior Intervention Plan (BIP) [34 C.F.R. 300.346(a)(2)(i)]. A BIP should include services and modifications that address the student's behavior in a manner designed to extinguish the negative behaviors. Services and modifications that might be included in a BIP include, but certainly are not limited to, seating arrangement, reduced or increased contact with other students, reward systems, and counseling with behavior specialists.

Procedural Due Process

In addition to the requirement that disabled children are to receive a free and appropriate education, strong IDEA procedural guidelines have been established to ensure IDEA compliance. Within the three critical components of procedural due process (informing the person of the allegations against them; the opportunity for the accused to present a defense; and a fair, unbiased hearing), the courts have recognized that procedural due process is somewhat nebulous and that the amount of procedural due process owed to a person is dependent upon the magnitude of the substantive right to be taken away if the accused is found guilty. When comparing the amount of procedural due process owed a child who is about to lose a week's worth of recess to a student who is about to be expelled, it becomes easier to understand the court's rationale that not all situations require the same level of procedural due process.

As a result of current legislation and court cases, parents or other persons having legal standing and who have exhausted their administrative remedies (e.g., the school board) may seek mediation. During mediation, it is hoped that the parents and the district can come to agreement on the issue at hand. Should the parties be unable to reach consensus during the mediation process, either party may request a due process hearing. While states have different titles for the "judges" who preside over special education due process hearings, the ruling of the "judge" is enforceable. However, should either the parents or the district disagree with the ruling of the due process "judge," they may file suit in either a state or a federal trial court.

In a due process hearing, parents have the right to be accompanied by a lawyer or an individual with special knowledge of the problems of special needs children to present evidence, to confront and cross-examine witnesses, and to obtain a transcript of the hearing and the "judge's" written decision.

Some of the most highly contested issues regarding procedural due process are:

- failure to notify parents of a change in their child's placement,
- failure to provide explanations of documents,
- failure to provide information in primary language,
- lack of access to school records,
- lack of compliance with stay-put provision during due process proceedings.

Free and Appropriate Public Education

IDEA requires that services delivered to special education students must be provided at public expense. Further, school districts may not refuse to furnish special education services due to district budget constraints. While IDEA mandates that special education services are to be without cost, districts are allowed to charge for incidentals such as art fees and field trips as long as the same fees are also charged to non-disabled children (OSEP Policy Letter, 1992).

Additionally, special education services must be under public supervision and must meet state education agency requirements. However, minimal state standards cannot provide less protection than those established by federal regulations.

In order to provide a truly Free and Appropriate Public Education (FAPE), IEPs must outline special education placement and related services. However, it should be noted that IEPs do not guarantee students will attain the goals stated in the document. The IEP document does commit the district to make a good faith effort to help the student reach the stated goals. In *Springdale School District v. Grace* (1981), the Eighth Circuit Court of Appeals determined that FAPE was more than the mere offering of special education services and that FAPE did not require the district to provide the best possible education. Similarly, in *Age v. Bullitt County Public Schools* (1982), the First Circuit Court of Appeals ruled that the existence of better programs did not make a school's proposed program inappropriate (as cited in Yell, 1998).

Referral and Placement

REFERRAL PROCESS

Similar to the referral process for Section 504, federal regulations place an affirmative duty on public school districts to find those students in their district who have a disability and who may require special services (Nondiscrimination, 2003, 34 C.F.R. § 104.32). Frequently, school districts use free hearing and vision tests, letters to the community, preschool programs, advertisements, surveys, etc. to locate students who qualify for IDEA status. Students who are believed to be in need of services may be referred for evaluation by any person, including a parent/guardian, teacher, staff member, or even persons outside the school system (Puget Sound ESD, 2002, p. 10). Appendix B contains a chart showing the flow of the referral and placement process.

PROCEDURAL SAFEGUARDS

School districts must obtain parental permission to test a child with suspected disabilities. Should the parent(s) not consent to testing, schools may petition the courts for the necessary consent. In the event independent educational evaluations are required during the pre-placement phase of the evaluation process, the district will most likely be required to pay. In the course of obtaining parental permission to test, school districts are required to provide parents/guardians with procedural safeguards such as notice, an opportunity to examine relevant records, information pertinent to requesting impartial hearings, and special education review procedures (Nondiscrimination, 2003, 34 C.F.R. § 104.369).

Subsequent to obtaining permission (parental or court mandated) to evaluate and after the parents or guardians have been duly notified of their rights, qualified persons may begin the evaluation process.

IDENTIFICATION AND EVALUATION

Evaluation of a special needs child must be "full and individual." Evaluations must be conducted in all areas of suspected disability including health, vision, hearing, social and emotional status, general intelligence, academic performance, communicative status and emotional disabilities [34 C.F.R. § 300.532(g)]. Also, evaluations must draw from a variety of sources and no single procedure or test may be used as the sole criterion for determining whether a child is a "child with a disability" [34 C.F.R. § 300.534(a)(1)]. Sources such as aptitude and achievement tests, parental input, teacher recommendation, physical condition, background, and adaptive behavior may be used to gather pertinent evaluation information. In addition to the use of multiple assessment techniques, the evaluations must be conducted in the child's primary (or native) language or using the child's primary mode of communication. The tests must be racially and culturally nondiscriminatory in both the way they are selected and the way they are administered. A final determination of special education identification must be made by a "panel of experts" (i.e., the IEP team).

INDIVIDUALIZED EDUCATION PLANS

Individualized education programs (IEP) are the cornerstone of IDEA. It is from these documents that parents, students, and school districts come to consensus on the educational placement and services. Constructing an IEP can be complicated and stressful. However, when an IEP is constructed in a logical, linear manner, the outcome is a document designed to meet the needs of the child.

Steps for Developing a Good IEP

1. Select the category of disability most appropriate for the child based on the results of the evaluations.
2. Determine the areas of the general curriculum that will be adversely affected by the child's disability.
3. Determine the way the child's disability will adversely affect progress in those parts of the general curriculum noted in step #2.
4. Determine the student's current level of performance and establish how far he or she is expected to advance during the year.
5. Identify the tools, instruments, and methodologies that will be used to measure progress. (It is important to determine how progress will be measured early in the IEP development process!)
6. Decide where the team expects the student to be in one year. This is the annual goal and should be reasonable, observable, measurable, and achievable. On the other hand, the goals should have sufficient rigor that achievement of the annual goals will take more than minimal effort on the part of the school and/or the student.
7. Establish short term goals so that all involved will be able to see that progress, albeit it in small steps, is occurring.
8. Decide which special education instruction services the student will need to achieve the goals outlined in the IEP. Ask if adaptations to the content delivery, testing procedures, the physical classroom, etc. will be needed. (Remember, the team only needs to address those curricular areas outlined in step #2.)
9. Decide which related services will be needed to achieve the annual goals. Per Federal law 20 U.S.C. 1401 (a)(17), qualifying related services include:
   - transportation
   - psychological services
   - speech/language pathology and audiology
   - physical and occupational therapy
   - recreation
   - early identification and assessment of disabilities
   - counseling, including rehabilitation counseling
   - orientation and mobility
   - medical services for diagnostic or evaluation purposes
   - school health services
   - social work services
   - parent training and parent counseling

10. Decide on the least restrictive environment. First write the IEP, **then** determine placement. Where is it most likely that the needs already spelled out in the IEP can be provided?

11. Determine the supplementary aids and services necessary to help the student achieve the annual goals in the least restrictive environment. You should think in terms of needs of the student as well as the supports needed by the teacher(s). Supplementary aids and services are defined as "aids, services and other supports that are provided to enable children with disabilities to be educated with non-disabled children to the maximum extent appropriate" (34 C.F.R. 300.26).

12. Explain any exclusions from the regular classroom or from extracurricular activities due to the student's disability.

13. Be specific in outlining the involvement of the student in any classroom, state, or federally mandated testing program.

14. Identify when services begin and when they end. While this would seem obvious, write it down so there are no misunderstandings.

15. Identify how you will report on the student's progress. The law says that parents of special needs children are entitled to be informed of progress at least as often as parents of regular education students.

(adapted from J. Walsh, *Writing a Good IEP,* n.d.)

Yearly Evaluation

Districts are required to convene an IEP meeting for individual students at least once a calendar year. However, IEP teams are required to meet as frequently as necessary to assure the needs of the student are being met.

WHO IS REQUIRED TO BE IN ATTENDANCE AT IEP MEETINGS?

As a rule, an IEP meeting should consist of persons who hold the following job descriptions:

- Special education representative
- Regular education representative
- Administrator or designee who has the authority to commit district resources
- Assessment professional
- Parent or person with legal standing
- Additional support staff (ex., OT, PT, Speech pathologist, etc.)
- Student (if appropriate)
- Other persons as appropriate (e.g., lawyers, advocates, etc.)

Of interest is a recent court case from Kansas (*Johnson v. Olathe Dist. Sch. Unified Sch. Dist No. 233,* 2003) where it was determined that a regular education teacher must be present at the IEP meetings only if the student will be participating in regular education programming and that a person with the designation of "special education teacher" does not need to be present at IEP meetings if there is a representative who is responsible for teaching and working directly with the child.

Minutes of IEP meetings are not required but are advisable. For IEP teams that create minutes, the minutes should be read back to the IEP team at the conclusion of each IEP meeting. Following the reading, persons present at the meeting should sign the signature page acknowledging the content of the minutes. Should a parent or other person disagree with the IEP document or the minutes of the IEP meeting, they may attach an addendum to the minutes.

Related Issues

PLACEMENT IN PRIVATE SCHOOLS

Under IDEA, public schools are required to provide a free and appropriate education (FAPE) to all qualifying students. Should a school district be unable to provide FAPE, and a private institution is able to provide the necessary services, the school district maintains responsibility for the services the student receives and is required to pay the educational costs (e.g., tuition and transportation) necessary for the child to attend the private school (*Florence County School Dist. Four v. Carter,* 1993). However, parents who unilaterally place their child in a private institution run the risk of bearing the burden of the tuition and other educational costs should it be determined that the public school district provided FAPE.

LEAST RESTRICTIVE ENVIRONMENT

Least restrictive environment (LRE) is a legal term found repeatedly throughout IDEA literature. When Congress included LRE in IDEA, the intent was to guarantee that handicapped children be educated with non-handicapped children to the maximum extent appropriate. In recognizing students' varied levels of disability and need, legislators and the courts have acknowledged that LRE is a continuum, a range of programs with a variety of services with institutionalization on the more restrictive end and full inclusion in the regular classroom on the other. It is the responsibility of the IEP team to determine which program delivery style and which services combine to create the least restrictive environment for each individual student. (Note: The words mainstreaming and inclusion are educational terms and represent possible points on the special education least restrictive environment continuum. Mainstreaming and inclusion are not required under IDEA . . . least restrictive environment is!) When determining LRE, IEP teams must factor in the opportunity for special needs children to socialize and whether provided services meet the portability test, i.e., could be provided within a less restrictive environment (*Roncker v. Walters,* 1983).

ZERO REJECT

Under IDEA, all children are entitled to a free and appropriate education regardless of the severity of their disability. The concept of zero reject is based on the *PARC* (1972) ruling that "education" is more than academics, and therefore even the most severely disabled students are able to benefit from appropriately designed education. In a court case where the school district claimed a student was too severely disabled to benefit from education and moved to exclude the child from school, the First Circuit Court of Appeals upheld the concept of zero reject by ruling that **all** children are entitled to a public education (*Timothy W. v. Rochester, New Hampshire, School District,* 1989).

Conclusion

The courts and society, as a whole, currently recognize that students with disabilities have a right to a public education, but while the right to an education is no longer an issue, considerable angst exists on a number of issues within the arena of special education. Every year the courts hear a plethora of cases where parents and districts seek guidance in identifying the parameters of FAPE and claim discrimination based on their child's disability. It is expected that the reauthorization of IDEA will provide additional direction and guidance to administrators as they continue to take the lead in providing a free and appropriate educational environment for all students.

Applying Your Knowledge

Adam, a student at Utopia High School, has Down's Syndrome and is eligible for special education services. Adam is a junior who for the past two years has participated in the fine arts program as a special helper with the marching and symphonic bands. His duties are to help load and unload the large trucks that carry equipment and instruments. In the past, Adam has had adult chaperones assist him with his duties because his hyperactivity generally leads to inappropriate interactions between himself and the other band members.

Adam's parents are very active in his educational life and have made sure that his IEP includes participation in the extra-curricular activities. While the IEP addresses the issue of participation, it does not require adult supervision.

Recently, the band announced its intention to travel on a three-day, two-night trip to Atlanta to participate in a contest. Adam would like to go on the trip. Adam's parents, who are refusing to go on the trip as chaperones, are adamant that this trip will be an important milestone in Adam's education and are requesting that he stay in a hotel room with other students who would be responsible for monitoring Adam's behavior. The band director is wary of having Adam on the trip without proper adult supervision and has asked for your thoughts.

QUESTIONS

1. Can the district deny Adam access to the field trip? Why or why not?
2. If the district allows Adam to travel without adult supervision, what is the extent of the district's liability if Adam creates a problem in Atlanta?
3. If Adam travels with the band and is housed in a room with regular education students, what responsibilities, if any, can the district impose on those students?
4. How does the wording in Adam's IEP affect the district's decision to allow or deny Adam's participation in the trip?

QUESTIONS FOR THOUGHT

1. Describe how society's view of persons with physical or mental handicaps has changed over time.
2. Why do you think the federal government felt it was necessary to mandate that individual school districts be held accountable for identifying handicapped children in their districts (child find)?
3. Think about the children in your school who are identified as special needs and those who although not identified may need special assistance. Are the 13 categories of disability sufficiently broad (or narrow) to meet the needs of all school age children?
4. As administrators, what steps can you take to assure that teams make appropriate decisions at a manifestation determination meeting?
5. Describe the role "related services" play in a special needs child's IEP.
6. Assume that because the district is unable to provide FAPE to a special needs child, the child is placed in a private institution. Do a financial comparison of the cost to educate the student at the private institution and in the public school. In addition to the financial ramifications, are there considerations other than money that might make placing a child in a private institution appropriate?

References

Age v. Bullitt County Public Schools, 673 F.2d 141 (6th Cir. 1982).

Alexander, K., & Alexander, M. D. (2001). *American public school law.* Belmont, CA: Wadsworth/Thompson Learning.

Beattie v. Board of Education, Wisconsin, 172 N.W. 153 (Wis. 1919).

Brown v. Board of Education, 347 U.S. 483, 74 S.Ct. 686 (1954).

Council for Exceptional Children & National Association of Elementary School Principals (2001). *IDEA: A guide for principals.* Alexandria, VA: Council for Exceptional Children.

Department of Public Welfare v. Haas, 154 N.E. 2d 265 (Ill.1958).

Florence County School Dist. Four v. Carter By and Through Carter, 510 U.S. 7 (1993).

Honig v. Doe, 479 U.S. 1084 (1987).

Johnson v. Olathe Dist. Sch. Unified Sch. Dist No. 233, 316 F. Supp.2d 960 (D. Kan 2003).

Markowitz, J. (2001, April) *Synthesis brief: Student discipline and IDEA-Synthesis of GAO report.* Retrieved July 3, 2004, from *http://www.nasdse.org/FORUM/PDF%20files/ student_discipline_idea.PDF*

Mills v. Board of Education of the District of Columbia, 348 F.Supp. 866 (D.D.C. 1972).

Office of Civil Rights. (n.d.). *Frequently asked questions about Section 504 and the education of children with disabilities.* Retrieved July 7, 2004, from *http://www.ed.gov/about/offices/list/ocr/504faq.html*

OSEP Policy Letter, 20 IDELR 1155 (1992). Office of Special Education Programs.

Pennsylvania Association of Retarded Citizens (PARC) v. Commonwealth of Pennsylvania, 343 F.Supp. 279 (E.D. Pa. 1972).

Puget Sound ESD. (2002). *A parent & educator guide to free appropriate public education.* Retrieved July 6, 2004, from *http://www.psesd.org/specialservices/pdfs/504manual.pdf*

Roncker v. Walters, 700 F.2d 1058 (6th Cir. 1983).

Springdale School District v. Grace, 494 F.Supp. 266 (W.D. Ark 1980), aff'd, 656 F.2d 300 (8th Cir. 1981), vacated, 102 S.Ct. 3504 (1982), on remand, 693 F.2d 41 (8th Cir. 1982), cert. den. 461 U.S. 917 (1982).

Timothy W. v. Rochester, New Hampshire, School District, 875 F.2d 954 (1989).

Walsh, J. (n.d.). *Writing a good IEP.* Walsh, Anderson, Brown, Schulze & Aldridge, P.C., Austin, TX. (handout at presentation, no page number or date available.)

Watson v. City of Cambridge, Massachusetts, 157 Mass. 561, 32 N.E. 864 (Mass. 1893).

Yell, M. (1998). *The law and special education.* Upper Saddle River, NJ: Merrill.

20 U.S.C. 1401(a)(1)(A)(i)

20 U.S.C. 1401 (a)(17)

34 C.F.R. § 104.32

34 C.F.R. § 104.369

34 C.F.R. § 300.125(a)(1)(i)

34 C.F.R. § 300.346(a)(2)(i)

34 C.F.R. § 300.532(g)

34 C.F.R. § 300.534(a)(1)

34 C.F.R. § 330.526(c)(1)

Appendix A

Current Status of IDEA Reauthorization

IDEA was due to be reauthorized in March of 2004. As of the writing of this chapter the reauthorization has not occurred. To date, there does not seem to be a clear indication of when the reauthorization will be finalized. Therefore, the information contained in this Appendix is speculative.

Both houses of Congress drafted reauthorization bills (S. 1248 and H.R. 1350). On May 12, 2004, S. 1248 was considered in the Senate and on May 13, 2004 it became part of H.R. 1350. We are awaiting the outcome of H.R. 1350.

The National School Board Association's *Impact on IDEA Legislation* issued May of 2004 indicates the following proposals currently part of H.R. 1350:

TEACHER RECRUITMENT AND RETENTION

- provides for professional development grants of 1–5 years
- significantly reduces paperwork requirements. (Pilot paperwork reduction programs will be established in 10 states.)

PAPERWORK AND ADMINISTRATIVE PROCESS

- significantly reduces mandated parent notification
- general education teachers have the discretion of participating in the IEP meeting or providing input through alternative methods

IEP PROCESS

- parents may opt out of attendance at IEP meetings where minor changes are made
- parents may waive attendance of IEP members who become unavailable at the last minute
- greater flexibility as to who should be required at an IEP meeting

IMPACT ON IDEA LEGISLATION

- issues not disclosed prior to the hearing are barred
- some limitation on attorneys' fees
- permission to amend IEPs without total rewrites

PRIVATE PLACEMENTS

- schools must be given opportunity to resolve differences before placement in private institutions
- vouchers are not addressed

DISCIPLINE

- 45-day interim placement retained
- schools have greater latitude to remove dangerous students

FINANCING

- increased authorizations that are geared to fully fund in 7 years but it is not mandatory that the funding be made available (Harkin-Hagel Bill required federal government to meet the 40% funding rate proposed 30 years ago was defeated.)
- use of social security funds for eligible students is not prohibited

Appendix B

Referral and Placement for Special Education

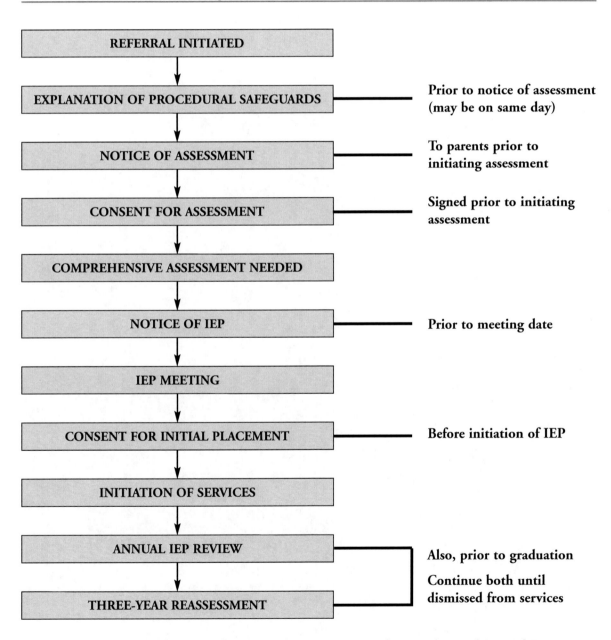

REFERRAL INITIATED

EXPLANATION OF PROCEDURAL SAFEGUARDS — Prior to notice of assessment (may be on same day)

NOTICE OF ASSESSMENT — To parents prior to initiating assessment

CONSENT FOR ASSESSMENT — Signed prior to initiating assessment

COMPREHENSIVE ASSESSMENT NEEDED

NOTICE OF IEP — Prior to meeting date

IEP MEETING

CONSENT FOR INITIAL PLACEMENT — Before initiation of IEP

INITIATION OF SERVICES

ANNUAL IEP REVIEW — Also, prior to graduation

THREE-YEAR REASSESSMENT — Continue both until dismissed from services

Schroth, G. and Littleton, M. (2001). *The Administration and Supervision of Special Programs in Education.* Dubuque, IA: Kendall/Hunt Publishing.

Section 504 of the Rehabilitation Act of 1973

2

Richard T. Geisel

Brenda R. Kallio

" . . . administrative competence and vigilance is necessary to ensure that students with disabilities have the opportunity to receive their federally granted right to a free and appropriate education."

—*Richard T. Geisel & Brenda R. Kallio*

Objectives

1. Overview the history of Section 504 legislation
2. Describe eligibility for services, the identification process, and services delivery processes for 504
   - Discuss the administrator's roles in implementing Section 504
   - Compare and contrast major elements of Section 504 and IDEA
   - Provide sample forms for use in implementing Section 504

Introduction

In addition to the educational rights mandated by IDEA, administrators are also bound by legislation emanating from Section 504 of the Rehabilitation Act of 1973 (hereinafter referred to as Section 504) wherein Congress made a commitment to citizens that "to the maximum extent possible, [persons with disabilities] shall be fully integrated into American life." The combination of IDEA and Section 504 currently define the educational entitlements for disabled children. While IDEA and Section 504 appear to provide many of the same opportunities to special needs persons, the two pieces of legislation are distinctly different. A comparison of major provisions of IDEA and Section 504 can be found in Appendix A. Additionally, Appendix B details the relationship between special education students (IDEA) and Section 504 students.

History of Section 504

Section 504 of the Rehabilitation Act of 1973 (2002) is a federal civil rights law that, among other things, prohibits organizations receiving federal funds from discriminating against individuals with disabilities. As a result, public elementary and secondary schools, as well as private schools accepting federal funds, must comply with the provisions of Section 504. In part, Section 504 provides that "no otherwise qualified individual with a disability in the United States...shall, solely by reason of her or his disability, be excluded from the participation in, be denied the benefits of, or be subjected to discrimination under any program or activity receiving federal financial assistance." The United States Department of Education has issued administrative regulations for the purposes of clarifying the educational applications of Section 504 and enforcing the nondiscrimination provisions of Section 504 (Nondiscrimination, 2003). These regulations make it clear that Section 504 applies "to preschool, elementary, secondary, and adult education programs or activities that receive federal financial assistance" (Nondiscrimination, 34 C.F.R. § 104.31). Consequently, school administrators must be alert to the affirmative obligations Section 504 imposes on their schools.

Qualifying for Section 504

Section 504 is a legislative attempt to put students with disabilities on the same level playing field as students without disabilities in order to ensure that all students have the opportunity to receive a Free and Appropriate Public Education (FAPE). To comply with the provisions of Section 504, it is imperative that school administrators know what qualifies as a legal disability. The federal regulations define a person with a Section 504 disability as one who "(i) has a physical or mental impairment which substantially limits one or more major life activities, (ii) has a record of such an impairment, or (iii) is regarded as having such an impairment" [Nondiscrimination, 2003, 34 C.F.R. § 104.3(j)].

DEFINING A "PHYSICAL OR MENTAL IMPAIRMENT"

The first issue, then, is whether a student has a legally defined impairment. The regulations define a "physical or mental impairment" as any physiological disorder or condition, cosmetic disfigurement, or anatomical loss affecting one or more of the following body systems: neurological; musculoskeletal; special sense organs; respiratory, including speech organs; cardiovascular; reproductive, digestive, genito-urinary; hemic and lymphatic; skin; and endocrine; or any mental or psychological disorder, such as mental retardation, organic brain syndrome, emotional or mental illness, and specific learning disabilities [Nondiscrimination, 2003, 34 C.F.R. § 104.3(j)(2)(i)].

A student who has an impairment that meets the above stated requirements, however, will not necessarily qualify for Section 504 accommodations. Further investigation is required to determine whether the disability substantially limits one or more life activities.

SUBSTANTIAL LIMITATION OF A MAJOR LIFE ACTIVITY

Once it has been established that a student has a legal disability (or is regarded as having a disability or has a record of a disability as explained in the federal regulations), the inquiry shifts to whether the disability substantially limits a major life activity (e.g., learning). A "major life activity" is defined as "functions such as caring for one's self, performing manual tasks, walking, seeing, hearing, speaking, breathing, learning, and working" [Nondiscrimination, 2003, 34 C.F.R. § 104.3(j)(2)(ii)].

Some students may have a legal disability that, nonetheless, does not substantially limit a major life activity [ex. attention deficit disorder (ADD) or obsessive compulsive disorder (OCD)]. In *Bercovitch v. Baldwin School, Inc.* (1998) the parents of a student diagnosed with attention deficit-hyperactivity disorder (ADHD) argued that their child should not have been suspended from school for behavioral problems because he was disabled based upon a doctor's diagnosis of ADHD. However, the First Circuit Court of Appeals noted that the student's academic achievement was not substantially below average (or below average at all) during his worse periods of misbehavior. Accordingly, the court refused to recognize the student's disability as a substantial impairment of his ability to learn.

Once a disability is confirmed, school administrators are required to determine whether the disability substantially limits a major life activity. Failure to go beyond simply establishing the existence of a disability could lead to the over-identification of Section 504 students, accompanied by unwarranted increases in the costs of providing special services.

The Process of Identification

Section 504 students are identified using a referral process similar to that used to identify students with IDEA disabilities and likewise Section 504 students may be referred for evaluation by any person, including a parent/guardian, teacher, staff member, or person outside the school system (Puget Sound ESD, 2002, p. 10). Once a Section 504 referral is received, the building or district coordinator (usually this is the special education director or a building principal in small districts) should assemble a review team to determine whether the child is eligible for Section 504 status. (For greater detail on the referral process, see the "Referral and Placement" section of the Special Education chapter. Appendix C of this chapter contains an example of a Section 504 referral form.)

Procedural Safeguards

"Public elementary and secondary schools must employ procedural safeguards regarding the identification, evaluation, or educational placement of persons who, because of disability, need or are believed to need special instruction or related services" (Office of Civil Rights, n.d.). Upon receipt of a 504 referral, the school district must provide parents/guardians with procedural safeguards that include parental notice before any formal identification, evaluation or placement action takes place (Yell, 1998, p. 112). "Section 504 requires districts to provide notice to parents explaining any evaluation and placement decisions affecting their children and explaining the parents' right to review educational records and appeal any decision regarding evaluation and placement through an impartial hearing officer" (Office of Civil Rights). (See Appendix D for a sample notice of rights under Section 504.) Additionally, a school district must secure parental permission prior to conducting an evaluation of eligibility under Section 504.

Evaluation for Section 504 Eligibility

Once the evaluation is complete, the 504 team meets to consider the results and to make a determination as to whether the student qualifies for Section 504 services. The 504 team must base its determination of eligibility or non-eligibility upon information gathered from several different sources, including input submitted by the child's parents/guardians (Puget Sound ESD, 2002, p. 10). Based upon the information gathered, the 504 team must determine whether the student has a physical or mental impairment that substantially limits a major life activity. Once the 504 team has made its determination, the child's parents/guardians should be notified of the team's decision and, once again, be provided a copy of their rights under Section 504. (See Appendix E for a sample determination of Section 504 eligibility.)

The Accommodation Plan

If the 504 team has determined that a student is eligible for Section 504 services or accommodation, the next step is for the team to develop the student's 504 accommodation plan. (See Appendix F for an example of a Section 504 individualized accommodation plan.) Accommodation plans should be designed to provide students access to a free and appropriate public education in spite of their disability. The Section 504 Federal regulations state that public schools "shall provide a free appropriate public education to each qualified handicapped person who is in the recipient's jurisdiction, regardless of the nature or severity of the person's handicap" [Nondiscrimination, 2002, 34 C.F.R. § 104.33(a)]. Accordingly, the 504 individual accommodation plan must provide "regular or special education and related aids and services that are designed to meet individual educational needs of handicapped persons as adequately as the needs of non-handicapped persons are met" [Nondiscrimination, 34 C.F.R. § 104.33(b)]. Once the 504 team has developed an appropriate accommodation plan to address the student's disability, the plan must be submitted to the child's parents/guardians for their approval and consent (Puget Sound ESD, 2002, p. 11). Note, students identified under IDEA are required to have an individual education plan (IEP). However, students identified under Section 504 are not required to have an IEP. The district may choose to develop an individual accommodation plan instead.

The Role of the Building Administrator

To stay in compliance with Section 504, the 504 coordinator will need to: (1) make sure staff understand the essence of Section 504 and the importance of adhering to a student's 504 accommodation plan; (2) hold the staff accountable for using and following the terms of a student's 504 accommodation plan; (3) facilitate the 504 identification, evaluation and accommodation process in a timely manner; (4) provide parents/guardians with required notices in a timely manner; and (5) make sure to reevaluate students, "periodically" such as when there is a change in placement (e.g., elementary to middle school), when a parent requests it, or when conditions appear to warrant it (e.g., the accommodation plan is not working effectively or there has not been a reevaluation for three years).

Enforcement of Section 504

The federal regulations for Section 504 require that each public school district create "a system of procedural safeguards that includes notice, an opportunity for the parents or guardian of the person to examine relevant records, an impartial hearing with opportunity for participation by the person's parents or guardian and representation by counsel, and a review procedure" [Nondiscrimination, 34 C.F.R. § 104.36]. If a parent/guardian has exhausted the school district's "review procedure" and is still convinced the school district is failing to provide a free and appropriate public education to their disabled child, the parent has two options. First, the parent/guardian can file a complaint with the Office of Civil Rights (OCR), which is the agency charged with the responsibility of enforcing Section 504. Generally, the OCR supports the use of informal negotiations and voluntary action to bring school districts into compliance with Section 504. However, federal funds may be terminated for a district that fails to correct its discriminatory practices (Cambron-McCabe, McCarthy, & Thomas, 2004, p. 191). The second option available to parents or guardians is to file a lawsuit in federal court (Office of Civil Rights, n.d.). However, in order to recover damages and attorney fees, a plaintiff must show gross misjudgment or bad faith on the part of school officials (*Smith v. Special Sch. Dist. No. 1,* 1999).

Conclusion

Both the IDEA and Section 504 were created to guarantee students with disabilities a free and appropriate public education. The similarities and subtle differences between the two laws can be confusing for even the most seasoned administrator. For example, not all students who qualify for Section 504 services qualify under IDEA; however, all students who qualify for services under IDEA qualify under Section 504. It is imperative that administrators understand how students with disabilities are appropriately identified, referred, evaluated and placed. Additionally, administrators must hold teachers accountable for implementing the IEP or the 504 Accommodation Plan and must ensure that those plans are revisited and revised when it becomes apparent a change is required. In short, administrative competence and vigilance is necessary to ensure that students with disabilities have the opportunity to receive their federally granted right to a free and appropriate education.

Applying Your Knowledge

LeeAnna experienced a severe injury to her arm as the result of a fall from a swing set. She was in a cast for a period of time following some surgery to assist with bone placement and mending. This incident occurred nearly six years ago, when LeeAnna was still in elementary school. It appeared that the bones had healed and LeeAnna was doing well as she completed elementary school and junior high. However, about midway through her freshman year in high school, LeeAnna began to experience severe joint pain in the arm she had broken six years earlier. LeeAnna's parents took her to the doctor, but no apparent cause could be diagnosed at the time. The pain continued in the arm but also began to spread to other parts of LeeAnna's body (feet, legs, shoulders); all of the pain was only on the side of LeeAnna's body on which the arm had been broken. Additional problems such as extreme cold on the one side of LeeAnna's body, hypersensitivity of her skin, and painful leg aches began to occur and did not subside over time. Finally, a diagnosis was made of a rare joint disease resulting from the trauma experienced during the injury six years ago. Though some medications provided temporary relief, this condition would be chronic and increase and decrease in pain at different times. The strain of walking from one class to another in a large, comprehensive high school seemed to increase LeeAnna's leg pain; additionally, being in the halls during the passing periods with 2,300 other students assured that she would be bumped by others. When her hypersensitivity of the skin was occurring, the pain from these unavoidable contacts drove LeeAnna to tears. As the freshman year came to a close LeeAnna begged her parents not to make her go back to school in the fall—it hurt too much.

QUESTIONS

1. From what you know here, is LeeAnna eligible for Section 504 accommodations?
2. Who should make the referral?
3. What might be some accommodations that would allow LeeAnna to remain in school without suffering?
4. Should LeeAnna be referred for special education services? Why or why not?

QUESTIONS FOR THOUGHT

1. What did the authors mean when they said . . . all special education students qualify as Section 504, but not all Section 504 students qualify for special education?
2. Why does "substantial limitation of a major life activity" play a critical role in determining whether a student qualifies as Section 504?
3. Why is it important to understand the distinctions between IDEA and Section 504?
4. What are some ways in which classroom teachers can be helped to understand their roles and responsibilities for 504 accommodations?
5. Is it important that non-certified staff understand Section 504? Why or why not?
6. Who has the responsibility for 504 referrals? As the building principal, how would you make sure that referrals are done?
7. When disciplining a child who receives Section 504 services, are they entitled to the same considerations and procedures as students covered by IEPs? Why or why not?

For Additional Information Online

Federal Regulations for Section 504 *http://www.ed.gov/policy/rights/reg/ocr/edlite-34cfr104.html#D*

Frequently Asked Questions about Section 504 and the Education of Children with Disabilities published by the Office of Civil Rights *http://www.ed.gov/about/offices/list/ocr/504faq.html*

A Parent & Educator Guide to Free Appropriate Public Education published by the Puget Sound ESD *http://www.psesd.org/specialservices/pdfs/504manual.pdf*

Meeting the Needs of All Students published by The Teacher's Guide
http://www.theteachersguide.com/504.html

504 Resources published by the Council of Educators for Students with Disabilities, Inc. *http://www.504idea.org/504resources.html*

Understanding and Working with the Office for Civil Rights (OCR) prepared by David M. Richards & Jose Martín, Attorneys at Law with Richards, Lindsay & Martin, L.L.P. *http://www.504idea.org/OCR.pdf*

References

Bercovitch v. Baldwin School, Inc., 133 F.3d 141 (1st Cir. 1998).

Cambron-McCabe, N. H., McCarthy, M. M., & Thomas, S. B. (2004). *Legal rights of teachers and students* (5th ed.). Needham Heights, MA: Allyn and Bacon.

Nondiscrimination on the Basis of Handicap in Programs or Activities Receiving Federal Financial Assistance, 34 C.F.R. § 104 (2003).

Office of Civil Rights. (n.d.). *Frequently asked questions about Section 504 and the education of children with disabilities.* Retrieved July 7, 2004, from *http://www.ed.gov/about/offices/list/ocr/504faq.html*

Puget Sound ESD. (2002). *A parent & educator guide to free appropriate public education.* Retrieved July 6, 2004, from *http://www.psesd.org/specialservices/pdfs/504manual.pdf*

Rehabilitation Act of 1973, 29 U.S.C. § 794 (2002).

Smith v. Special Sch. Dist. No. 1, 184 F.3d 764 (8th Cir. 1999).

Yell, M. (1998). The law and special education. Upper Saddle River, NJ: Merrill.

Appendix A

A Comparison Chart: IDEA and Section 504

	IDEA	*Section 504*
Purpose	To ensure that all children with disabilities have available to them a free, appropriate public education.	To prohibit discrimination on the basis of disability in any program receiving federal funds.
Who is Protected	Students who are eligible under the 13 categories of qualifying conditions.	Much broader. A student is eligible if s/he meets the definition of "qualified handicapped person," i.e., has or has had a physical or mental impairment that substantially limits a major life activity, has a record of or is regarded as disabled by others. Parents are also protected.
Duty to Provide a Free Appropriate Education	Both require the provision of a free appropriate education, including individually designed instruction, to students who qualify.	
	Requires the district to provide an individualized education program. "Appropriate education" means a program designed to provide "educational benefit."	"Appropriate" means an education comparable to the education provided to students without disabilities.
Special Education vs. Regular Education	A student is eligible to receive special education services only if a multidisciplinary team determines that the student has one of the handicapping conditions and needs special education.	A student is eligible if s/he meets the definition of "qualified handicapped person," i.e., has or has had a physical or mental impairment that substantially limits a major life activity, or is regarded as disabled by others. The student is not required to need special education in order to be protected.
Funding	YES	NO

	IDEA	*Section 504*
Accessibility	Not specifically mentioned although if modifications must be made to provide a free appropriate education to a student, IDEA requires it.	Detailed regulations regarding building and program accessibility.
General Notice	Require child find activities	Require child find activities
	Requires notification of parental rights.	Districts must include notice of nondiscrimination in its employee, parent, and student handbooks and, if the district has more than 15 employees, must specify the district's 504 coordinator(s).
Notice and Consent	Both require specific notice to the parent or guardian about identification, evaluation, and placement.	
	Requires written notice. Notice requirements are more comprehensive and specify what the notice must provide.	Requires notice. (A district would be wise to give notice in writing.)
	Written notice is required before any change in placement.	Requires notice before a "significant change in placement."
	Requires consent for initial evaluation placement.	Consent not required, but if a handicapping condition under IDEA is suspected, those regulations must be followed.
Evaluations	The regulations are similar.	
	Requires consent before an initial evaluation is conducted.	Requires notice, not consent.
	Reevaluations must be conducted at least every 3 years.	Requires "periodic" reevaluations.
	No provisions.	Requires a reevaluation before a significant change in placement.
	Provides for independent evaluations.	No provisions.

	IDEA	*Section 504*
Determinations of Eligibility, Program, and Placement	Done by admission, review, and dismissal committee. Parent is a member of the committee.	Done by a group of persons knowledgeable about the child, the evaluation data, and placement options. While parental participation is not mentioned in the regulations, parental notice is required.
Grievance Procedures	IDEA does not require a grievance procedure or a compliance officer.	Districts with more that 15 employees must designate an employee to be responsible for assuring district compliance with Section 504 and provide a grievance procedure (an informal hearing before a district staff member) for parents, students, and employees.
Due Process	Both require districts to provide impartial hearings for parents or guardians who disagree with the identification, evaluation, or placement of a student with disabilities.	
	Hearings conducted by a state hearing officer (who is an attorney). Decisions may be appealed to court.	Hearings conducted at the local level by an impartial person not connected with the school district. Person need not be an attorney. Decisions may be appealed to courts.
Enforcement	Compliance is monitored by the state's Education Agency which also receives and resolves complaints regarding IDEA. Office for Civil Rights does not enforce.	Enforced by the Office for Civil Rights by comprehensive investigation and monitoring activities.
Employment	No provisions.	Employment of persons with disabilities . . .

Appendix B

504

**Serving Students
with Needs**

504

ADD
Dyslexia
Substance Abuse
Depression

ADHD
Conduct Disorder
Identity Disorder
Alcoholism

I
D
E
A

Autism
Mental Retardation
Visual Impairments
Hearing Impairments
Other Health Impairments
Emotional Disturbance
Speech or Language Impairments
A Specific Learning Disability
Orthopedic Impairments
Traumatic Brain Injury
Multiple Disabilities
Deaf-Blindness
Deafness

Suicidal
Encopresis
Enuresis
AIDS/HIV

TB
Asthma
Dystmia
Diabetes

Reprinted with permission from G. Schroth & M. Littleton, *The Administration and Supervision of Special Programs in Education,* p. 16, Dubuque, IA: Kendall/Hunt (2001).

Appendix C

Referral for Section 504

Student: _____ Birthdate: ____/____/____ Grade: _____
           Last Name   First Name

Parent/Guardian: _____

   Work Phone: _____

   Home Phone: _____

Address: _____
      Street Number   Street Name   City   Zip Code

Today's Date: _____ Person Making Referral: _____

Date of Receipt of Request ____/____/____

Signature: _____

Reason(s) for Referral (list specific concerns/behaviors): _____

_____

_____

To date, what accommodations or special provisions have been made to assist the student? _____

_____

_____

Is the student currently receiving special education or other services? Yes ☐ No ☐

If yes, what services is the student currently receiving? _____

_____

_____

Please submit completed referral to the building principal or Section 504 building coordinator.

Reprinted with permission from *A Parent & Educator Guide to Free Appropriate Public Education,* Puget Sound ESD, Office of Special Services, November 2002.

Appendix D

Section 504 Notice of Parent/Guardian and Student Rights

This is a notice of your rights under Section 504. These rights are designed to keep you fully informed about the district's decisions about your child and to inform you of your rights if you disagree with any of the district's decisions.

You have the right to:

1. Have your child participate in and benefit from the district's education program without discrimination based on disability.
2. An explanation of your and your child's rights under Section 504.
3. Receive notice before the district takes any action regarding the identification, evaluation, or placement of your child.
4. Refuse consent for the initial evaluation and initial placement of your child.
5. Have your child receive a free appropriate public education. This includes your child's right to be educated with non-disabled students to the maximum extent appropriate. It also includes the right to have the district provide related aids and services to allow your child an equal opportunity to participate in school activities.
6. Have your child educated in facilities and receive services comparable to those provided to non-disabled students.
7. Have your child receive special education services if she/he needs such services.
8. Have evaluation, educational, and placement decisions for your child based upon information from a variety of sources, by a group of persons who know your child, your child's evaluation data, and placement options.
9. Have your child be provided an equal opportunity to participate in non-academic and extracurricular activities offered by the district.
10. Have educational and related aids and services provided to your child without cost except for those fees imposed on the parents/guardian of non-disabled children.
11. Examine your child's education records and obtain a copy of such records at a reasonable cost unless the fee would effectively deny you access to the records.
12. A response to your reasonable requests for explanations and interpretations of your child's education records.
13. Request the district to amend your child's education records if you believe that they are inaccurate, misleading, or otherwise in violation of the privacy rights of your child. If the district refuses this request, you have the right to challenge such refusal.
14. Request mediation or an impartial due process hearing to challenge actions regarding your child's identification, evaluation, or placement. You and your child may take part in the hearing and have an attorney represent you.
    Hearing requests can be made to the district's Section 504 coordinator.
15. Ask for payment of reasonable attorney fees if you are successful on your claim.
16. File a local grievance or complaint with the U.S. Department of Education Office [for] Civil Rights.

The person in this district who is responsible for ensuring that the district complies with Section 504 is:

_____

Reprinted with permission from *A Parent & Educator Guide to Free Appropriate Public Education,* Puget Sound ESD, Office of Special Services, November 2002.

Appendix E

Section 504 Student Eligibility Determination Form

Name: _____ Date of Meeting: _____

D.O.B. _____ School: _____ Grade: _____

1. Describe the nature of the concern:
   _____
   _____
   _____

2. What is the student's mental or physical disability?
   _____
   _____
   _____

3. Describe the basis for the determination of disability:
   _____
   _____
   _____

4. Describe the educational impact of the disability on the student's learning:
   _____
   _____
   _____

5. The student is eligible under Section 504: Yes: _____ No _____
   - If no, team recommendations:
     _____
     _____
     _____

   - If yes, recommended accommodations/services:
     _____
     _____
     _____

Participants' Names   Title   Date

_____
_____
_____
_____
_____
_____

Reprinted with permission from *A Parent & Educator Guide to Free Appropriate Public Education,* Puget Sound ESD, Office of Special Services, November 2002.

Appendix F

Section 504 Plan Accommodation Form

Student's Name: _____ Date: _____

Disability: _____ D.O.B. _____

School: _____ Grade: _____

Describe the educational and related aids and services that the student needs to receive a free appropriate public education.

Instructional:

_____

_____

_____

Environmental/Accessibility:

_____

_____

_____

Behavioral/Social:

_____

_____

_____

Assessment/Testing:

_____

_____

_____

Other:

_____

_____

_____

Implementation Date: _____ Review Date: _____

Participant/Title	Title	Date

Attach: Notice of Action/Consent and Notice of Parent/Guardian/Student Rights

Reprinted with permission from *A Parent & Educator Guide to Free Appropriate Public Education,* Puget Sound ESD, Office of Special Services, November 2002.

Title I and No Child Left Behind Act 3

Mark Littleton

Federal funding of Title I programs represents the largest single investment in public education by the federal government. Beginning with President Johnson's War on Poverty in 1965, Title I has reached millions of students in thousands of classrooms across the nation. Since the advent of the reauthorization of Title I with the No Child Left Behind Act, the law has become a powerful tool, raising standards for all children.

—Mark Littleton

Objectives

1. Describe the role of the federal government as it pertains to compensatory programs
2. Explain the evolution of the Elementary and Secondary Education Act to the No Child Left Behind Act
3. Identify the critical components of the No Child Left Behind Act
4. Illustrate the different Title I program designs and delivery options available to schools
5. Describe how current issues related to the No Child Left Behind Act affect the operation of public school campuses

Introduction

The U.S. Constitution is silent on public education. Rather, the legal development for public schools, and the subsequent funding of the schools, is left to the individual states (Alexander & Alexander, 2001). Given these circumstances, one would assume that federal involvement is minimal, at best. Yet, the federal government has been engaged in subsidizing various aspects of public education since the 19th Century, and the federal government's role in public education was substantially shaped in the mid–1960s by the Elementary and Secondary Education Act (ESEA) (Finn, 1995). Within the 1965 ESEA, Title I was enacted to assist in America's war on poverty by directing federal funds to assist students from low-income families. Now authorized under the No Child Left Behind Act (NCLB) of 2001, Title I provides $11 billion in federal funds to education (Education Funding Research Council, 2004). These funds target schools in which the student population is "disproportionately poor" (Puma & Drury, 2000, p. 2).

NCLB was bipartisan legislation that incorporated four key principles 1) accountability for results, 2) flexibility in the use of funds, 3) greater parental choice, and 4) an emphasis on scientifically-based teaching methods (U.S. Department of Education, 2004). However, what began as a show of legislative solidarity to improve a failing educational system, NCLB became a hotbed of political debate (Mizell, 2003) with some claiming that the law "is in serious disrepair" (Cuban, 2004, p. 1).

Although it is more of a federal subsidy than a program in the strictest sense (Puma & Drury, 2000), the success of Title I is open to debate (Puma & Drury, 2000; Le Tendre, 1999; Fashola & Slavin, 1998; Ravitch, 1997; Jendryka, 1993). Proponents argue that the federal subsidy has provided assistance to millions of children in approximately 13,000 districts across the United States (Le Tendre, 1999). Detractors argue that standardized test scores for targeted students show no improvement and Title I schools deliver a curriculum that lacks challenge (Puma & Drury, 2000). In fact, NCLB proponents justify the massive overhaul of Title I as a mechanism to fix a seriously troubled educational system (Mizell, 2003).

Regardless, Title I funds affect over 46,0000 schools (Le Tendre, 1999), and remain a substantial portion of the budget for many of these campuses. It would be prudent of school leaders to understand the mechanism for funding Title I programs and to know what practices enhance the success of those programs at the campus level.

HISTORY

If only in a political sense, the federal government has been reluctant to become directly involved in public education. Congress specifically prohibits intrusion into public education.

> No provision of any applicable program shall be construed to authorize any department, agency, officer, or employee of the United States to exercise any direction, supervision, or control over the curriculum, program of instruction, administration, or personnel of any educational institution, school, or school system. (20 U.S.C. Section 1232a)

However, the federal government has retained a strong interest in education. At the onset, the federal government took an indirect role in public education choosing to affect policy with subsidy. (Refer to Table 1 for a summary of legislation affecting education.) This indirect control was performed in two ways. First, grants were offered to states with the stated intent of supporting the common good for the general public. Second, grants with conditions (or strings) were offered to help subsidize special programs. Until the mid–1960s, federal funding focused on issues of national interests such as land grants

Table 1 Federal Legislation Assisting Education
Selected from the National Center for Education Statistics, 2004

Morrill Act of 1862—provided land grants for colleges specializing in the agricultural and mechanical arts.

Smith-Hughes Act of 1917—federal aid for vocational programs in public schools below the college level.

Lanham Act of 1940—federal aid to local governments for the construction of facilities, including schools.

National Defense Education Act (NDEA) of 1958—provided federal funds to promote scholarship in the sciences.

Economic Opportunity Act of 1964—provided federal funds for the War on Poverty, including Head Start.

Elementary and Secondary Education Act of 1965—authorized grants for elementary and secondary school programs for children of low-income families.

Education Consolidation and Improvement Act (ECIA) of 1981—consolidated 42 federal programs to be funded under the ESEA block grant authority.

Augustus F. Hawkins-Robert T. Stafford Elementary and Secondary Improvement Amendments of 1988—reauthorized ESEA and other programs through 1993.

Goals 2000: Educate America Act of 1994—formalized education goals and established a National Education Standards and Improvement Council providing for voluntary national board certification.

Improving America's School Act of 1994—Reauthorized ESEA.

Education Flexibility Partnership Act of 1999—allows states to participate in the Education Flexibility Partnership program.

No Child Left Behind Act of 2002—comprehensive reauthorization of ESEA and adding specific proposals related to accountability, assessment, and parental choice.

and national defense projects. (Alexander & Alexander, 2001) More recently, federal funds have been directed toward specific educational programs. Although there had been several previous attempts to provide subsidies for general education programs, the passage of ESEA was a significant policy statement showing the federal government's interest in education (Cross, 2004).

According to Spring (2002), it was a stroke of political genius that President Johnson directly addressed religious squabbles and concerns of educational lobbyists with a single piece of legislation. Proponents of federal aid to education wanted to pass a general aid to education bill, but ESEA, with its more narrow focus of alleviating economic imbalances, survived the legislative process (Roeber, 1999). The Act focused on providing aid to children of poor families instead of general aid to public and private schools (Spring, 2002). Contrary to popular opinion, ESEA was not designed to target "low-income students per se, but to all students, regardless of income, who suffered from poverty's deleterious effects upon their schooling" (Zamora, 2003, p. 419).

Of the eight titles in ESEA (see Table 2), the most significant piece is Title I, a section of law designed to assist educationally and economically deprived children. It is interesting to note the clarity of purpose of Title I as stated in Section 201 of ESEA. The initial purpose of the law was to address the special educational needs of low-income families, and to improve the instructional programs affecting schools impacted by low-income families.

Table 2 Elementary and Secondary Education Act of 1965

Title I	Educationally deprived children
Title II	Libraries and textbooks
Title III	Supplementary education
Title IV	Cooperative research
Title V	State education departments
Title VI	Handicapped children
Title VII	Bilingual education
Title VIII	Dropout prevention & Adult education

Title I quickly became a popular federal subsidy with near-unanimous approval upon each reauthorization (Jendryka, 1993). As often happens with federal subsidy programs, federal controls increased with each reauthorization (Fowler, 2000). Elmore and McLaughlin (1982) note that these escalating compliance requirements were to amplify the federal government's presence in defining "certain specific responses at the local level" (p. 165). Sometimes called "a skillfully constructed package of compliance and assistance measures" (Elmore & McLaughlin, 1982, p. 162), procedural requirements and fiscal accountability increased dramatically during the first 15 years of Title I's existence. Designed to assist with reading and mathematics instruction, federal regulations required that Title I funds be used to supplement, not supplant, state and local funds (Puma & Drury, 2000).

Yudof, Kirp, and Levin (1992) note that ESEA "exhibited the difficulties as well as the potential of federal involvement in education" (p. 698). Congress commissioned a study of ESEA in the 1974 reauthorization. Because of the perceived intrusion into public education by the federal government, program evaluation was a critical component of Title I (Fowler, 2000). In the extensive review, the National Institute of Education was very critical of the implementation of Title I at the federal and state levels. Apparently, the "federal preoccupation with compliance objectives" had occupied so much of state administrators' time that little attention was given to assistance (Elmore & McLaughlin, 1982, p. 168). Subsequent legislation reflects the concern with compliance requirements by providing options for schools to Title I and non-Title I programs.

The increased emphasis on fiscal accountability led schools to focus on a particular curriculum option called "pull out." (Program design options will be discussed in more detail later in the chapter.) Puma and Drury (2000) note that "pull outs came under increasing fire for their lack of coordination with regular classroom instruction and, in 1978, the 'schoolwide' option was introduced" (p. 3).

The size of Title I along with its complex set of regulations, "made it a prime target for the Reagan administration, which hoped to eliminate the program entirely" (Yudof, et al., 1992, p. 698). Congress resisted the temptation to eliminate Title I, but then provided for fewer federal restrictions in the 1981 Education Consolidation and Improvement Act (ECIA). In the ECIA, Title I was renamed Chapter 1, a name that remained until the 1994 reauthorization (Elmore & Rothman, 1999; Goldberg, 1987).

The Hawkins-Stafford amendment to the ESEA in 1988 required that federally funded programs be gauged by *opportunity to learn* measures. These measures were designed to describe the educational process. Each district receiving Chapter 1 funds was to use the indicators to assess the quality of the program. The Hawkins-Stafford amendment signaled the return of administrative guidance as well as the beginning of parental involvement (Schwartz, 1995).

The 1994 reauthorization of the Title I in the Improving America's Schools Act (IASA) represented a significant shift in the compensatory program. Although the most significant change (again renamed Title I) was the increase in parental involvement (Yudof, Kirp, & Levin, 1992), IASA required states to establish identical challenging standards and benchmarks for Title I and non-Title I students (Elmore & Rothman, 1999). Congress recognized that

> Although the achievement gap between disadvantaged children and other children has been reduced . . . the most urgent need for educational improvement is in schools with a high concentration of children from low-income families and achieving the National Education Goals will not be possible without substantial improvement . . . [and] educational needs are particularly great for low-achieving children in our Nation's highest-poverty schools . . . (20 U.S.C.S. 6301[1–3])

IASA attempted to align federal policies with state and local policies (Wirt & Kirst, 1997). According to Puma and Drury (2000), three programmatic themes emerged during this alignment. Under the umbrella of a standards-based reform theme, IASA required states to develop "challenging standards of performance and assessments that measure student performance against the standards" (Elmore & Rothman, 1999, p. 9). Upon identifying the struggling schools, states were then to provide additional assistance to the schools.

The second programmatic theme signaled a significant operational shift. Prior to 1978, Title I provided for targeted assistance programs that addressed the needs of individually identified students. In 1978 an additional program design was offered (Wang, Wong, & Kim, 1999). Schools were allowed the option of the school-wide design provided that the district matched federal funds with their own funds. Few schools opted for the school-wide design due to the matching funds requirement until the passage of the 1988 Hawkins-Stafford amendment eliminated this barrier. Schools in which at least 75% of the student population were identified as low-income qualified for the school-wide design. This design let the school co-mingle federal, state, and local funds to provide a comprehensive, coherent program of instruction. Under the IASA, the poverty-rate for the funding of school-wide programs was adjusted from 75% to 50%, allowing a considerably larger number of schools the freedom to combine funding sources (Puma & Drury, 2000).

Finally, IASA provided for more program management flexibility than previous reauthorizations of ESEA. In the Education Flexibility Partnership Act of 1999 (Ed Flex) federal and state officials were given authority to waive some federal requirements if those requirements were viewed as inhibiting school improvement (U.S. Department of Education, 2001; Puma & Drury, 2000). Prior to IASA, a large number of public schools received Title I funds—approximately 70% of elementary schools. Although IASA, through its funding provisions, reduced the percentage of schools receiving aid, there was "a precipitous increase in the percentage of high-poverty secondary schools receiving funding"—61 % to 93% (Puma & Drury, 2000, p. 6).

Many of the provisions in IASA set the stage for dramatic changes with the No Child Left Behind (NCLB) Act. On January 8, 2002, President George W. Bush signed into law the NCLB Act, a bipartisan reauthorization of ESEA. NCLB symbolizes a historic extension of the federal government in public education (Wenkart, 2003). Based upon the four principles of accountability, local control, parental choice, and scientifically-based teaching (Sclafani, 2003), the major provisions of NCLB include a) state accountability systems, b) adequate yearly progress of schools, c) local district and school improvement, d) increased emphasis on school-wide programs, e) teacher and paraprofessional qualifications, and f) participation of eligible children in private schools (U.S. Department of

Education, 2002). Former U.S. Secretary of Education Rod Paige noted the country's commitment, through NCLB, to "educate every child, regardless of skin color, spoken accent or zip code" (Paige, 2004). NCLB is a massive law, consequently only the highlights of current NCLB as it pertains to the operation of Title I in the public schools will be presented in this chapter.

FEDERAL COMPENSATORY GUIDELINES

As has already been mentioned, federal guidelines for Title I are complex. Covering the minutia of program guidelines is beyond the scope of this book. However, an understanding of some of the broad fiscal and procedural guidelines may assist in effective program implementation and supervision.

Fiscal Guidelines

In the $11 billion Title I program, federal funds are distributed to the state education agencies (SEA). The SEAs then distribute the funds to the qualifying local districts. According to Puma and Drury (1999) "Title I funds are distributed to counties, districts, and schools—generally in proportion to the number of poor school-age children in those jurisdictions" (p. 5).

In targeted assistance programs, Title I funds may be used only to supplement state and local resources (20 U.S.C. Section 6321(b)(1)). There is no single definition of "supplement, not supplant." However, the supplement not supplant standard usually applies if school personnel can show that the program would continue with local funds in the event that federal funds were to cease.

Funds for school-wide programs may be used in combination with other federal, state, and local funds. Supplement not supplant applies to school-wide programs, as well, but the determination of use is made at the school level instead of the program level. The funds must be used to support activities identified by a comprehensive school reform plan, which is developed with the involvement of community and school personnel. Although the Title I funds may be co-mingled, schools are admonished to maintain an accurate record of how Title I funds are distributed.[1]

Funding of the provisions added by NCLB created considerable discontent between state and federal officials and members of the Bush administration. In January, 2004, 10 U.S. Senators sent a letter to U.S. Secretary of Education, Rod Paige, blasting the administration for, among other things, underfunding NCLB (Kennedy, et al., January 8, 2004). Eight states seriously considered "opting-out" of NCLB, but very few bar state funding of NCLB (Education Funding Research Council, 2004). Choosing to opt-out is attractive to some states primarily because it would take more state and local funds to comply with NCLB requirements than the state would receive in federal assistance (Tirozzi & Ferrandino, 2004). In response, federal government officials warn state officials of the dangers of opting-out, which may include funding losses in programs other than those funded through NCLB (Education Funding Research Council, 2004).

PROCEDURAL GUIDELINES

Although the fiscal structure of the distribution of Title I funds varies from state to state and the federal guidelines often are complex, the goal of Title I remains the same. In a

[1]See, for example, Under Secretary Hickok's letter to the Honorable Sandy Garrett, Superintendent of the Oklahoma Department of Education, March 6, 2003.

2001 report published by the U.S. Department of Education, the Planning and Evaluation Service noted that

> The primary purpose of the program has not changed since the time when it first became law—to ensure equal educational opportunity for all children regardless of socioeconomic background and to close the achievement gap between poor and affluent children, by providing additional resources for schools serving disadvantaged students. (p. 2)

Yet, NCLB has taken the purpose of Title I a step further. Section 6301 of the Act provides that

> The purpose of [Title I] is to ensure that all children have a fair, equal, and significant opportunity to obtain a high-quality education and reach, at a minimum, proficiency on challenging state academic achievement standards and state academic assessments. This purpose can be accomplished by:
>
> 1. Ensuring that high-quality academic assessments, accountability systems, teacher preparation and training, curriculum, and instructional materials are aligned with challenging state academic standards so that students, teachers, parents, and administrators can measure progress against common expectations for student academic achievement;
> 2. Meeting the educational needs of low-achieving children in our nation's highest-poverty schools, limited-English proficient children, migratory children, children with disabilities, Indian children, neglected or delinquent children, and young children in need of reading assistance;
> 3. Closing the achievement gap between high- and low-performing children, especially the achievement gaps between minority and nonminority students, and between disadvantaged children and their more advantaged peers;
> 4. Holding schools, local educational agencies, and states accountable for improving the academic achievement of all students, and identifying and turning around low-performing schools that have failed to provide a high-quality education to their students, while providing alternatives to students in such schools to enable the students to receive a high-quality education;
> 5. Distributing and targeting resources sufficiently to make a difference to local educational agencies and schools where needs are greatest;
> 6. Improving and strengthening accountability, teaching, and learning by using state assessment systems designed to ensure that students are meeting challenging state academic achievement and content standards and increasing achievement overall, but especially for the disadvantaged;
> 7. Providing greater decisionmaking authority and flexibility to schools and teachers in exchange for greater responsibility for student performance;
> 8. Providing children an enriched and accelerated educational program, including the use of schoolwide programs or additional services that increase the amount and quality of instructional time;
> 9. Promoting schoolwide reform and ensuring the access of children to effective, scientifically based instructional strategies and challenging academic content;
> 10. Significantly elevating the quality of instruction by providing staff in participating schools with substantial opportunities for professional development;
> 11. Coordinating services under all parts of this subchapter with each other, with other educational services, and, to the extent feasible, with other agencies providing services to youth, children, and families; and
> 12. Affording parents substantial and meaningful opportunities to participate in the education of their children. (20 U.S.C. Section 6301)

PARENT INVOLVEMENT

Parent involvement is key to an effective Title I program. Section 6318 of NCLB specifies the parameters of parent involvement for the participating school districts. These guidelines require that each school served by NCLB funds establish a policy that involves parents in the planning, development, implementation, and evaluation of the Title I program. In the spirit of local control, NCLB does not mandate how parent involvement will be achieved, but school personnel would be well-advised to heed subparagraph (e)(3) of section 6318 which states that each participating school district

> shall educate teachers, pupil services personnel, principals, and other staff, with the assistance of parents, in the value and utility of contributions of parents, and in how to reach out to, communicate with, and work with parents as equal partners, implement and coordinate parent programs, and build ties between parents and the school.

Due, in part, to the fact that quality parental involvement has not been achieved in most Title I schools (Wang, Wong, & Kim, 1999), section 6316 of NCLB provides a "choice plan" for school districts. The U.S. Department of Education notes that the lack of parent involvement is particularly noticeable from poor families (U.S. Department of Education, 2001). Previous re-authorizations of Title I strengthened the "emphasis on school/family community partnerships by: (1) specifying partnerships . . . linked to student learning; (2) asking schools to develop . . . a 'compact' . . . ; and (3) allowing funds to be commingled to create unified programs that serve all parents" (Puma & Drury, 1999, p. 27). However, NCLB's choice option sends a clear signal to participating schools of the necessity to involve parents to the greatest extent.

Contemporary Issues

Regardless of its bipartisan beginnings, the implementation of NCLB has led to numerous, hotly-debated controversies. For some states, the cost of implementing the law is more than the federal subsidy they would receive through the program. However, the detrimental effects of opting-out of the program may be too severe. Some of the controversial issues related to NCLB include accountability, student testing, adequate yearly progress, and high quality teachers.

ACCOUNTABILITY

Each state must develop a single accountability system based on the state's academic standards, and include a system of punishments and rewards to hold each public school accountable for the performance of all students (34 C.F.R. Section 200.12).[2] Although accountability may be the most controversial provision in NCLB (Price, 2003), there are those who view it as "among the most race-conscious legislative remedies to racial inequity in K–12 education" (Losen, 2004, p. 246). NCLB requires each participating state to disaggregate student scores by gender, racial and ethnic group, English proficiency status, migrant status, students with disabilities, and economically disadvantaged (34 C.F.R. Section 200.2). This provision is a far-cry from previous testing programs that reflect a school, district, or state average. Sclafani (2003) notes that under NCLB, "it will not be enough to raise the average score by raising the performance of the best students even higher" (p. 46).

Proponents argue that accountability systems are necessary to obtain improvement. Additionally, accountability empowers parents and policymakers with the ability to

---

[2]U.S.C. is an acronym for United States Code, the actual law passed by Congress. C.F.R. is an acronym for Code of Federal Regulations, the U.S. Department of Education's rules for implementing the law.

ensure that schools provide a quality education. Furthermore, the disaggregation of the testing data will force schools to address the issues of the *neediest* of students. Opponents of accountability programs contend that poor and inadequate accountability systems will fail to accurately assess schools, and redirect valuable resources from necessary programs (Kucerik, 2002).

STUDENT TESTING

Sclafani (2003) commented that "assessment is critical to making schools accountable and to identifying practices that make schools and teachers successful" (p. 45). Federal regulations require each state receiving funds to implement a system of student assessment in mathematics, reading/language arts, and science. The assessments must be aligned with state standards, and must provide for the assessment of all students, including limited English proficient students and students with disabilities (34 C.F.R. Section 200.2). The assessment results must be made available to parents (34 C.F.R. Section 200.8), and the results must be disaggregated by gender, racial and ethnic group, English proficiency status, migrant status, students with disabilities, and economically disadvantaged (34 C.F.R. Section 200.2).

Controversy regarding this aspect of the law stems from a) inclusion of all students, even those students not served by federal funds, and b) the arguable bias of standardized tests (Price, 2003), i.e., testing opponents contend that standardized testing does not adequately measure a student's or school's achievement level or progress (Kucerik, 2002). Testing is an expensive activity, and testing programs that involve every child are costly, in terms of time and money. Additionally, testing of limited English proficient students and students with disabilities can adversely affect a school's adequate yearly progress. (Of course, the counter-argument and a crucial component of NCLB is that all children should be tested so that none are "left behind.")

ADEQUATE YEARLY PROGRESS

The backbone of the accountability system is adequate yearly progress (AYP). AYP is defined by the state, but must include a student assessment system that considers all public school students, and specific data on economically disadvantaged students, students from major racial and ethnic groups, limited English proficient students, and students with disabilities (34 C.F.R. Section 200.13). In addition, graduation rates must be used to determine AYP. The states may use retention rates, attendance rates, and participation in academically-advanced programs (e.g., gifted-talented, advanced placement, and college preparatory) (34 CFR Section 200.19).

Controversy stems from the fact that some school districts report strong student performance on the assessment, but fail to have an adequate number of students to meet AYP (Robelen, 2004). Polls indicate that what the law defines as AYP is not popular with the general public (Robelen, 2004). Former Secretary Paige noted that for a school to be considered making AYP, the school must assess 95% of its students and students in each subgroup (Paige, 2002). For example, an ethnically and socially homogeneous school might need to meet student performance requirements based on the totality of the student population because the sub-groups do not apply. On the other hand, an ethnically and socially diverse school will need to meet performance requirements of the total student population and the applicable sub-groups of race, ethnicity, and limited English proficiency.

HIGHLY QUALIFIED TEACHERS

NCLB requires that all participating states have *highly qualified* teachers in the core academic subject areas by the end of the 2005-06 school year (34 C.F.R. Section 200.57). The U.S. Department of Education defines a highly qualified teacher as one who has a bachelor's degree, state certification, and who has demonstrated competency in a core academic area (34 C.F.R. Section 200.56). In school-wide programs, all teachers teaching one or more academic subjects must be highly qualified. In targeted assistance programs, any teacher whose salary is partially or fully paid by Title I funds must be highly qualified (Texas Education Agency, 2003).

Many schools find it difficult to meet this demanding new standard. As a result, the U.S. Department of Education has provided local districts with some flexibility in meeting the highly qualified teacher standard (Texas Education Agency, 2003). For example, federal policy changes have made it easier for rural school districts and for science teachers to meet the highly qualified mandate (*Changing the Rules,* 2004).

Program Design and Delivery Options

TARGETED ASSISTANCE

Implementation of Title I programs takes one of two different designs. The predominant pattern has been the targeted assistance plan which are "pull-out programs that deliver supplementary instruction to low-achieving students during the time they would have spent in their regular classes" (Puma & Drury, 2000, p. 7). In-class instruction is another aspect of the targeted assistance design. The in-class model allows for isolated groups within the academic classroom. Often the in-class model was little more than the pull-out model located within the academic classroom. As mentioned earlier, the targeted assistance model was the exclusive design until 1978.

One state agency directs districts to develop targeted assistance programs that

1. Help students meet the state's performance standards,
2. Are based on improving student achievement,
3. Incorporate a plan considering the needs of the students served,
4. Utilize effective instructional strategies,
5. Support the regular instructional program,
6. Provide for a well qualified staff, supported by professional development, and
7. Increase parental involvement. (Texas Education Agency, 2001)

Targeted assistance programs have proven to be a "target" for many Title I critics. Anstrom (1995) warns that "curricular fragmentation resulting from Chapter 1 [now Title I] students missing out on core academic instruction while attending remedial reading and math classes has been a frequently occurring side effect" (p. 3).

SCHOOL-WIDE

Prior to NCLB, school-wide programs required that 50% of the student population qualify as low-income. Wang, Wong, and Kim (1999) note that "although Title I legislation has permitted school-wide programs since 1978, these programs were rarely implemented prior to the passage of the IASA, partly due to the requirement that school districts match federal grants with their own funds" (p. 5). IASA further encouraged the school-wide program by reducing the low-income student population requirement to 50% (from 75%). As a result the number of schools moving to the school-wide design increased. Under NCLB, the required low-income student population requirement was reduced to 40%, providing opportunities for additional schools to operate on a school-wide basis.

The core elements of a school-wide program include a comprehensive needs assessment based upon the achievement of the children on the state assessment. From that needs assessment, reform strategies for the school must a) provide opportunities for all children (not only Title I identified students) to meet proficient levels on the state assessment, b) use effective instructional methods that strengthen the core academic areas and increase the amount of instructional time, and c) provide for the needs of low-achieving children through counseling services, college and career awareness, and integration of vocational and technical education programs (20 U.S.C. Section 6314).[3]

Private School Participation

As it was originally passed, the Elementary and Secondary Education Act of 1965 was designed to benefit children from low-income families. It was designed to improve instruction for *all* children. In all reauthorizations, as with the original bill, private school children are included under the provision of helping all children. However, the federal government does not send federal funds directly to private schools. As the funds are granted to the local educational agencies (school districts), the agencies become responsible for serving eligible students within the boundaries of their district. Often, private school administrators and public school officials work closely to generate requests for federal funds. After consultation with private school administrators, public school officials must provide for equitable participation in the Title I program for eligible private school students (20 U.S.C. Section 6320).

There has been considerable discussion and some litigation regarding the use of public funds to assist private schools. However, the courts have determined that Title I funds can be used to assist eligible students in private schools. Anyone interested in further discussion is encouraged to investigate the cases of *Agostini v. Felton* (1997) and *Mitchell v. Helms* (2000).

VOUCHERS

Rosenthal (1999) points out that the current Republican leadership wants to provide greater flexibility in the Title I program. Combining the large ESEA monies (of which Title I is the largest portion) into block grants was one way to do this. Under the voucher concept, the federal government would provide parents of Title I eligible students with vouchers. These vouchers would be taken to the school of parental choice (private or public). The school, in turn, would send the voucher to the state for reimbursement for educating the child. However, such a move makes it difficult to ensure that low-income students benefit from Title I funds. The use of vouchers in the Title I program has already prompted political debates, and is sure to generate court challenges. Recently, the U.S. Supreme Court upheld an Ohio law that provided tuition vouchers for students in poor performing schools to attend public or private schools of their choice (*Zelman v. Simmons-Harris,* 2002). Regardless of the federal constitutionality of such programs, state constitutional provisions may be more restrictive.

Supervision

As with many federal programs, Title I is reauthorized periodically. As a result, rules and policies change regularly. Fowler (2000) notes that "these are important policy issues for . . . districts, and should be followed closely" (p. 220). An astute supervisor will follow the changes closely to ensure that his or her school is not in danger of losing funds.

---

[3]See 34 C.F.R. Section 200.26 et seq. for additional, specific information from the U.S. Department of Education. Additionally, state-specific information can be obtained from each state agency of the participating states.

Supervisors also need to know what works. Fortunately, Title I programs have been thoroughly researched, and there is ample information concerning indicators of a successful program. Wang, Wong and Kim (1999) suggest that school-wide programs are more effective than targeted assistance schools. Also, U.S. Department of Education (2001) research suggests that when teaching reading, teachers should:

- Give children access to a variety of reading and writing materials.
- Present explicit instruction for reading and writing, both in the context of authentic and isolated practice.
- Create multiple opportunities for sustained reading practice in a variety of settings.
- Carefully choose instructional-level text from a variety of materials.
- Adjust the grouping and explicitness of instruction to meet the needs of individual students. (p. 35)

The same study (U.S. Department of Education, 2001) suggests that effective teaching of mathematics include

- Focusing on problem solving. Students need conceptual understanding to deal with novel problems and settings and to become autonomous learners. Instruction should encourage multiple solutions to problems.
- Defining basic skills to involve more than computation.
- Emphasizing reasoning and thinking skills, concept development, communicating mathematically, and applying mathematics. Students must learn mathematics with understanding, building new knowledge from experience and prior knowledge.
- Presenting content in a logical progression with an increasing emphasis on higher-order thinking skills, such as problem-solving and mathematical reasoning, and mathematical communication.
- Integrating topics of numeration, patterns and relations, geometry, measurement, probability and statistics, algebra, and algorithmic thinking. Instruction should broaden the range of mathematical content studied, an aspect of teaching in which low-income children are often short-changed.
- Taking advantage of calculators and computers to extend students' mathematical reach. (p. 36)

Understanding the research regarding effective reading and mathematics instruction is not sufficient. The instructional staff (teachers, teacher's aides, etc.) need continual staff development and training to hone their instructional skills and to stay abreast of current effective instructional methodology (U.S. Department of Education, 2001; Puma & Drury, 1999). Teachers are, after all, the most effective resource in improving student achievement (Darling-Hammond, 2000; Greenwald, Hedges, & Laine, 1996). Quality professional development programs for Title I teachers will be strong in content, be distributed over an extended period of time in which teachers are actively engaged, utilize study groups and mentoring, and be aligned with the standards and assessment instruments used to measure student progress (U.S. Department of Education, 2001).

Summary

Federal funding of Title I programs represents the largest single investment in public education by the federal government. Beginning with President Johnson's War on Poverty in 1965, Title I has reached millions of students in thousands of classrooms across the nation. Since the advent of the reauthorization of Title I with the No Child Left Behind Act, the law has become a powerful tool, raising standards for all children.

However, the best of tools will not work if they are not used properly. There is evidence to suggest that Title I programs operate best on a school-wide basis, particularly when class sizes are reduced and quality instruction is implemented. All children, those receiving Title I services included, should be held to high standards of performance, and taught by a qualified staff who engage in appropriate professional development activities. Teachers should utilize instructional strategies known to be effective and focus on improving student performance. Last, but certainly not least, parents need to be involved in every phase of the process. Parental involvement is often the key to student engagement and, consequently, student learning.

The shrewd supervisor is not only knowledgeable of effective programs and instructional practices, but she or he is cognizant of the rules and regulations associated with implementing a Title I program. As a result, professional development is important for the supervisor as well as the teacher. Only when supervisors are aware of effective program design, instructional practices, and program requirements and limitations can they ensure that the Title I program supports the entire instructional program of the school.

Applying Your Knowledge

A bedroom community is located in a suburb of a large metropolitan area. The district is located conveniently near the headquarters of several large corporations, but it is rapidly becoming an industrial center. The elementary school has a student population of 610. The demographics of the school are quite interesting. Approximately 15% of the students live in homes where the household income exceeds $200,000. These students live in a neighborhood that is stable, where the parents drive to manage major divisions of large corporations. The data reveal that students from the high-income households are the top students and have instructional needs addressed through honors and gifted programs. Interestingly, during the previous school year, 48% of the students at the elementary school were from low-income households. However, due to the rapid immigration of low-income families to the industrial region, the projected low-income population is expected to reach 53%. Student scores are declining as the number of students from low-income households increase.

QUESTIONS

1. What is the best program design for the campus? Why?
2. What can the campus principal do to ensure that the school maintains adequate yearly progress?
3. What should the campus principal do to attain participation from low-income and high-income parents?

QUESTIONS FOR THOUGHT

1. How has federal involvement in education changed from the enactment of ESEA to NCLB?
2. What are the major differences between targeted assistance programs and school-wide programs?
3. Do you view vouchers as deleterious to the public school system? Why or why not?

4. What are the positive and negative aspects to standardized testing programs for students?
5. How can schools involve parents in a significant way?

For Additional Information Online

Council of Chief State School Officers (CCSSO)—*http://www.ccsso.org/*

Education Commission of the States (ECS)—*http://www.ecs.org/*

Internet Education Exchange—*http://www.iedx.org/*

National Center for Education Statistics—*http://www.nces.ed.gov/*

Texas Education Agency—*http://www.tea.state.tx.us*

U.S. Department of Education—*http://www.ed.gov*

References

STATUTES

Title I, Improving the Academic Achievement of the Disadvantaged, 34 Code of Federal Regulations (C.F.R.), Part 200.
Helping Disadvantaged Children Meet High Standards, 20 United States Code (U.S.C.), Chapter 70, Subchapter I, Section 6301 et seq.
Elementary and Secondary Education Act, Public Law 89-10 (April 11, 1965).
Fiscal Requirements, 20 U.S.C. Chapter 70, Subchapter I, Section 6321.
Parental Involvement, 20 U.S.C. Chapter 70, Subchapter I, Section 6318.
Participation of Children Enrolled in Private Schools, 20 U.S.C. Chapter 70, Subchapter I, Section 6320.
Prohibition against Federal control of education, 20 U.S.C. Section 1232(a).
Statement of Purpose, U.S.C. Chapter 70, Subchapter I, Section 6301.
Strengthening and Improvement of Elementary and Secondary Schools Helping Disadvantaged Children Meet High Standards, 20 United States Code (U.S.C.), Chapter 31, Section 1232a.

COURT CASES

Agostini v. Felton, 521 U.S. 203; 117 S.Ct. 1997 (1997).
Mitchell v. Helms, 530 U.S. 793; 120 S.Ct. 2530 (2000).
Zelman v. Simmons-Harris, 536 U.S. 639; 122 S.Ct. 2460 (2002).

OTHER

Alexander, K., & Alexander, M.D. (2001). *American public school law.* Fifth edition. Belmont, CA: West/Thomson Learning.
Anstrom, K. (1995). New directions for Chapter 1/Title I. *Directions in Language and Education, 1.* National Clearinghouse for Bilingual Education. Retrieved September 23, 2000 from *http://128.164.90.197/ncbepubs/directions.*
Changing the rules. (2004, April 7). *Education Week* on the Web. [On-line Serial]. Available at *http://www.edweek.org.*
Cross, C. (2004). *Political education.* New York: Teachers College Press.
Cuban, L. (2004, March 17). The contentious 'No Child' law: Who will fix it? And how? *Education Week on the Web.* Retrieved March 22, 2004 from *http://www.edweek.org.*
Darling-Hammond, L. (2000, January 1). Teacher quality and student achievement: A review of state policy evidence. *Education Policy Analysis Archives* [On-line Serial], *8,* Available: *http://olam.ed.asu.edu/epaa.*

Education Funding Research Council. (2004, March). *Title I Monitor, 9* (3).

Elmore, R.F., & Rothman, R (Eds.). (1999). *Testing, teaching, and learning: A guide for states and school districts* (National Research Council). Washington, D.C.: National Academy Press.

Elmore, R.F. & McLaughlin, M.W. (1982). In A. Lieberman & M.W. McLaughlin (Eds.), *Policy Making in Education: Eighty-first Yearbook of the National Society for the Study of Education.* Chicago: The University of Chicago Press. pp. 159–194.

Fashola, O.S. & Slavin, R.E. (1998, January). Schoolwide reform models, *Phi Delta Kappan, 79* 370–380.

Finn, C. (1995). Towards excellence in education. *Public Interest,* 120, 41–54.

First, P.F. (1992). *Educational policy for school administrators.* Boston: Allyn and Bacon.

Fowler, F.C. (2000). *Policy studies for educational leaders.* Columbus, OH: Merrill.

Goldberg, K. (1987, December 9). Lawsuit challenges Chapter 1 and 2 aid to church schools. *Education Week on the Web.* [On-line serial]. Available: *http://www.edweek.org.*

Greenwald, R. Hedges, L., & Laine, R. (1996). The effect of school resources on student achievement, *Review of Educational Research, 66,* 361–396.

Jendryka, B. (1993). Failing grade for federal aid. *Policy Review, 66,* 77–81.

Kennedy, E., Dodd, C., Harkin, T., Mikulski, B., Bingaman, J., Murray, P., Reed, J., Edwards, J., Clinton, H.R., & Miller, G. (2004, January 8). *Letter to Secretary Paige on the Bush administration's failure to properly implement No Child Left Behind Act.* Retrieved from *http://edworkforce.house.gov/democrats/paigenclbletter.html* on February 25, 2004.

Kucerik, E. (2002). The No Child Left Behind Act of 2001: Will it live up to its promise? *Georgetown Journal on Poverty Law and Policy, 9,* 479–487.

Le Tendre, M.J. (1999). *Title I must be #1 now!* Speech presented at the National Association of State Title I Directors in New Orleans, LA. Retrieved August 31, 2000 on *http://www.ed.gov/offices/OESE/CEP/neworlea2.html.*

Losen, D. (2004). Challenging racial disparities: The promise and pitfalls of the No Child Left Behind Act's race-conscious accountability, *Howard Law Journal, 47,* 243–298.

Mizell, H. (2003, July). *NCLB: Conspiracy, Compliance or Creativity.* Paper presented at the "Learn and Lead" Week of the National Staff Development Council, St. Louis, MO.

Paige, R. (2002, July 24). *Letter from the Secretary on Adequate Yearly Progress.* Retrieved April 8, 2004 from *http://www.ed.gov/policy/elsec/guid/secletter/020724.html.*

Paige, R. (2004, March 11). *Memo to editorial writers.* Retrieved March 22, 2004 from *http://www.ed.gov/news/opeds/edit/edit/2004/03112004.html.*

Price, D. (2003). Outcome-based tyranny: Teaching competency while testing like a state, *Anthropological Quarterly, 76,* 4, 715–729.

Puma, M.J., & Drury, D.W. (2000). *Exploring new directions: Title I in the year 2000.* Alexandria, VA: National School Board Association.

Ravitch, D. (1997, June 2). Success in Brooklyn, but not in D.C. *Forbes, 159,* 90.

Robelen, E.W. (2004, September 1). Poll: Public still on learning curve for Federal school law. *Education Week on the Web.* [On-line serial]. Available: *http://www.edweek.org.*

Roeber, E.D. (1999). Standards initiatives and American educational reform, in G.J. Cizek (Ed.) *Handbook of Educational Policy,* pp. 151–181. Boston: Academic Press.

Rosenthal, I. (1999). ESEA debate heats up. *Technology and Learning,* 20, 43.

Schwartz, W. (1995). Opportunity to learn standards: Their impact on urban students. *ERIC Clearinghouse on Urban Education.* New York. (ERIC Document Reproduction No. ED 389 816).

Sclafani, S. (2003). No Child Left Behind, *Issues in Science and Technology 19,* 2.

Spring, J. (2002). *Conflicts of interests: The politics of American education* (4[th]ed.). Boston: McGraw-Hill.

Texas Education Agency. (2003). *NCLB Bulletin, 1* (1). Retrieved April 8, 2004 from *http://www.tea.state.tx.us/nclb/bulletin.html.*

Texas Education Agency. (2001). Division of Student Support Programs. Retrieved on February 7, 2001 from *http://www.tea.state.tx.us/support/titleia.*

Tirozzi, G., & Ferrandino, V. (2004, March 31). *Improving NCLB.* Message posted to Principals.org, archived at *http://www.principals.org/advocacy/views/ImprovingNCLB.cfm.*

U.S. Department of Education. (2004). Retrieved on April 5, 2004 from *http://www.ed.gov/nclb/*.

U.S. Department of Education (2002). *The No Child Left Behind Act: Summary of final regulations.* Retrieved February 12, 2004 from *http://www.No ChildLeftBehind.gov.*

U.S. Department of Education, Planning and Evaluation Service. (2001). *High standards for all students: A report from the national assessment of Title I on progress and challenges since the 1994 reauthorization.* Washington, DC: 2001. Doc. No. 2001–16.

Wang, M.C., Wong, K.K., & Kim, J.R. (1999). *A national study of Title I school-wide programs: A synopsis of interim findings.* A research report supported by the Office of Educational Research and Improvement, U.S. Department of Education, and the Laboratory for Student Success, Temple University Center for Research in Human Development and Education. (ERIC Document Reproduction Service No. 436 596).

Wenkart, R. (2003, July). *Contracting for supplemental educational services under the No Child Left Behind Act.* Paper presented at the Tenth Annual Education Law Conference, Portland, ME.

Wirt, F.M., & Kirst, M.W. (1997). *The political dynamics of American education.* Berkely, CA: McCutchan Publishing Corp.

Yudof, M.G., Kirp, D. L., & Levin, B. (1992). *Educational policy and the law.* St. Paul, MN: West Publishing Company.

Zamora, P. (2003). In recognition of the special educational needs of low-income families: Ideological discord and its effects upon Title I of the Elementary and Secondary Education Acts of 1965 and 2001, *Georgetown Journal on Poverty Law and Policy, 10,* 413–447.

Ensuring Success for Migrant Students

Velma D. Menchaca

Alejo Salinas, Jr.

It is important that teachers create a positive classroom environment for migrant students. Migrant students often find themselves in new classrooms. The challenges of adjusting to strange, new learning and home environments often contribute to feelings of isolation and loneliness.

—*Velma Menchaca & Alejo Salinas, Jr.*

Objectives

1. Present demographics of the migrant population in the U.S.
2. Describe some of the unique educational experiences of migrant students
3. Discuss the issue of culturally relevant teaching as it relates to migrant students
4. Describe involvement of parents of migrant students
5. Discuss how schools can assist and support migrant students to succeed

Introduction

Migrants are defined in the U.S. Department of Education (1994) guidelines as "migratory workers, or the children of migratory workers who move for the purposes of obtaining seasonal or temporary work in agriculture or fishing" (p. 4). Each year approximately three to five million farmworkers and their families leave their homes to follow the crops (National Center for Farmworker Health, 2001). Their lives revolve around working and moving from one harvest to another with the hope of improving their finances.

Migrants in the United States are extremely diverse. Approximately 92% of all migrants are culturally and linguistically diverse, with 85% being Hispanic. Of the Hispanic migrant population, 60% are Mexican American and are the largest subgroup followed by Puerto Ricans, Cubans, Central and South Americans (Kissam, 1993). While white Americans make up 8% of the migrant population, the remaining 7% is comprised of black Americans, Jamaicans, Haitians, Laotians, Thais, and other racial and ethnic minorities (National Center for Farmworker Health, 2001).

Migrants who have immigrated to the U.S. from Mexico and parts of Central America primarily harvest fruits and vegetables (Fix & Passel, 1994; Oliveira, Effland, & Hamm, 1993). In the summers, they may harvest tomatoes or broccoli in Texas or apricots, peaches, or grapes in California. They tend to migrate up and down along three known geographic routes: the East Coast stream, the Mid-continent Stream, and the West Coast Stream following seasonal crops.

Educating migrant students is one of the solutions to changing their lives in a positive manner. Whether a family decides to continue with yearly migration or relocates permanently in proximity to their seasonal work, the task of educating the migrant student remains of paramount importance. The dynamics which shape the migrant students' environment provides parameters for understanding the migrant educational context.

This chapter is organized around several broad categories: educational experiences of migrant students, culturally relevant teaching, migrant parental involvement, and the challenges of secondary schools. An array of information on the lives of migrant children, and hardships they encounter in the fields is provided. Also discussed are the challenges migrants encounter in schools because of their mobile lifestyles, the obstacles that keep them from graduating, and the hurdles they must successfully jump to get into college.

Instructional strategies that have been successful with migrant students and strategies for educational leaders to incorporate to ensure positive parental involvement; the involvement of migrant parents in the schools; and diversification of the curriculum by implementing culturally relevant content are also addressed. Finally, the authors have provided several lessons with examples relevant to the lives of migrant students.

PROFILE OF THE MIGRANT FAMILY

Over 80% of migrants and seasonal farmworkers are U.S. citizens or are legally in the United States (Fix & Passel, 1994). The average annual income for these families is less than $7,500 per year, far below the federal poverty level (Oliveira, Effland, & Hamm, 1993). The work of migrant farmworkers tends to be seasonal and often very inconsistent. The number of farmworkers needing housing exceeds the number of available substandard housing units (National Center for Farmworker Health, 2001). Therefore, farmworkers, particularly migrants, confront obstacles in obtaining housing. Agricultural employers recognize that lack of adequate housing is a serious challenge.

They resort to temporary housing such as labor camps; however, construction and maintenance of these labor camps can be expensive, especially since labor camps are only occupied during harvest season. The housing that is readily available for most migrant families may not meet the minimum inspection standards, posing a national health problem. Migrant families tend to live without adequate restroom facilities and clean drinking water in substandard houses, which are usually barrack-like structures, run-down farmhouses, trailer homes, or small shacks (Shotland, 1989). Some migrants may be forced to sleep in tents, cars, or even ditches when housing is not available.

Many migrant families face occupation-related health problems such as risk of injury from farm machinery and equipment and from pesticide poisoning (Menchaca & Ruiz-Escalante, 1995). Respiratory problems caused by pesticide poisoning, natural fungi, and dusts are common. Lack of safe drinking water contributes to dehydration, heat strokes, and heat exhaustion. Dermatitis, a skin rash, is often intensified because of the sun, sweat, and lack of sanitary facilities. Other health concerns are attributed to poor sanitation and poverty. Thus, the intensity of health problems for migrant farmworkers is greater than for the general population (National Center for Farmworker Health, 2001).

The census indicates that among Hispanic migrant children, 38% lived in poverty in 1990 as compared to 18% of non-Hispanic children (U.S. Bureau of Census, 1993). Some commonly reported health problems among migrant children include: lower height and weight, respiratory diseases, parasitic conditions, chronic diarrhea, and congenital and developmental problems. Poverty, hunger, fear, and uncertainty fill the lives of migrant children.

Educational Experiences of Migrant Students

Children of migrant farmworkers have not been academically successful in public schools. Poverty and migration make it difficult for migrant children to create a different life and future than that of their parents. Their schooling may be interrupted several times throughout one school year; a high mobility rate places an enormous stress on migrant children and on the schools. The challenges they confront may multiply as they progress through the grades. These challenges must be addressed in order for students to fully develop their intellectual potentials. For example, their educational needs vary considerably; some lack literacy skills in Spanish while English language abilities are limited for others. The quality of instruction for migrant students may be hampered if the curriculum does not adequately address their needs or provide supplemental instructional services to overcome academic difficulties that result from frequent educational disruptions. Most school personnel are not prepared to adequately serve the academic needs of Hispanic students, in general, nor migrant students in particular (Menchaca, 1996).

Migrant students have the lowest graduation rate of any population group in the U.S. public schools (Johnson, Levy, Morales, Morse, & Prokop, 1986). The drop-out rate among children of migrant farmworkers is almost twice that of children from non-migrant families. This rate is conservatively estimated at 45%, well above the national average of 25% (National Program for Secondary Credit Exchange and Accrual, 1994). Data from other studies show that the dropout rates for migrant students range from 45% to 65% (Levy, 1987; Vamos Inc., 1992). These longitudinal studies focused on Hispanic students identified while they were in sixth grade; however, these students were not tracked for long because of a high disappearance rate. They either moved, disappeared, dropped out, or no longer qualified for services.

Approximately 50% of migrant students are one or more years below grade level. Thus, half of all migrants could be at risk of dropping out of school (Migrant Education Secondary Assistance Project, 1989). Research indicates that several factors influence the students to leave school before graduating. Living in poverty leads to dropping out of school because an additional family member contributing to the household income is welcomed. Students also tend to drop out of school if they are not proficient in English, even though learning English for all migrants is an economic asset. These students generally have suffered academically due to their mobile lifestyles, dislike school, participate little in school activities, have no home base, are economically disadvantaged, and have low motivation and low persistence (Rasmussen, 1988). Some teachers become disinterested in migrant students due to their diverse academic, social, and economic needs; consequently, the students leave school.

In a study conducted by the Migrant Youth Program (1985), some students indicated that their needs were not met by school personnel, although teachers and counselors believed the students' needs were met. Martinez (1994) reported that according to principals and teachers, factors that influence the school performance of migrant children are: (a) social prejudice, (b) lack of communication, (c) mobility, (d) no educational continuity, (e) education not valued, (f) inappropriate home environment, and (g) lack of knowledge of how educational systems operate. Yet, migrant advocates such as mentors, counselors, or advisors had a more holistic perspective on reasons migrant students leave school. Many of them indicated that poverty contributed to school absences because these students needed to work, care for younger siblings or stay home due to illnesses (Martinez & Cranston-Grigras, 1996; Martinez, Scott, Cranston-Grigras & Platt, 1994).

Migrant children must be assisted in adjusting to new environments. These children transfer to several schools during the span of their education, sometimes as often as three times a year. These experiences are not pleasant, and at times can be uncomfortable because the students never feel grounded or that they truly belong. When some students do feel a sense of belonging or have made friends, they are soon uprooted to go to the next harvest site. What may compound the situation even more is that these children may not be proficient in English and therefore, may not be accepted by some of their classmates (Dyson, 1983). These children tend to withdraw, are not noticed, and thus are overlooked. They experience isolation for not being accepted for who they are, intensifying their sense of low self-esteem. Consequently, educators would be wise to provide an environment for migrant students that aids rapid adjustment. For example, the Jackson County Migrant Education Program (1981) in Medford, Oregon produced a handbook titled *MIGRANT EDUCATION—HARVEST OF HOPE*. This handbook covers several topics including knowledge of children for whom English is a second language (ESL). The handbook also addresses how migrant students relate to teachers, and provides suggestions for meeting the needs of ESL students. Most important is the message that the migrant students need the teachers to care, respect, understand and encourage them.

Another site that provides migrant children rich learning experiences is Waitz Elementary in Mission, Texas, located in the southern-most part of Texas about six miles north of the Texas-Mexico border. Approximately 30% of the children at Waitz Elementary are from migrant families who live in tar paper shacks or in trailer homes along dirt roads. With a 99% Mexican-American student population, Waitz Elementary annually rates among the top 10% of all Texas schools in reading and mathematics achievement. The school "defies predictions of low achievement by a sustained focus on multiple factors" (Cawelti, 1999, p. 1) that remarkably improve student performance. The principal and teachers are committed to high expectations and make every effort to ensure high student achievement. They are committed to quality implementation of multiple changes that contribute to student achievement. Teachers use bilingual education approaches with students who enter with limited English skills. The teachers focus on making sure that all students pass the state-mandated assessment. The school strongly emphasizes regular attendance and recognizes classrooms with all children present; good citizenship is recognized and rewarded.

Culturally Relevant Teaching

Culturally relevant teaching (Ladson-Billings, 1990; 1995) is a pedagogy that empowers students intellectually, socially, emotionally, and politically to examine critically educational content and processes. It uses the students' home culture to help create meaning and understanding of the children's world. Thus, not only is academic success emphasized by the culturally relevant teacher, so are social and cultural successes (Ladson-Billings, 1992). Migrant students can be empowered through the school curricula if they see connections between their home culture and their school, thus encouraging pride in who they are.

Culturally relevant teaching rests on three criteria: (a) academic success, (b) cultural competence, and (c) cultural consciousness (Ladson-Billings, 1995). Teachers must direct, reinforce, and cultivate academic success and excellence in their migrant students. They must attend to students' academic needs, not just make them feel good. Teachers who use culturally relevant strategies believe that academic success is possible for all students when they help students make connections with their community. Making this connection allows migrant students to learn from a familiar cultural base which acknowledges their ancestors and develops understanding in their culture, thus empowering them to build on their personal backgrounds (Banks, 1994; Barba, 1995). Teachers who use culturally relevant teaching believe that migrant students have special strengths that need to be explored and utilized in the classroom.

Teachers who embrace culturally different strategies utilize the migrant students' culture as the vehicle for learning. Historically, textbooks have failed to address the cultures of Hispanic students in general, and Hispanic migrant students in particular. Consequently, Hispanic students encounter concepts taught in culturally unfamiliar fashions (Barba, 1995). Thus, many students never acquire the desired level of understanding. Teachers using culturally relevant strategies encourage migrant students to use their home language while they acquire the second language, English.

Culturally relevant teaching allows students to develop a "sociopolitical cultural consciousness that allows them to critique the cultural norms, values, mores, and institutions that produce and maintain social inequalities" (Ladson-Billings, 1995, p. 162). They know that students must have opportunities to make decisions and to take actions related to the topic, issue, or problem they are studying. Students can gather data, analyze their values and beliefs, synthesize their knowledge and values, identify alternative courses of action, and decide what actions need to be taken, if any. Students are taught thinking and decision-making skills that empower them and provide a sense of political efficacy (Banks, 1988). In other words, when students identify a problem and are given the freedom to make decisions on what action needs to be taken to remedy the problem, they will gain a sense of pride and satisfaction.

Integrating Relevance for Migrant Students

Teachers validate the cultures of students by integrating culturally relevant content into the curriculum (Menchaca, 2000). Teachers legitimize Hispanic migrant students' real life experiences as part of the formal curriculum. In a science lesson, for example, the use of culturally familiar plants, flowers, and fruits prevalent to the Hispanic culture could be presented along with the content in the textbook. Or, studying the production of plants, fruits, and vegetables gives teachers an excellent opportunity to introduce the mobile lifestyle of migrant students. Because of their mobile lifestyles, migrant students bring rich experiences to the classroom. Teachers can build on students' strengths by embracing and incorporating their experiences in the lessons. When studying the food pyramid in a health lesson, the use of culturally familiar foods and examples of diseases that are prevalent in migrant family households will enhance concept acquisition (Marines & Ortiz de Montellano, 1993).

In a language arts lesson, teachers can incorporate a variety of Hispanic children's books. Much of the Hispanic literature focuses on the life and experiences of migrant students. Teachers can encourage positive ethnic affiliation for migrant students. Nurturing ethnic affiliation helps migrant students learn about and respect cultural groups' heritage and histories while retaining the value of their own culture instilled in their hearts and minds. There are many young children's books that can easily be incorporated in language arts or history classes. Some examples of these books are: *In My Family-En Mi Familia* (Garza, 1996), *Pepita Finds Out-Lo que Pepita descubre* (Lachtman, 2002), *Uncle Chente's Picnic-El picnic de Tío Chente* (Bertrand, 2001a), and *The Bakery Lady-La señora de la panaderia* (Mora, 2001).

The following adolescent novels can be used at the middle or high schools with migrant students: *White Bread Competition* (Hernández, 1997), *Spirits of the High Mesa* (Martinez, 1997), *The Summer of El Pintor* (Lachtman, 2001), and *Trino's Time* (Bertrand, 2001b). These novels explore conflict, friendships, loyalties, romances, racial identities, death, and Hispanic traditions. Other novels such as *Ya Será Hora?—Is It Time?* and *Qué Será? What Is It?* (Salinas, 1999, 2004) depict the successes of Mexican American families. With humor and sensitivity, the authors shed light on the lives of middle school and high school Hispanic adolescents. Migrant students can read about their own life experiences as they read the mysteries, challenges, dreams, and conflicts of other young Hispanic adolescents. Teachers can incorporate both their own personal experiences and the experiences of migrant students in the lessons. Teachers can personalize the curriculum by using the foods, places, locations, and names familiar to these students. It is always important that teachers build on the richness of all students' experiences and culture to make learning more meaningful. For example, it is important for white students to read about the successes, challenges, and dreams of Hispanic students or of black students, to view the various ethnic perspectives, and to understand the ways in which the histories and cultures of our nation are inextricably bound.

Hispanic students, and migrants in particular, possess a source of emotional, physical, moral, and spiritual strength. While they travel to different parts of the country during the harvest season, they ameliorate differing cultural values. What they lack is a consistent base of role models who project success. The literature and curricula have omitted meaningful Mexican American figures as a source of inspiration and motivation for success. Instead, textbooks have given token attention to the Hispanic culture (Escamilla, 1996a; Nieto, 1996; Revett, 1986). Historically, textbooks have presented foreign-born Hispanics as role models or heroes instead of native-born Hispanic role models like Jamie Escalante, a very successful Mexican American teacher from East Los Angeles who had a movie made because of his success with Latino students; Federico Peña, a Mexican American from Brownsville, Texas who was elected Mayor of Denver and eventually appointed by President Clinton as Secretary of Transportation; or Ellen Ochoa, a Latina astronaut born in Los Angeles who has logged over 978 hours in space and has flown on four NASA space shuttle missions. Escamilla (1987) investigated the cultural exclusion of Mexican Americans in the school curricula. She concluded that neither Mexican American students nor students of other ethnic groups had a thorough understanding of the history, culture, or contributions of Mexican Americans.

The lack of recognizable role models at the national level is limited and oftentimes overlooked in the schools. Migrant students of Hispanic origin would benefit from recognizing their unsung heroes; their foundations, trials, tribulations and success stories should be included as part of the curriculum. Students tend to be motivated by persons they recognize, who live within their midst, and who are successful local products of their communities.

Instructional Strategies for Migrant Students

Instructional strategies, such as cooperative learning, developing metacognitive skills, enhancing self-concept, creating a positive environment, building on migrant students' strengths, and personalizing lessons with migrant students' experiences, are recommended to help teachers understand migrant students. Research supports cooperative learning as an effective instructional strategy (Johnson, Johnson & Maruyama, 1983). Migrant students do well in cooperative learning settings because they sense other students are encouraging and supporting their efforts to achieve. Cooperative learning lowers anxiety levels and strengthens motivation, self-esteem, and empowerment by using students as instructional agents for migrant students (Platt, Cranston-Gingras, & Scott, 1991). Students take responsibility for both their own learning and the learning of their peers. By becoming active group participants, they gain equal access to learning opportunities.

Metacognitive skills help students become independent learners by helping them comprehend concepts, monitor their success, and make the necessary adjustments when they have difficulty understanding concepts. Students learn to recognize when they are approaching an obstacle, make necessary corrections, and proceed. Teachers instruct students to employ alternative strategies once they have recognized and determined a breakdown in comprehension. For example, if a student is reading and has difficulty understanding the text, he or she could apply some "fix-it" strategies (Baker & Brown, 1984), such as ignore and read on, anticipate the problem to be resolved by future information, make an educated guess based on prior knowledge, reflect on what has already been read, re-focus on the current sentence or paragraph, and consult the glossary, encyclopedia or teacher.

It is important that teachers create a positive classroom environment for migrant students. Migrant students often find themselves in new classrooms. The challenges of adjusting to strange, new learning and home environments often contribute to feelings of isolation and loneliness. Teachers can help students overcome these feelings by modeling respect and eliminating any form of threat or ridicule. Teachers can further foster a sense of safety and trust by sharing some of their own experiences, and by assigning older students to act as mentors or buddies to new immigrant students when appropriate. When students have faith in their own abilities, they are more likely to persist and succeed despite the many obstacles they encounter in schools. When necessary, teachers can modify assignments to allow for success in meaningful activities that are valued by the migrant student and by others, such as family and friends.

Teachers reach out to migrant students when they build on their strengths. Most migrant students have lived, traveled, and studied in several states. Teachers can incorporate into lessons these diverse experiences and the richness of students' cultures and languages. Examples include recognizing migrant children for their travel experiences, their knowledge of geography, and their ability to overcome crisis situations. Building on these experiences and capabilities serves to validate students' knowledge, which in turn, enhances students' self-images and sense of self-worth (Gonzales, 1991). Drawing from students' home and work experiences in lessons helps students understand ideas and transfer them to other content. To find out about students' experiences, teachers can have them write or tell about their migrant trajectory and experiences. Later, teachers can incorporate both their own experiences and those of the children into content lessons such as language arts, social studies, and science. Teachers can personalize content by using familiar places and names in addition to using analogies to connect new concepts to students' experiences.

Extracurricular Activities

Since schooling for migrant students is interrupted with each move, most are not involved in any form of extracurricular activity. Many migrant children do not participate in after school activities because they lack transportation, have after-school responsibilities, or their parents are not aware of the extracurricular activities available. Yet, participating in extracurriculuar activities can provide enriched learning experiences. These experiences provide migrant students opportunities to develop social skills, talents, and promote positive attitudes about themselves and their schools. Some of these challenges can be overcome by providing transportation since many school-sponsored sports and activities are held after classes are over and by informing parents of all before and after-school activities. In some communities, after-school recreation programs are sponsored by clubs, organizations, or local parks and recreation departments. In Florida, the Dade County Park and Recreation Department has activities specifically designed for migrant students since the enrollment of these students has increased dramatically in that area (Dyson, 1983). The facility, located close to a migrant camp, offers adult supervision and activity coordination including bilingual explanations for games and planned activities. The goal of this facility is to contribute to the total well-being of children regardless of language or ethnicity.

The possibilities of migrant students participating in organized sports such as football, baseball, basketball, golf, etc. is limited by their constant mobility. Their brief attendance at various schools, or lack thereof, precludes participation. Recognition of athletic abilities is partly attributed to engagement in local sports and school team sports. Because migrant students arrive late and leave early during the school year, their competitive attributes in the sports realm are usually overlooked. In isolated cases, coaches attempt to persuade parents to allow the student to enroll at the beginning of the school year or remain until the spring sports are concluded. Most of the parents refuse these requests because they value their family work over a sports program. Leaving their children behind with relatives to participate in sports while parents migrate for work is considered an undue burden for all involved. Students that are exempted from the migrant stream rituals of late arrivals and early withdrawals prove to be outstanding athletes.

Extra-curricular participation in academic areas, such as spelling bees, University Interscholastic League, and literary competition, are more accessible to migrant students. The periods of competition are usually held in the early spring and allow more opportunities for migrant students to participate. Late enrollment is compensated by longer practice sessions and preparation time. Such activities provide migrant students recognition for their academic capabilities and success, and serve to further motivate academic challenges.

Migrant Parental Involvement

Educating students is not the sole responsibility of the schools. Parents play an important role in the education of their children. Yet, schools are not always clear about developing or defining their expectations for parental involvement. However, educators can understand how migrant parents define schooling and education and their perceptions of how schools operate (Martinez & Velasquez, 2000). Historically, school districts have lacked coherent policies or practices for attending to parental needs, specifically those of migrant parents. On the other hand, parents are often preoccupied with other concerns and do not become actively involved in their children's schools unless the activity satisfies a particular personal interest. The hardships migrant parents confront are much greater than those of most parents. Their lives revolve around work and moving from place to place, making it difficult to be involved in their children's education.

Often schools limit parental involvement to attending open house, parent-teacher conferences, monitoring children's homework, and reinforcing school discipline policies. These traditional approaches are one-way communications from school to home, rather than respecting the home situation and recognizing that all parents have something valuable to contribute. Migrant parents tend to be intimidated if they did not have positive school experiences as youngsters. A directed, authority-based form of communication that lacks a sense of closeness and mutual interest intensifies feelings of nonparticipation. Many migrant parents have not been sure how best to be involved in schools, nor the degree of involvement that is appropriate. They do not possess the skills necessary for successful participation. Moreover, the language used in educational settings is not always clear to them. Quite often, they struggle to understand education jargon. Migrant parents have not played an active role in the school system in the past, but educators could increase their involvement by taking the initiative to ensure that migrant parents feel safe and welcome.

Many intervention programs tend to be "prescriptive" instead of real and inclusive (Valdes, 1996). However, the following parent involvement strategies can be adopted and incorporated to develop strong relationships between the school and community (Ruiz-Escalante & Menchaca, 1999) that support and empower migrant parents to become more involved in schools. Schools at all grade levels should:

- rethink how to attract language minority parents and migrant parents to their campuses,
- provide training in the language which parents understand and speak,
- train parents to explore the processes of decision-making,
- help parents improve their parenting skills and provide them the necessary tools to assist their children with homework,
- inform parents of trainings through communication in their home language,
- train parents to work within the system to bring about positive change,

- identify what support services are offered for children of different cultures or different languages,
- design in-service training to learn how to empathize with parents and recognize their strengths while making the most of parent-teacher conferences,
- respond to the multicultural needs of parents and the community to effectively facilitate this relationship.

Developing a variety of strategies to contact and reach out to migrant parents can be helpful. Educators who continuously make connections with parents can positively affect the children's academic performance. Sometimes, someone other than parents, such as teachers or counselors, can inspire students to complete school and graduate. Some migrant parents believe it is the sole responsibility of the school to educate children (Chavkin, 1991), and believe their involvement in the schools might be construed as interference. The following are parent involvement strategies that can help dispel such myths and foster healthy relationships between the school and community (Ruiz-Escalante & Menchaca, 1999). These strategies usually require a moderator or central person such as a community or church official to lead the charge by:

- inviting educators to community centers or church meetings,
- sharing the social and cultural dimensions of the migrant community with educators,
- inviting educators to the community to talk about the school's goals or answer parents' questions,
- exploring ways parents can become volunteers in schools,
- working actively with the school system to bring about positive change.

The Challenges for Public Schools

High drop-out rates, low achievement test scores, poor attendance, and over-aged students in classes are problems common to migrant students (Salerno, 1991). High mobility, cultural differences, and limited proficiency in English are also challenges migrant students encounter. From the school's standpoint these challenges can be overwhelming. Most teachers have not been trained to teach the culturally or linguistically disadvantaged student, the migrant student, and/or the limited-English speaking student. Thus, schools must hire, train, and retain competent staff to provide appropriate instruction to migrant students.

Schools have begun to seek assistance from external entities to respond to the needs of migrant students by establishing, for example, bilingual or dual-language programs in elementary schools and English-as-a-second language (ESL) programs. Instruction in bilingual programs is in the native language and instruction in dual-language programs is in English and Spanish. In most bilingual programs, students are transitioned to English usually by third grade; in dual-language programs, students continue to learn in both languages each year as they advance in grade level. ESL classes are typically found in secondary schools and instruction is in English. In some programs, migrant students receive additional help when needed. For example, some ESL classes have a teacher aide or a tutor to assist with the instruction because ESL classes enroll students whose native languages vary greatly. Flexible instructional programs and support programs are needed to facilitate their schooling through reading and writing and critical thinking skills. Such support programs include tutorial services, counseling services, enrichment activities, career awareness, health services and medical referrals. Intervention must be provided to these highly mobile students. There must be an emphasis on high expectations and excellence. Placing migrant students in small classrooms, where instruction is more personalized, is also important. Personal contact with teachers allows students to "exhibit competence, initiative, and responsibility" (Druin, 1986, p. 2). Since many migrant students enter school after the school year has begun, teachers tend to pre-judge them unfavorably (Neuman, 1988). Therefore, having a staff that sets high expectations for all students is necessary. Assigning classroom buddies for late-enrolling migrant students gives them a warm and receptive welcome.

The needs of migrant students that are seniors in high school are numerous in nature, and schools must plan solutions for their success. There are more Hispanic seniors in vocational or general education programs than in the college preparation programs. There are fewer numbers of Hispanic seniors in courses such as trigonometry, calculus, physics, chemistry, or English. Fewer Hispanics take the Scholastic Aptitude Test (SAT) and the American College Test (ACT) which are examinations used for college admissions. These deficits exclude Hispanics and more specifically, Hispanic migrant students, from opportunities for admission into colleges. Public schools need to nurture a supportive environment in which staff express expectations that migrant students will attend college and be successful. Schools should provide academic opportunities for making up credits, tutoring, taking appropriate courses, and test-taking skill development. School counselors should assist migrants in applying to and preparing for college. This type of involvement increases college attendance rates (Horn & Chen, 1998). Other forms of support services could be in the form of: (a) early identification of college-bound students which enhances the chances for better preparation, (b) transition services that provide migrants with study skills for taking the SAT and ACT, (c) tutorials for academic courses, (d) a system to alert students about visits from college recruiters, test deadlines, college fairs, scholarship deadlines, etc., and (e) information related to college admission and financial aid.

Other more personal services that schools can provide migrant students are academic assistance such as counseling, extended day/week/year programs, and special summer schools. Career awareness and vocational education has also been successful with migrant students. Even successful migrant students are at-risk in high school. For this reason, the following programs have been designed for continued support (Rasmussen, 1988).

- The College Assistance Migrant Program (CAMP) is a title IV program that provides tutoring, orientations, and counseling for migrants planning to enter college. CAMP programs are found on many university campuses and have been successful for migrant students. They have lowered freshmen dropout rates by offering academic support work options to students during their first year of college (National Commission on Migrant Education, 1992).
- The College Bound program is a summer program for seniors to assist them in the transition from high school into college. Students work, study, and receive assistance and counseling at a college campus; approximately 90% of College Bound students enroll in colleges the following semester.
- Graduation rates of migrant students have risen from 10% to more than 40%. This increase is attributed to the U.S. Department of Education's Migrant Education Program, which for more than twenty years has worked with states to prepare migrant students for a successful transition to postsecondary education or employment (Morse & Hammer, 1998). Admission into college requires migrant students to have completed high school with the appropriate courses for postsecondary education, knowledge of application requirements and financial aid deadlines, and strategies and skills to progress through a system that was not created for migrant students. Factors that have contributed and facilitated migrant

students' college attendance are: access to counseling centers that offer an array of options; exercise of their personal motivation and sense of self-efficacy; access to financial aid and scholarships, loans, and work-study programs; support from family, friends, and educational personnel; and parental involvement in decisions about their children's education. Thus, schools can take an active role in ensuring that migrant students receive assistance in preparing and applying for college by providing opportunities for migrants to make up credit, being receptive of work transferred from other schools, providing assistance through tutoring, and developing study skills and test-taking skills (Morse & Hammer, 1998).

The Principal's Role

The principal's role in migrant education has changed from the inception of the program. Principals were responsible for implementing a program designed by central office staff with built-in assurances. The principal provided campus monitoring to ensure that only migrant students were served with designated funds. The migrant program, in essence, was a duplicate of the regular program in a segregated setting. The ultimate goals were to comply with the migrant application guidelines and to avoid supplanting programs.

At the present time, the principal is guided by district personnel responsible for migrant education. In identification and recruitment, the principal may select an enrollment day for migrant parents and students. This can be done prior to the start of the school or on any given date during the school year. Recruitment of migrant students can also take place at community-based sites; house to house recruitment is also available.

Identification of migrant students is important in order to provide services on a priority basis. Technically, the migrant students with the most need receive more services. The New Generation System (NGS) provides data storage concerning enrollments, academic progress and health updates. Certificates of Eligibility are also encoded in the NGS. Parents are responsible for certifying eligibility as per compliance with state and federal guidelines. The principal has access to all information in order to assure adequacy of services.

The principal is on the front line of recruitment and services for migrant students; every effort must be made to provide instructional services to students. Students who do not qualify for school-related programs can be referred to programs such as Head Start, Even Start or State Migrant Head Start. A home-based program can be provided to three and four year olds not enrolled in an early childhood program. Student development is a priority for principals once migrant identification has occurred.

The principal must also ensure that the campus is providing culturally, developmentally, and linguistically appropriate programs and materials. The promotion of research-based programs and curricula that are culturally appropriate is also part of a principal's responsibility. Additionally, the principal is also involved in adequate staff development that emphasizes training on culturally and linguistically appropriate practices.

Coordination of information is a crucial job for school leaders; the principal must communicate with other administrators, counselors, teachers and parents concerning interpretation of progress reports and test data utilized to assess student needs. Compliance with opportunities for students to participate in extra-curricular activities is also important. The principal serves as an advocate for migrant students and their families by promoting the evaluation and modification of instructional programs to meet student needs.

Secondary school principals have additional responsibilities; they must inform students, parents and staff about local and state requirements for promotion and graduation as well as pre-requisites for post secondary education. Adequate placement of students and documentation of local and out-of-district credit completion are ultimately responsibilities of the principal. The principal also plays a significant role in ensuring that students have an opportunity to complete their credits or make up work. Besides focusing on students graduating under the Recommended or Distinguished Achievement Plan (in applicable states), the principal also refers students for Advanced Placement Courses, Bilingual/ESL, Gifted and Talented, Magnet programs, Special Education and Title I programs.

The principal is involved in numerous migrant related activities that ensure student success. Ultimately, the graduation rate, test data and post secondary attendance serve as gauges indicative of the combined efforts of numerous persons to transform the education of migrant students into a positive and productive experience.

Conclusion

This chapter has provided an array of information on the lives of migrant children. These students encounter hardships in the fields, including health aliments they suffer because of the serious type of work they and their families undertake. The poverty that surrounds the lives of these students is a way of life. Also, migrant students encounter many challenges, generally due to their mobile lifestyles. Consequently, many migrant students fail to graduate. A supportive school environment can serve to overcome some of the barriers migrant students encounter.

This chapter also provided information on how schools can nurture a positive environment for parental involvement. Several examples of lessons, diversified with culturally relevant content, were discussed. Examples of instructional strategies that have been successful for migrant students were also presented.

The authors ask that all educators keep one thing in mind: migrant students dream of being successful and of not having the same lifestyles as their families. Many want to work hard, graduate, and be successful. They, more than other students, know about work ethics. Educators have the power to help make their dreams come true. This can be done by training teachers to set high expectations for students, being sensitive to their needs, and providing opportunities for them to be successful.

Applying Your Knowledge

You are the principal of Ochoa Elementary School. A parent informs you that her child, Teresa, feels uncomfortable in Ms. Henry's fifth grade class. You begin to question the parent and as the dialog continues, you realize that Teresa was asked several questions about her experience picking apricots when she returned to school in late September. The parent reports that this had also happened to three other students in Teresa's class. The children were embarrassed by the approach Ms. Henry used to have these migrant students share their summer experiences with the rest of the students. The other students were surprised that Teresa and the three other migrant students actually worked to help support their families or took care of their younger siblings while both parents worked in the fields. You decide to meet with Ms. Henry to discuss how the migrant students felt while they were asked to discuss some very private experiences. Ms. Henry stated that she was trying to empower the migrant students by portraying them as heroes to the rest of the class. Not realizing what she was doing, Ms. Henry had been singling out or profiling the migrant students.

QUESTIONS

1. Why did the migrant students feel different from the rest of the students?
2. As the principal, what would you tell Ms. Henry?
3. As the principal, what approaches would you suggest to Ms. Henry?
4. How can Ms. Henry better understand migrant students?

QUESTIONS FOR THOUGHT

1. How can principals ensure that the educational experiences of migrant students will be more positive on their campuses?
2. How can migrant students overcome the challenges they encounter in schools because of their mobile lifestyles?
3. Explain why principals must support culturally relevant teaching for all students.
4. Discuss how the hardships migrant families encounter in the fields can be detrimental to their children's success in school.
5. What are the obstacles that often keep migrant students from graduating?
6. What approaches can principals implement so migrant parents feel more welcomed on their campuses?

For Additional Information

Migrant Education Program, U.S. Department of Education *www.ed.gov/ programs/mep/index.html*

Office of Elementary and Secondary Education, U. S. Department of Education *www.edlgov/about/offices/list/oese/ome/index.html*

Resources for Migrant Education, AEL, Inc. *www.ael.org*

The Best Migrant Education Resources *www.lone-eagles.com/migrant.html*

References

Baker, L., & Brown, A. (1984). Metacognitive skills and reading. In P. D. Pearson, R. Barr, M. L. Kamil, & P. Mosenthal, (Eds.), *Handbook of reading research, Vol. I* (pp. 353–394). New York: Longman.

Banks, J. A. (1988). Approaches to multicultural curriculum reform. *Multicultural Leader, 1*(2), 1–2.

Banks, J. A. (1994). *Multicultural education: Theory and practice.* Boston, MA: Allyn & Bacon.

Barba, R. H. (1995). *Science in the multicultural classroom: A guide to teaching and learning.* Boston, MA: Allyn & Bacon.

Bertrand, D. G. (2001a). *Uncle Chente's Picnic-El picnic de Tío Chente.* Houston, TX: Arte Público Press.

Bertrand, D. G. (2001b). *Trino's Time.* Houston, TX: Arte Público Press.

Cawelti, G. (1999). Improving achievement. *American School Board Journal, 186,* 34–37.

Chavkin, N. F. (1991). *Family lives and parental involvement in migrant students' education.* Washington DC: U.S. Department of Education, Office of Educational Research and Improvement. (ERIC Document Reproduction Service No. ED335174)

Druin, G. (1986). *Effective schooling and at-risk students: What the research shows.* Portland, OR: Northwest Educational Laboratories. (ERIC Document Reproduction Service No. ED275926)

Dyson, D. S. (1983). *Utilizing local resources at the local level.* Fact Sheet. Las Cruces, NM: ERIC Clearinghouse on Rural Education and Small Schools. (ERIC Document Reproduction Service No. ED286702)

Escamilla, K. (1996). *Do they really know their culture?* Paper presented at the annual conference of the Arizona Association for Bilingual Education. Flagstaff, Arizona, February.

Escamilla, K. (1987). *Incorporating Mexican American history and culture in the social studies curriculum.* (ERIC Document Reproduction Service No. ED393645)

Fix, M. & Passel, J. S. (1994). *Immigration and immigrants: Setting the record straight.* Washington DC: The Urban Institute.

Garza, C. L. (1996). *In my family-En mi familia.* San Francisco, CA: Children's Book Press.

Gonzales, F. (1991). *Validating the students' culture in the classroom.* San Antonio, TX: Intercultural Development Research Association.

Hernández, J. Y. (1997). *White bread competition.* Houston, TX: Arte Público Press.

Horn, L. J., & Chen, X. (1998). *Toward resiliency: At risk students who make it to college.* Washington, DC: U.S. Department of Education Office of Educational Research and Improvement.

Jackson County Migrant Education. *MIGRANT EDUCATION—HARVEST OF HOPE.* Medford, OR: Jackson County Educational Service District, 1981. (ERIC Document Reproduction Service No. ED212441)

Johnson, D., Johnson, R., & Maruyama, G. (1983). Interdependence and interpersonal attraction among heterogeneous and homogeneous individuals: A theoretical formulation and a meta-analysis of the research. *Review of Educational Research, 53*(1), 5–54.

Johnson, F. C., Levy, R. H., Morales, J. A., Morse, S. C., & Prokop, M. K. (1986). *Migrant students at the secondary level: Issues and opportunities for change.* Las Cruces, NM: ERIC Clearinghouse on Rural Education and Small Schools. (ERIC Document Reproduction Service No. ED270242)

Kissam, E. (1993). Formal characteristics of the farm labor market: Implications for farm labor policy in the 1990s. In *Migrant Farmworkers in the United States.* Briefing of the Commission on Security and Cooperation in Europe, Washington, DC: U.S. Government Printing Office.

Lachtman, O. D. (2002). *Pepita finds out-Lo que Pepita descubre.* Houston, TX: Arte Público Press.

Lachtman, O. D. (2001). *The summer of el pintor.* Houston, TX: Arte Público Press.

Ladson-Billings, G. (1990). Like lightning in a bottle: Attempting to capture the pedagogical excellence of successful teachers of Black students. *International Journal of Qualitative Studies in Education, 3*(4), 335–344.

Ladson-Billings, G. (1992). Liberatory consequences of literacy: A case of culturally relevant instruction for African American students. *Journal of Negro Education, 61*(3), 378–391.

Ladson-Billings, G. (1995). But that's just good teaching! The case for culturally relevant pedagogy. *Theory into Practice, 34*(3), 159–165.

Levy, R. (1987). *Migrant attrition project.* Oneonta, NY: Eastern Stream Center on Resources and Training.

Marines, D. & Ortiz de Montellano, B. (1993). *Multiculturalism in science: Why and how?* Presented at National Science Teacher Association Conference, Oaxpec, Mexico.

Martinez, F. (1997). *Spirits of the high mesa.* Houston, TX: Arte Público Press.

Martinez, Y. G. (1994). *Narratives of survival: Life histories of Mexican American youth from migrant and seasonal farmworkers who have graduated from High School Equivalency Program.* Unpublished. University of South Florida.

Martinez, Y. G., Scott, J., Cranston-Gingras, A., & Platt, J. S. (1994). Voices from the field: Interviews with students from migrant farmworker families. *Journal of Educational Issues of Language Minority Students, 10,* 333–348.

Martinez, Y. G., & Cranston-Gingras, A. (1996). Migrant farmworker students and the educational process: Barriers to high school completion. *The High School Journal, 80,*(1), 28–38.

Martinez, Y. G., & Velazquez, J. A. (2000). *Involving migrant families in education.* Charleston, WV: ERIC Clearinghouse on Rural Education and Small Schools. (ERIC Document Reproduction Service No. ED448010)

Menchaca, V. D. (1996). The missing link in teacher preparation programs. *Journal of Educational Issues of Language Minority Students, 17,* 1–9.

Menchaca, V. D. (2000). Culturally relevant curriculum for limited-English proficient students. *The Journal of the Texas Association for Bilingual Education, 5*(1), 55–59.

Menchaca, V. D., & Ruiz-Escalante, J. A. (1995). *Instructional strategies for migrant students.* Charleston, WV: Appalachia Educational Laboratory, ERIC Clearinghouse on Rural Education and Small Schools. (ERIC Document Reproduction Service No. ED388491)

Migrant Education Secondary Assistance Project. (1989). *MESA National MSRTS Executive Summary.* Geneseo, NY: BOCES Geneseo Migrant Center.

Migrant Youth Program. (1985). *Perceptions of why migrant students drop out of school and what can be done to encourage them to graduate.* Albany, NY: Upstate Regional Offices and Migrant Unit, State Education Department.

Mora, P. (2001). *The bakery lady-La señora de la panaderia.* Houston, TX: Arte Público Press.

Morse, S. & Hammer, P. C. (1998). *Migrant students attending college: Facilitating their success.* Charleston, WV: ERIC Clearinghouse on Rural Education and Small Schools. (ERIC Document Reproduction Service No. ED423097)

National Center for Farmworker Health. *About America's farmworkers.* Available *http://www.ncth.org/abouttws.htm, 2001.*

National Commission on Migrant Education. (1992). *Invisible children: A portrait of migrant children in the United States.* Final Report. Washington DC: U.S. Department of Education. (ERIC Document Reproduction Service No. ED348206)

National Program for Secondary Credit Exchange and Accrual. (1994). *Options and resources for achieving credit accrual for secondary-aged migrant youth.* Washington DC: U.S. Department of Education. Office of Migrant Education.

Neuman, J. (1988). *What should we do about the highly mobile student? A research brief.* Mount Vernon, WA: Educational Service District 189. (ERIC Document Reproduction Service No. ED305545)

Nieto, S. (1996). *Affirming diversity: The sociopolitical context of multicultural education* (2[nd]ed.). White Plains, NY: Longman.

Oliveira, V., Effland, J. R., & Hamm, S. (1993). *Hired farm labor use of fruit, vegetable, and horticultural specialty farms.* Washington DC: U.S. Department of Agriculture.

Platt, J. S., Cranston-Gingras, A., & Scott, J. (1991). Understanding and educating migrant students. *Preventing School Failure, 36*(1), 41–46.

Rasmussen, L. (1988). *Migrant students at the secondary level: Issues and opportunities for change.* Las Cruces, NM: ERIC Clearinghouse on Rural Education and Small Schools. (ERIC Document Reproduction Service No. ED296814)

Revett, K. H. (1986). *Mexico and Mexican Americans in US history textbooks.* Unpublished master's thesis, The University of Texas at Austin.

Ruiz-Escalante, J. A., & Menchaca, V. D. (1999). Creating school-community partnerships for minority parents. *Texas Teacher Education Forum, 24,* 45–49.

Salerno, A. (1991). *Migrant students who leave school early: Strategies for retrieval.* Geneseo, NY: BOCES Geneseo Migrant Center. (Eric Document 335 179)

Salinas, A. (1999). *Ya será hora?-Is it time?* Hidalgo, Texas: Hidalgo ISD Permanent Scholarship Foundation.

Salinas, A. (2004). *Qué será? What is it?* Hidalgo, Texas: Hidalgo ISD Permanent Scholarship Foundation.

Shotland, J. (1989). *Full fields, empty cupboard: The nutritional status of migrant farmworkers in America.* Washington DC: Public Voice for Food and Health Policy. (ERIC Document Reproduction Service No. ED323076)

U. S. Bureau of Census. (1993). *The foreign-born population in the United States, 1990 census of population.* Washington, DC: U.S. Department of Commerce.

U. S. Department of Education. (1994). *Improving America's Schools Act,* 103–382 statute, Title 1, part C, (Migrant Education) Program Purpose, Section 1301–(4). Washington, DC: Office of Educational Research and Improvement.

Valdes, G. (1996). *Con respeto: Bridging the distance between culturally diverse families and schools: An enthnographic portrait.* New York: Teachers College Press.

Vamos, Inc. (1992). *National migrant student graduation rate formula, for the national program for secondary credit exchange and accrual.* Geneseo, NY: BOCES Geneseo Migrant Center.

Academic Enhancement, Intervention, and Preparation Programs

5

Karen M. Watt
Mary Alice Reyes

You can't control the choices students
make for post-secondary education,
but you can control the opportunity
for preparation.

—*Martha Salmon (2004)*

Objectives

1. Provide the historical background that led to the creation of selected academic enhancement, intervention and preparation programs
2. Discuss the basic components of selected academic enhancement, intervention and preparation programs
3. Highlight the similarities and differences between the programs
4. Show how school staff can contribute to the success of each of the programs

Introduction and Background

Of the billions of dollars spent to ensure educational opportunity for America's children, very little is spent on programs that encourage students to prepare for, enter and graduate from college. Many programs focus on dropout prevention, remediation, and after-school academic support activities. This chapter highlights programs that address the large gaps in academic performance and disparity in college enrollment rates between students from economically disadvantaged families and more advantaged students. One of the goals of early intervention programs is to provide at-risk student groups with the college preparation skills and knowledge needed to enter and succeed in college (Perna & Swail, 2001). While existing preparatory programs offer a variety of services, those that have the potential to increase the number of underrepresented students who enroll and succeed in college offer high quality instruction, special services such as tutoring, or a redesigned curriculum that better suits the students' needs (Gandara & Bial, 2001; Gandara & Moreno, 2002).

In 1954, the Supreme Court's ruling in Brown v. Board of Education recognized the urgency for equitable educational opportunities for all students. For disadvantaged students a college education remained unattainable because of academic, economic, cultural and social barriers (Moore, 1997). By the early 1960's Congress realized that the nation's commitment to economic circumstance extended beyond high school. In support of this commitment, Congress established a series of programs to help low-income Americans enter college, graduate and move on to participate more fully in America's economic and social life (Upward Bound, 1999 as cited in Schroth, 2001).

Johnson's War on Poverty spurred the passing of the Economic Opportunity Act of 1964, legislation that increased attention to the country's large disadvantaged population and raised an awareness of the social and economic advantages of educating all children. Johnson's legislation provided funds for a number of programs, several of which provided funds for the pursuit of postsecondary degrees. Out of this legislation, Upward Bound and Talent Search were born (Schroth, 2001).

In 1968, the Special Services for Disadvantaged Students Program was created and later termed Student Support Services (SSS). Authorized by the Higher Education Amendments, SSS became the third in the series of educational opportunity programs. SSS programs provide disadvantaged college students with academic and motivational support to enable them to complete their postsecondary education and pursue graduate studies. These three initiatives, Upward Bound, Talent Search, and SSS, became known as the TRIO Programs (Federal TRIO Programs, 2000 as cited in Schroth, 2001).

Recently, the Office of Postsecondary Education which houses Federal TRIO programs, developed Educational Opportunity Centers (EOC). These centers provide counseling and information on college admissions to qualified adults who want to enter or continue a program of postsecondary education. The goal of EOC is to increase the number of adult participants who enroll in postsecondary education institutions by providing financial-aid counseling and assisting in the application process. Some of the services provided by the program include academic advice, career workshops, information on financial assistance, tutoring and mentoring *(http://www.ed.gov/programs/trioeoc/purpose.html)*.

Since the birth of TRIO, several other programs have been designed to increase college attendance and success rates of underrepresented groups of students. These include SCORE, Project GRAD, GEAR UP and AVID. All four of these programs are "distinctive in their focus on ensuring that promising Latino and other minority students do what is necessary to attend college" (Slavin & Calderon, 2001, p. 79). These initiatives will be discussed in this chapter.

Upward Bound

Upward Bound is a federally funded program that provides low income students with extra instruction, study skills and tutorials, usually after school or on Saturdays, and an intensive six-week summer program on a college campus. Upward Bound students enroll in college at a higher rate than their comparison peers (Burkheimer, Riccobono, & Wisenbaker, 1979). Myers and Schirm (1999) also found that Upward Bound students received more academic credits in math and social studies than did a comparison group.

Upward Bound represents the largest federal intervention aimed at helping students attain a postsecondary education, until GEAR UP grants were established as part of the High Education Amendments of 1998 (Myers & Schirm, 1999). In 1966, $2 million were allocated to support 42 Upward Bound projects, and in 1989–90, $426.1 million were awarded to support 177 projects around the country (Hexter, 1990 as cited in Schroth, 2001).

All Upward Bound projects must provide the following services:

- instruction in reading, writing, study skills, and other subjects necessary for success in education beyond high school,
- academic, financial, or personal counseling,
- exposure to academic programs and cultural events,
- tutorial services for Upward Bound classes as well as those taken in the student's local school,
- mentoring programs (Students are closely monitored so staff can intervene should the students experience problems),
- information on postsecondary education opportunities,
- assistance in completing college entrance and financial aid applications,
- assistance in preparing for college entrance examinations,
- work study positions to expose participants to careers requiring a postsecondary degree (Upward Bound, 2000 as cited in Schroth, 2001).

Natriello, McDill, and Pallas (1990) concluded that Upward Bound is successful in getting students to graduate from high school and enter college, but it does little to ensure that students who enter college will persist in attaining a college degree. This lack of encouragement for student persistence is attributed to too little time devoted to academic instruction during high school, and no definite strategy for intervention once an Upward Bound student enters college (U. S. Department of Education, 1991).

Talent Search

Talent Search serves students in grades six through twelve who are low-income and potential first-generation college students. A 1968 amendment to Title IV of the Higher Education Act of 1965 that created Talent Search stipulated that participants must have "exceptional potential" for postsecondary education (Hexter, 1990). By the year 2000, over 300,000 students were enrolled in a Talent Search program (Schroth, 2001).

Rosenbaum (1992) summarized the three major goals of Talent Search:

1. Identifying youth of extreme financial and cultural need with an exceptional potential for postsecondary education and encouraging them to complete secondary school and undertake further education.
2. Publicizing existing forms of student financial aid, including aid furnished under the Higher Education Act.

3. Encouraging secondary school or college dropouts of demonstrated aptitude to reenter educational programs (p. 104 as cited in Schroth, 2001).

Agencies receiving Talent Search dollars may provide the following services:

1. Academic, financial, career, or personal counseling including advice on entry or re-entry to secondary or postsecondary programs,
2. Career exploration and aptitude assessments,
3. Tutorial services to help students achieve in their academic classes,
4. Information on postsecondary education,
5. Information on student financial assistance,
6. Assistance in completing college admissions and financial aid applications,
7. Assistance in preparing for college entrance exams,
8. Mentoring programs to give students personal attention when problems arise,
9. Special activities for 6th, 7th, and 8th graders,
10. Workshops for the families of participants (Talent Search, 1999 as cited in Schroth, 2001).

By providing this wide array of services, Talent Search is able to increase the students' chances for entering and completing college. One drawback is that Talent Search directors often attempt to provide interventions with a limited number of program staff (Hexter, 1990 as cited in Schroth, 2001).

Student Support Services (SSS)

The third of the group of TRIO programs is Student Support Services (SSS) which centers on students while they are in college or other postsecondary educational programs. The goals of SSS are to increase the college retention and graduation rates of its participants and to facilitate the transition of students from one level of higher education to the next (Student Support Services, 1999 as cited in Schroth, 2001).

The government requires that SSS provide students with:

1. Instruction in basic study skills,
2. Tutorial services,
3. Academic, financial, or personal counseling,
4. Assistance in securing admission and financial aid for enrollment in four-year institutions,
5. Assistance in securing admission and financial aid for enrollment in graduate and professional programs,
6. Information about career options,
7. Mentoring,
8. Special services for students with limited English proficiency (U. S. Department of Education, 1994 as cited in Schroth, 2001).

Only institutions of higher education may sponsor SSS programs and must insure that SSS participants are offered financial aid packages to meet their full financial needs. In 2000, 796 colleges and universities nationwide hosted SSS programs (U.S. Department of Education, 1994 as cited in Schroth, 2001).

In 1994, 43% of the SSS budget was for two-year colleges and 57% was for four-year colleges, with an estimated annual expenditure per student of approximately $860. According to a national study of SSS programs, after three years of program implementation, the SSS programs were found to be effective in targeting disadvantaged students and providing help beyond the typical services that students normally accessed (U.S. Department of Education, 1998).

After three years of implementation, approximately 58% of the students who began at two-year institutions were still enrolled at a college (either the same institution where they began or another college). Retention (for SSS participants) at the same institution from the first to second year increased by 7%, and by 9% from the second year to the third year. The effective processes, activities, and services helping SSS participants included peer tutoring, instructional courses and workshops, and cultural events. In particular, peer tutoring showed a statistically significant positive effect on student retention levels (U.S. Department of Education, 1998).

SCORE

SCORE, or Score for College, (Johnson, 1983, as cited in Fashola & Slavin, 1998) is a dropout prevention/college preparatory program that was developed in partnership with the Orange County Department of Education and the University of California, Irvine. The program staff conducted a comprehensive, ongoing formative evaluation during the first three years of operation (1979–1982). Data gathered in the formative phase of the program was used to make programmatic changes to more effectively accomplish the goals and objectives of the program *(http://www.scoreed. com/presenting/record.htm).*

The program targets at-risk students in grades 9–12 whose likelihood of graduating from high school or enrolling in college is perceived to be low by their teachers. Students receive career counseling, tutoring, opportunities to join clubs, and a summer academic program focusing on college preparatory courses. SCORE also focuses on moving students out of English as a Second Language classes and into the mainstream (Fashola & Slavin, 1998).

In several case studies conducted on SCORE schools, findings revealed that the number of Latino students enrolled in algebra, chemistry and physics increased, as well as participation in SAT taking (Wells, 1981). University of California eligibility rates of the first group of SCORE students were compared to a random sample of high school African American and Latino graduates. Eligibility rates for SCORE students were 40% as compared to the random sample's 5.2%; SCORE students also enrolled in 4-year colleges at a higher rate (41%) than the other group (11%) (Wells, 1981, as cited in Fashola & Slavin, 1998).

SCORE was awarded Exemplary Status in 1982 by the Elementary and Secondary Education Act (ESEA), Title IV-C, based on a comprehensive summative evaluation conducted by an outside evaluator. The comprehensive evaluation yielded statistically significant data (P<.001) in all major areas *(http://www.scoreed.com/presenting/record.htm).* The comprehensive evaluation revealed that all major program goals and objectives were met or exceeded, in addition to the following:

1. Of the first SCORE class in 1981, 40% were eligible to attend the University of California by having completed the A-F course requirements with a high enough combination of grade point average and test score. This finding was statistically significant (P<.001).
2. Of this same senior class, 40. 8% enrolled in a four-year college or university. This finding was statistically significant (P<.001).
3. Of those students who participated in a Summer Residential Program and received school year assistance through the guidance, tutoring, motivation, and parent programs, 56% enrolled in a four-year college or university. This finding was statistically significant (P<.001).

By the end of the third year, 100% of SCORE students were enrolled in two or more college preparatory courses at their local high schools as compared to 52% at a comparison high school *http://www.score-ed.com/presenting/record.htm.*

Project GRAD

Project GRAD (Graduation Really Achieves Dreams) is also a dropout prevention/college preparation program developed by the former CEO of Tenneco and the University of Houston in 1989. GRAD provides scholarship incentives for students who graduate on time with at least a 2.5 GPA. The effectiveness of this program was demonstrated in one study that showed the percentage of students graduating (50%) and attending college (10%) rose to 78% and 60% respectively (Ketelsen, 1994; McAdoo, 1998).

Project GRAD has expanded into a private, not-for-profit organization that works in partnership with high schools and their feeder middle schools to implement multiple reform models that lead to higher graduation rates and college attendance rates. Nationally in 1999, Project GRAD served over 68,000 students in 92 schools (Opuni, 1999).

Project GRAD implements a series of interventions to assist a school in preparing more students to graduate from high school and enter post-secondary educational institutions. First, Project GRAD uses Consistency Management and Cooperative Discipline that facilitate classroom management and student/teacher cooperation. Second, Project GRAD implements educational initiatives to supplement basic elementary and middle school reading and math curricula. Third, the initiative works through Communities in Schools to improve the quality and level of parental and community support for school activities. Finally Project GRAD implements a comprehensive outreach program which includes a community-wide Walk for Success to recruit students and their parents.

One of Project GRAD's primary goals is to raise the college enrollment rates of graduates from its high schools. In addition, Project GRAD provides scholarships to students who graduate on time, take a minimum of three years of mathematics, maintain a 2.5 grade point average, and complete a minimum of two summer institutes provided by local universities (Opuni, 1999).

GEAR UP

The GEAR UP (Gaining Early Awareness and Readiness for Undergraduate Programs) program was established under the Higher Education Amendments of 1998 to support programs which provide information on early college awareness, academic support, and financial assistance to disadvantaged students to encourage them to enter and succeed in post-secondary education. The awards are competitive for up to five years in duration, and the grants are available to states and partnerships between middle schools, high schools, colleges and universities, community organizations, and businesses. The intent is to positively impact low-performing schools serving low-income and minority students. The uniqueness of the program is that it serves entire cohorts of low-income students rather than those chosen based upon some pre-determined criteria. The grant stipulates that at least 50% of the participants must be eligible for free or reduced lunch or rank at 150% of the poverty level *(http://www.ed.gov/offices/OPE/gearup).*

In addition, the program serves students as early as 6th or 7th grade when they are beginning to form their academic aspirations and developing their plans regarding future careers. GEAR UP continues to support the students throughout their high school years to ensure that they are prepared to succeed once enrolled in college. GEAR UP differs from other programs in that it is a working partnership between public and private entities engaged in a common purpose: to significantly increase the number of low-income students prepared to enter and succeed in post-secondary education. Schools, universities, community colleges, business and community partners share in this responsibility. More importantly, the program focuses on local and sustainable initiatives that will continue to prepare new cohorts of students as they reach middle school (National Council for Community and Education Partnerships, 2004).

The GEAR UP initiative provides support for schools to develop a college-going culture through engagement in systemic reform that provides all students, not just a select few, an opportunity to prepare for college. Reform initiatives may include aligning of the K–16 curriculum, eliminating academic tracking, and implementing professional development models that prepare teachers to integrate technology and other innovations into the instructional program.

Comprehensive services offered to students such as mentoring, tutoring, and counseling are designed to raise students' educational aspirations and prepare them academically for success in college. Other services such as preparation for college admissions tests, dissemination of information concerning the college application process, and financial aid counseling, all serve to further increase college awareness and preparation. To demystify the college experience, students also participate in tours and engage in summer activities on college campuses.

Since parental expectations influence and are predictive of the educational aspirations of children (Looker & Pineo, 1983; Mau, 1995), GEAR UP focuses on providing parents with information in an effort to raise their awareness of college entrance requirements and their very important role in their children's preparation for post-secondary education. Financial constraints often present themselves as barriers to a post-secondary education for low-income parents; therefore every GEAR UP student receives the 21st Century Scholars Certificate indicating notification of eligibility for financial aid. Some programs also offer a scholarship component to provide college financial assistance to its participating students (Cunningham, Redmond, & Merisotis, 2003).

The program is currently implemented in 47 states and serves approximately 1.2 million students. Since its inception, funding has reached almost 1.2 billion which supports 280 partnerships and 36 state grants (*http://www.edpartnerships.org*).

AVID

AVID (Advancement Via Individual Determination) is a college preparatory program that was established in 1980 in one English teacher's classroom as a means to serve students who were recently bussed to a newly desegregated suburban high school. Mary Catherine Swanson began a social and academic support elective class called AVID to assist this group of students in their rigorous courses in which they were recently enrolled. Mrs. Swanson believed her students could succeed in the most rigorous curriculum, such as Advanced Placement classes, but only needed extra support provided by the AVID elective. Of the 30 students who began AVID in 1980, 28 went to college (Mehan, Villanueva, Hubbard, & Lintz, 1996).

AVID has since spread to many states, and in some cases, such as in Texas, has been used as a school reform model (Watt, Yanez, & Cossio, 2002). The Obey-Porter Comprehensive School Reform Demonstration Program (CSRD) legislation includes nine components that schools must use in order to implement a reform model. These nine components have been aligned with the AVID essentials that were developed by Swanson in 1980.

AVID has established indicators by which to measure the success of the program. Schools that implement AVID must successfully implement 11 essentials to be certified as an AVID school. The 11 AVID essentials include: 1) student recruitment and selection requirements; 2) voluntary participation agreements from student, staff and parents; 3) integration of the AVID elective class within the regular school day; 4) enrollment in rigorous curriculum that satisfies college requirements; 5) introduction of a strong writing and reading curriculum; 6) introduction of inquiry for critical thinking skills; 7) emphasis on collaborative instruction; 8) academic assistance through tutoring with trained college tutors; 9) evaluation of program implementation through data collection and analysis; 10) district/school commitment to AVID funding appropriations and compliance; and 11) interdisciplinary site team collaboration (Swanson, 2000). Implementation of the AVID essentials ensures a school environment conducive to empowering students to become more responsible for their learning, and thus increases their college preparation and educational expectations to pursue a college degree.

The significance of AVID in schools has been documented in studies conducted within the California school system. Students enrolled in AVID on a continuous basis demonstrated a greater propensity towards attempting and completing college-level courses, thereby producing a larger number of AVID students enrolling in colleges or universities than AVID student dropouts or students with no AVID background (Slavin & Calderon, 2001, p. 86). AVID's reputation for improving college rates and academic success in underserved minorities assisted in increasing its implementation in over 700 U.S. schools and its overseas implementation in U.S. government sponsored schools in Europe and Asia, subsequently earning an international status (Slavin & Calderon, 2001, p. 88).

Recently the AVID program was reviewed by the organization of Building Engineering and Science Talent (BEST). AVID was found to be "notable," which meant that there was at least one rigorous, independent study of AVID (BEST, 2004). In addition, Watt, Powell and Mendiola (2004) found that AVID students in Texas outperformed their peers in end-of-course exams, state assessments, and participation in advanced graduation plans over a three-year period.

Administrator's Role

For a high school or middle school principal, choosing an intervention program can be daunting. There are many opportunities available for principals seeking to decrease their dropout rates and increase the college-going rates of their students. Finding the best fit for an administrator's campus is the challenge.

Considerations administrators need to make when selecting a program for implementation include funding, technical assistance, links to other programs, sustainability and evaluation. Typically the administrator seeks out programs that are supported by a funding source so that technical support is available in the first two to three years. Throughout the first three years of implementation, administrators should work with staff members to develop a sustainability plan for when the initial funding source comes to an end.

In a recent study of AVID, Watt, Huerta, and Cossio (2004) found that the campus leaders had a direct impact on program implementation. Major findings included the need for the campus administrators to attend implementation training along with their teachers, as well as the need for administrators to provide ideological and financial support for the program. Shared responsibility, low teacher turnover, appropriate staff development, and appropriate resource allocation are critical to the success of any implemented program.

Summary

In summary, many models have been developed over the years that address issues of access and equity for students underrepresented in higher education. Most of these models have been developed because of federal legislation resulting in the allocation of millions of dollars for college preparation and career guidance and training. Though not all programs have resulted in the preparation of large numbers of students for college (Project GRAD, AVID), some have been used for school reform models (AVID) and for supplemental resources (GEAR UP, TRIO). Table 1 shows various characteristics of each model discussed in this chapter.

Applying Your Knowledge

You are the principal of a high school that has a diverse student body. The ethnic makeup is 70% Hispanic, 25% African American, and 5% White and Asian. Over 60% of the student body qualifies for free and reduced lunch and 25% are limited English proficient. Though your students have always done well on state-mandated tests resulting in a high accountability rating, only 3% are enrolled in Advanced Placement classes and only 17% attend four-year colleges and universities. Your freshman class typically has 800 students enrolled and in addition, most of your students are still graduating on the lowest graduation plans.

QUESTIONS

1. What are some steps you as the campus instructional leader will take to address the issue of low enrollment in Advanced Placement and low college-going rates?
2. Which intervention programs discussed in this chapter would be appropriate to implement to increase the number of students graduating on more rigorous graduation plans? How will you find out about these programs, and how are they funded?
3. Which intervention programs discussed in this chapter could be implemented to assist students in acquiring financial aid for college?
4. Describe your role as campus leaders in the implementation of the intervention program(s) you choose to address the issues stated above.

QUESTIONS FOR THOUGHT

1. What are the major advantages and disadvantages of each of the intervention programs discussed in this chapter?
2. What are the criteria for selecting students for each of the following programs: AVID, GEAR UP, Upward Bound, and Talent Search?
3. Should administrators rely on the government to offer funding for intervention programs? What are some alternatives for funding intervention programs?
4. How are intervention programs sustained, and is sustainability an important consideration?
5. Which intervention programs are supported by research? Why is it important to consider only programs that have a research base for implementation?

Table 1

	Year Established	Funding Source	Purpose	Main Services Provided
Upward Bound	1966	U.S. Department of Education—Amendment to Higher Education Act	Aimed at helping students attain a postsecondary education.	• Instruction • Counseling • Tutoring • Mentoring • Assistance in applying to college and completing financial aid forms
Talent Search	1968	U.S. Department of Education—Amendment to Higher Education Act	Encourage economically disadvantaged youth to complete secondary school and undertake further education. Encourage secondary school or college dropouts of demonstrated aptitude to reenter educational programs.	• Academic, financial, career, or personal counseling • Career exploration and aptitude assessments • Tutorial services • Assistance in completing college admissions and financial aid applications • Mentoring programs • Family workshops
SSS	1968	U.S. Department of Education—Amendment to Higher Education Act	Increase the college retention and graduation rates and facilitate the transition of students from one level of higher education to the next.	• Study skills • Tutorial services • Academic, financial, or personal counseling • Assistance in securing admission and financial aid for enrollment in four-year institutions • Information about career options • Mentoring • Special services for LEP students
SCORE	1979	Orange County Department of Education & University of California at Irvine	Dropout prevention/college preparatory program.	• Career counseling • Tutoring • Opportunities to join clubs • Summer academic program focusing on college preparatory courses • Moves students out of ESL classes and into the mainstream

	Year Established	Funding Source	Purpose	Main Services Provided
AVID	1981	Private, not-for-profit organization; Various funding sources: grants, local & state funding	To restructure the teaching methods of an entire school and to open access to the curricula that will ensure four-year college eligibility to almost all students.	• AVID elective class • Professional development • Enrollment of students in rigorous curriculum • Strong writing and reading curriculum • Inquiry for critical thinking skills • Collaborative instruction • Tutoring with trained college tutors
Project GRAD	1989	Tenneco & University of Houston; now private, not-for-profit organization	Dropout prevention/college preparation program. Series of interventions to assist a school in preparing more students to graduate from high school and enter post-secondary educational institutions.	• Provides scholarship incentives for students who graduate on time with at least a 2.5 GPA • Consistency Management and Cooperative Discipline • Supplement basic elementary and middle school reading and math curricula • Improve the quality and level of parental and community support
GEAR UP	1998	U. S. Department of Education	To provide information on early college awareness, academic support, and financial assistance to disadvantaged students to encourage them to enter and succeed in post-secondary education.	• Mentoring • Tutoring • Counseling • Preparation for college admissions tests • Dissemination of information concerning the college application process • Financial aid counseling

Additional Information

www.avidonline.org

www.ed.gov/gearup

www.projectgrad.org

www.score.org

www.trioprograms.org

References

BEST. (2004). *The talent imperative: Meeting America's challenge in science and engineering, ASAP.* San Diego, CA: BEST.

Burkheimer, G. J., Riccobono, J., & Wisenbaker, J. (1979). *Final report: Evaluation study of the Upward Bound program—a second follow-up.* Durham, NC: Research Triangle Institute, Center for Educational Research and Evaluation.

Cunningham, A., Redmond, C., & Merisotis, J. (2003). *Investing early. Intervention Programs in Selected U.S. States.* Montreal, Canada: Institute for Higher Education Policy.

Fashola, O. S., & Slavin, R. E. (1998). Promising programs for elementary and middle schools: Evidence of effectiveness and replicability. *Journal of Education for Students Placed at Risk, 2,* 251–307.

Federal TRIO Programs. (2000). U. S. Department of Education. *http://www.trioprograms.org.*

Gandara, P. & Bial, D. (2001). *Paving the way to postsecondary education: K–12 intervention programs for underrepresented youth.* Washington, DC: U.S. Department of Education, National Center for Educational Statistics.

Gandara, P., & Moreno, J. F. (2002). Introduction: The Puente Project: Issues and perspectives on preparing Latino youth for higher education. *Educational Policy, 16*(4), 463–473.

Hexter, H. (1990). *A description of federal information and outreach programs and selected state, institutional and community models.* Background paper number three. Washington, DC: Advisory Committee on Student Financial Assistance. (ERIC Document Reproduction Service No. ED 357 686)

http://www.ed.gov/offices/OPE/gearup

http://www.ed.gov/programs/trioeoc/purpose.html

http://www.score-ed.com/presenting/record.htm

Ketelsen, J. L. (1994). Jefferson Davis feeder school project. Houston, TX: Tenneco Corporation Project GRAD.

Looker, E. D. & Pineo, P. C. (1983). Social psychological variables and their relevance to the status attainment of teenagers. *The American Journal of Sociology, 88*(6), 1195–1219.

Mau, W. C. (1995). Educational planning and academic achievement of middle school students: A racial and cultural comparison. *Journal of Counseling and Development, 73*(5), 518–535.

McAdoo, M. (1998). Project GRAD's strength is in the sum of its parts. *Ford Foundation Report, 29*(2), 8–11.

Mehan, H., Villanueva, I., Hubbard, L., & Lintz, A. (1996). *Constructing school success: The consequences of untracking low-achieving students.* Cambridge, UK: Cambridge University Press.

Myers, D. E., & Shirm, A. L. (1999). *The national evaluation of Upward Bound. The short-term impact of Upward Bound: An interim report.* Washington, DC: U.S. Department of Education.

Moore, M. T. (1997). *A 1990's view of Upward Bound: Programs offered, students served, and operational issues.* Washington, DC: U.S. Department of Education.

Natriello, G., McDill, E., & Pallas, A. (1990). *Schooling disadvantaged children: Racing against catastrophe.* New York: Teachers College Press.

National Council for Community and Education Partnerships. (2004). *http://www.edpartnerships.org.*

Opuni, K. A. (1999). *Project GRAD: Program evaluation report, 1998–99.* Houston, TX: The University of Houston.

Perna, L. & Swail, W. (2001). Pre-College outreach and early intervention. *Thought & Action, 17*(1), 99–110.

Rosenbaum, J. E. (1992). *Review of two studies of Talent Search.* U.S. Department of Education Office of Policy and Planning's Design Conference for the Evaluation of the Talent Search Program (pp. 103–132). Washington, DC: U.S. Government Printing Office.

Schroth, G. (2001). Upward Bound and other TRIO programs. In G. Schroth and M. Littleton, (Eds.), *The Administration & Supervision of Special Programs in Education* (pp. 55–66). Dubuque, IA: Kendall/Hunt.

Slavin, R. E. & Calderon, M. (2001). Effective programs for Latino students. Mahwah, NJ: Lawrence Erlbaum Associates, Inc.

Student Support Services. 34 Code of Federal Regulations §646 (U.S. Government Printing Office, 1999).

Talent Search. 34 Code of Federal Regulations §646 (U.S. Government Printing Office, 1999).

Upward Bound. 34 Code of Federal Regulations §645 (U.S. Government Printing Office, 1999).

Upward Bound Math/Science Program. (2000). U. S. Department of Education. *http://www.trioprograms.org.*

U. S. Department of Education. (2004). *Proposal submitted to the Program Effectiveness Panel of the United States Department of Education SCORE.* Washington, DC: Author.

U.S. Department of Education. (1991). *Evaluation of Upward Bound: The basic approach.* Report prepared for the Office of Planning and Evaluation. Washington, DC: Author.

U.S. Department of Education. (1994). *Federal TRIO programs and the school, college, and university partnership program.* Washington, DC: U.S. Government Printing Office.

U. S. Department of Education. (1998). *National study of student support services: Third year longitudinal study results.* Washington, DC: Author.

Watt, K. M., Huerta, J., & Cossio, G. (2004). Leadership and AVID implementation Levels in four south Texas border schools. *Catalyst for Change, 33*(2), 10–14.

Watt, K. M., Powell, C. A., & Mendiola, I. D. (2004). Implications of one comprehensive school reform model for secondary school students underrepresented in higher education. *Journal of Education for Students Placed at Risk, 9*(3), 241–259.

Watt, K. M., Yañez, D., & Cossio, G. (2002). AVID: A comprehensive school reform model for Texas. *National Forum of Educational Administration and Supervision Journal, 19*(3), 43–59.

Wells, J. (1981). *SCORE: Final report presented for ESEA Title IVC.* Sacramento: California Department of Education.

Career and Technology Education

6

Norma T. Salaiz
Karen M. Watt

A new educational system is evolving throughout this nation to prepare our youth for rewarding, high-performance careers. It should become a first-class 'system of choice' that will support and strengthen the goals and standards set for all secondary and post secondary students . . . But, for this system to become a successful reality, educators, employers, and policy-makers must develop a common vision for the critical elements of the system and a plan to set all the elements in place in every community of our country.

—(Hull, 2000, p. 1)

Objectives

1. Discuss the history of career and technology education (CATE)
2. Discuss technical preparation (tech prep)
3. Identify types of career and technology education programs
4. Identify student leadership opportunities available in career and technology education programs
5. Identify the role of the administrator in the integration of Tech Prep into CATE reform

Introduction

The Carl D. Perkins Vocational and Applied Technology Education Act Amendment of 1990 defines vocational technical education as organized programs offering sequences of courses directly related to preparing individuals for paid or unpaid employment in current emerging occupations requiring training other than a baccalaureate or advanced degree (Public Law 101–392 § 521 [41]). These vocational technical education programs were designed to provide career awareness and skills that would enable students to find employment after leaving school (Imel, 1993).

Rapid changes in technology, a shortage of an adequately skilled workforce, and the call for school accountability have created some new challenges for educators, employers, and policy-makers. The need to link education and employment has been and will continue to be crucial in the United States' effort to develop a workforce that can compete in world markets. Consequently, the call for vocational technical education and workforce training reform has led to legislative action and funding for the Tech Prep reform initiative.

Historical Perspective

Social, economic, and political forces led to the development of vocational education through the *Smith-Hughes Act of 1917* for the purpose of preparing youth for jobs resulting from the industrial revolution. The *Smith-Hughes Act* provided an alternative from the general curriculum and called for a new one that would better meet the needs of the children of the working class. For the first time, working class children were attending high school but were not headed for professional careers (Gray, 1991). "Thus, the earliest vocational programs were grounded primarily in the need to prepare more blue-collar-type students with practical skills for the nation's farms, factories, and homes" (Lynch, 2000, p. 2).

This system of vocational education continued for the next seven decades. Enrollment in high school vocational programs continued to increase until the early 1980s when a decline in enrollment began. A few reasons blamed for the decline in vocational education enrollment included perceptions that the programs did not meet the needs of students, employers, and the community; programs competed against other curricular programs such as college preparatory; programs had an image of a dumbed-down curriculum; programs targeted primarily to educationally disadvantaged students; and that vocational programs inhibit rather than enhance youth's future career and educational choices (Lynch, 2000, p. 3).

Vocational Education Reform

The United States federal government has been aggressively involved in vocational education reform during the last 20 years. The 1983 report, *A Nation at Risk* (National Commission on Excellence in Education) addressed the threat of potential economic catastrophe that could occur without major elementary and secondary educational reform.

Policymakers and educators were made aware of the numbers of students emerging from high school without the skills to enter college or succeed in the world of work. The threat of technology replacing traditional jobs with new jobs that demanded higher skill and knowledge challenged U.S. communities to reevaluate the existing educational system.

A public document prepared by the National Commission on Secondary Vocational Education (1984), *The Unfinished Agenda,* introduced Tech Prep as an innovative concept for educational improvement. This commission recommended that the Tech Prep concept could be instrumental in restructuring school systems to address concerns on students' preparedness for college and the workforce through improved coordination between secondary and post-secondary education, integrated applied academics and technical studies, and assisted transition into two-year post-secondary education.

The Commission on the Skills of the American Workforce (1990) produced a report, *America's Choice: High Skills or Low Wages* calling for reform in work force preparation that centered on skill standards and the attainment of a certificate of mastery. The report mentioned the exportation of American low-skill jobs to workers in developing countries, where wages were 3 to 10 times lower. The report stressed the importance of developing high skills in U.S. workers in order to obtain and keep higher paying jobs. The report created the challenge for U.S. policy makers and educators to prepare students for higher skill, higher wage careers.

This urgent call for educational reform led to the first significant legislative act, *Carl D. Perkins Vocational and Applied Technology Education Act of 1990* (U.S. Congress, 1990). This act focused on vocational-technical education reform efforts by: a) promoting integrated vocational and academic curricula and instruction, b) developing technical preparation education (Tech-Prep) programs, c) promoting participation of special populations, especially the economically disadvantaged, d) developing state systems of performance standards and measures, and e) incorporating "all aspects of industry" into curricula and instruction.

Tech Prep initiatives were specified under Title II and IIIE of Public Law 101–392 of the *Perkins Act.* Tech Prep was defined as a combined secondary and postsecondary education program that focused on:

- an associate degree or two-year certificate,
- technical preparation in at least one field of engineering technology, applied science, mechanical, industrial, or practical art or trade, or agriculture, health, or business,
- student competence in mathematics, science, and communication (including applied academics) through sequential courses of study,
- and placement in employment (U.S. Congress, P.L. 101–392, 1990).

The federal government funded a study to identify the skills considered essential to building a high-performance economy characterized by high-skill, high wage employment (The Secretary's Commission on Achieving Necessary Skills, 1991; SCANS, 1992). This report stressed the need for a high-performance workplace with workers demonstrating solid foundation skills in basic literacy and computational skills, thinking skills, and personal qualities that make workers dedicated and trustworthy. Effective workers were also characterized as possessing interpersonal skills and the ability to manage resources, information, technology, and systems. Policy makers and educators were now encouraged to integrate skill standards such as the SCANS competencies into the curriculum.

A second critical legislative reform effort in vocational-technical education was the *Goals 2000: Educate America Act of 1994* (U.S. Congress, P.L. 103–227, 1994). *Goals 2000* centered on the adoption of content and student performance standards in elementary and secondary education. The National Skill Standards Board (NSSB) was created under *Goals 2000* to identify occupational clusters; establish a system of voluntary partnerships to develop standards; conduct research, disseminate and coordinate strategies; and endorse the skill standards systems. *Goals 2000* refocused the Perkins's established performance systems of career awareness and occupational skill development to student performance and emphasized accountability and reform.

A third piece of federal legislation, the *School-to-Work Act of 1994* (U.S. Congress, P.L. 103–239, 1994), was established to help states develop programs that broaden students' career options, make learning more relevant, and promote successful transition to college. According to Warnat (1997):

> The School-to-Work Act represents a significant philosophical shift in the focus of federal legislation that prepares young people for work. First of all, it focuses on all students, breaking down the tradition of individuals choosing either the college track or the vocational track. Secondly, it concentrates on preparing young people for both college and careers, so that they can choose which education-career path to take and when. No one is excluded from the opportunity to continue with further education. Third, education is no longer the sole domain of schools . . . workplaces are seen as education learning environments along with secondary and post-secondary schools (p. 34).

The *School-to-Work Act* introduced the concept of career majors/pathways and encouraged early career exploration as school-based learning components. Workplace mentoring and coherent sequence of courses focusing on the development of workplace competencies addressed the work-based learning component. Connecting activities were encouraged such as employer incentives to participate in school-based and work-based learning programs. *School-to-Work* expanded *Perkins's* innovations, reinforced *Goals 2000's* standards framework, and added the work-based learning component.

Reauthorization of Perkins

The latest legislative action resulting in educational reform is the reauthorization of *Carl D. Perkins Vocational and Technical Education Act of 1998* (U.S. Congress, P.L. 105–332, 1998). This act has often been referred to as *Perkins III* and primarily focuses on restructure and reform of programs from the *1990 Perkins Act*. *Perkins III* supports state and local educational reform that creates seamless education and workforce development systems. It also emphasizes the development of quality vocational and technical programs with academic integration. *Perkins III* reauthorizes Tech Prep and promotes the use of work-based learning and new technologies in Tech Prep programs. Partnership development is encouraged between Tech Prep programs and business, labor organizations, and postsecondary institutions that award baccalaureate degrees. *Perkins III* also attempts to align vocational and technical education program reform with state and local reform efforts that improve student achievement, prepare students for post-secondary education, and result in smooth transition to the workplace. This act clarifies the common goals and objectives of vocational-technical education and the Tech Prep reform initiative.

Perkins III supports the *Workforce Investment Act of 1998,* which restructures employment training, adult education, and vocational rehabilitation programs by promoting the development of integrated, one-stop education and workforce development systems for adults and youth. The restructured *Perkins III* sets out a new vision of student academic and technical achievement in postsecondary education and opportunities in high-skill, high-wage careers.

Implementation of Tech Prep

States are responsible for interpreting the Perkins Act and developing consistent and concrete definitions of a Tech Prep participant and program. Defining and describing local Tech Prep programs and participants has had ongoing concerns since the implementation of this reform initiative. Opposing views of what a Tech Prep program should consist of or exactly who should be considered a Tech Prep participant has led to different state (or even consortia within a state) definitions.

Some consortia believe Tech Prep should not be considered a distinct program because it will lead inevitably to the stigma associated with "tracking," particularly of vocational students. Consortia following this approach may not differentiate students in Tech Prep from the general student population or may count students as in Tech Prep if they happen to take any of the courses considered fundamental to the Tech Prep initiative (for example, articulated vocational courses). Students, however, are unaware of their participation in a "program." On the other hand, some consortia view Tech Prep as a true program; students apply for admission, enroll, and participate in a defined set of activities that set them apart from other students. These consortia often consider a cohesive Tech Prep program to have the added benefit of allowing students to feel that they are part of something special, and may encourage students to wear Tech Prep logos or take them on special field trips to reinforce this attitude (Silverberg & Hershey, 1995, p. 10).

Despite the fact that identification of Tech Prep students differs among consortia, most Tech Prep students meet common criteria. Tech Prep students identify and select a career pathway of interest; participate in the development of a four or six-year educational plan leading toward that career pathway; are enrolled in vocational courses in the selected career pathway; and participate in applied academic classes that reinforce real world skills (Silverberg & Hershey, 1995, Sec. V p. 10). The two most common elements of the definition of a Tech Prep student include participation in vocational or Career and Technology Education (CATE) and applied academic course work.

Parnell (1993) suggests that the most successful Tech Prep programs typically contain the following characteristics:

1. A structural and substance-rich Applied Academic curriculum that provides opportunities for all students to understand the relationship between academic subject matter and real-life application.
2. High standards for achievement, as well as thorough assessment policies.
3. Learning and guidance strategies that allow all students to acquire positive attitudes toward life skills, lifelong learning, and family-wage career opportunities.
4. Teacher-counselor pre-service and inservice programs about tech prep.
5. Collaboration among high school, college, and employer representatives.
6. Strategies aimed at changing attitudes about vocational-technical education community and technical college "bridge" programs that prepare adult students who have missed the high school portion of the sequence to move into and succeed in the tech prep program (p. 7).

Even though Tech Prep has been popular with business persons and educators, Lynch (2000) believes that no direct cause and effect quantifiable data is available on the effectiveness of Tech Prep. Lynch suggests that a major problem in assessing Tech Prep's impact on measured student achievement is the varied definition tech prep has developed by state consortia throughout the nation.

Assessing the effectiveness of nation-wide Tech Prep programs is complicated and multi-dimensional due to diverse and unique characteristics of local consortia. The

U.S. Department of Education intentionally allowed states considerable freedom to design Tech Prep systems to be responsive to local conditions and constraints (American Vocational Association, 1992). Due to the diversity of local Tech Prep programs, researchers have struggled to find consistent and clearly defined measurable outcomes on Tech Prep programs and participant achievement necessary in documenting systemic change.

Hershey, Silverberg, Owens, and Hulsey (1998) state in *Focus for the Future: The Final Report of the National Tech Prep Evaluation,* that the creation of Tech Prep consortia has strengthened local collaboration among educators, increased career guidance, emphasized applied academics, and increased employer involvement with schools. Since federal legislation specified the components of Tech Prep with local consortia discretion on implementation, Tech Prep has taken diverse forms emphasizing individual components. This study found that most consortia have not brought these individual aspects of Tech Prep together in a structured, challenging program of study that substantially change students' educational experience.

Evaluating Tech Prep Programs

Documenting continuous program improvement has not been easy and researchers continue to search for reform efforts that are making a difference. Lynch (2000) identifies Tech Prep as one of six components integral to high school reform in his report titled, *High School Career and Technical Education for the First Decade of the 21st Century.* The others are high school majors, contextual teaching and learning, work-based learning, authentic assessment, and career academies. Lynch states that:

> There isn't a lot of hard, statistical or other empirical data to support most school reform programs, or at least those programs that have a national agenda or focus. This is especially true if the fundamental goal of the reform is increased student achievement as measured by standardized test scores (p. 12).

Despite the lack of empirical data, Lynch believes that there are denominators common across the various reform initiatives and that their inherent components are reasonably well grounded in data. "The initial review by experts who have designed, engaged in, or studied high school reform believe that all of these common denominators or key elements of reform need to be included in the redesign or reform of the American high school" (p. 12).

Identifying which Tech Prep components are making an impact on local program improvement depends on the degree of implementation within individual high schools. Various studies (Hershey et al, 1998; Hayward & Benson, 1993) reported that the more experienced Tech Prep consortia, operating five years or longer, were ahead of most in accomplishing objectives by getting beyond just articulating existing courses and/or merely providing advanced placement in college for high school tech prep graduates. These consortia were involved with serious curriculum development, redirecting core academic courses along a career path, and addressing components designed to improve secondary and postsecondary programs.

Bragg (1995) identified six core concepts that formed and were continuing to form the basis for developing and implementing solid local Tech Prep programs:

1. Tech prep must be grounded in an integrated, authentic, and rigorous core curriculum at both the secondary and postsecondary levels.
2. Formal articulation between secondary and postsecondary schools must be present.

3. Work-based learning experiences must be integrated into the curriculum.
4. Tech prep must be established as a standards-driven, performance-based educational initiative.
5. Tech prep is to be an educational vehicle accessible to all students.
6. Collaboration among stakeholders is essential (p. 299).

The Strategic Planning, Evaluation of Curriculum, and Assessment Planning (SPECAP) study conducted by Texas Tech University (1996) found that Texas Tech Prep consortia have provided exemplary leadership in cooperative planning and implementation of local educational reform. According to this study this planning has had a direct and positive impact on Texas education, students, and the economy. In a five year Texas Tech Prep study (Brown, 2000; Tech-Prep Texas, 2001), the following data were documented:

> Results show 10th–12th grade cohorts of tech prep participants had slightly higher annual attendance rates and lower annual dropout rates than either of the non-tech prep groups. Moreover, tech prep students in their senior year had slightly higher graduation rates than the comparison groups, with an increasing percentage successfully completing college preparatory programs between 1994–95 and 1998–99. Certain ethnic, at-risk, and economically disadvantaged sub-populations demonstrated similar results (p. 1).

Student enrollment in Texas Tech Prep programs continues to increase and according to Brown, may be due to one or a combination of the following: the integration of Tech Prep into all graduation options; an increase in the number of Tech Prep programs; improved program marketing; and/or improved student identification.

Bragg (2000) refers to a four-year longitudinal study she is currently working on involving eight local consortia. Findings, thus far, indicate that the majority of Tech Prep participants are "engaged in substantial academic and career-technical course work at the secondary level, with the majority transitioning to two-year or four-year colleges" (p. 6). This study reports at least 70% of Tech Prep participants, in the eight participating consortia, entered a postsecondary institution within one to three years of high school graduation. Most students were also reported working part-or full-time jobs, often related to their chosen career field.

A study on Tech Prep's impact on student achievement in South Carolina (Donelan, 1999) found no significant changes had occurred. Student achievement was defined by the following three criteria: decrease in the dropout rate; improved scores on standardized tests; and increased postsecondary school attendance.

> These criteria have been recognized by the School to Work Opportunities Act as appropriate success measures for the Tech Prep program. However, these variables do not appear to be direct measures for assessing the effectiveness of the Tech Prep program. To determine if Tech Prep is providing students with relevant academic skills, marketable occupational skills, and appropriate work-place behaviors, other measures, such as rate of hire, starting wages or salaries, and wages or salary rates five years after graduation in an occupation consistent with training received in the Tech Prep program appear to be more direct measures of the effectiveness of the Tech Prep program (pp. 46–47).

Identifying appropriate measures for evaluating the success of a Tech Prep program appears to be a critical assessment issue.

Assessing the effectiveness of nation-wide Tech Prep programs is complicated and multi-dimensional due to diverse and unique characteristics of local consortia. The U.S. Department of Education intentionally allowed states considerable freedom to design Tech Prep systems to be responsive to local conditions and constraints (American Vocational Association, 1992). Researchers have struggled to find consistent and clearly defined measurable outcomes or processes on Tech Prep programs and participant achievement necessary in documenting systemic change.

Hershey, Silverberg, Owens, and Hulsey (1998) state in *Focus for the Future: The Final Report of the National Tech Prep Evaluation,* that the creation of Tech Prep consortia has strengthened local collaboration among educators, increased career guidance, emphasized applied academics, and increased employer involvement with schools. Since federal legislation specified the components of Tech Prep with local consortia discretion on implementation, Tech Prep has taken diverse forms emphasizing individual components. This study found that most consortia have not brought these individual aspects of Tech Prep together in a structured, challenging program of study that substantially change a student's educational experience.

Types of Career and Technology Programs

Career and Technology Education programs vary based on the extent of Tech Prep reform that has occurred at the local, regional, and state levels. Differences are evident even within consortia based on the local leadership efforts. Generally, CATE programs today will consist of vocational and academic courses organized into a coherent sequence and career pathways, majors, or clusters. Some of the most common career clusters include the following: Business, Marketing, and Management Occupations; Engineering and Science Related Occupations; Health Occupations; Consumer Service Occupations; Arts, Media, and Communication Occupations; Agriculture Occupations; Construction Occupations; and Manufacturing and Production Occupations (Hull & Grevelle, 1998, p. 92).

In recent years, CATE program reform has included integrating standards-based curriculum, such as industry certification. Some popular industry certification areas included in this integration are: Automotive Service Excellence certification in the automotive training programs; Certificed Nursing Assistant, Pharmacy Technician certification, and Dental Assistant certification in Health Science career training programs; A+, CISCO, and MOUS certification in computer technology programs; and Security Services in Law Enforcement training programs. These industry certification programs have resulted in clarifying the training objectives of the CATE programs through standards established by industry and measured by certification exams. Both teachers and students focus on learning the curriculum identified by industry as needed for entry-level employment.

CATE courses are often organized within a career cluster in three stages: introductory courses, pre-employment courses, and work-based learning courses. Students progress through the three stages as their interest increases and skill level develops. Introductory courses provide career awareness and opportunities within that career cluster and give the student general information on educational requirements necessary to focus on specific careers. The time frame for introductory courses is usually 45 minutes to one hour per day. The pre-employment courses provide hands-on training through simulated laboratory experiences or job shadowing. Work-based courses include internships or cooperative work experience in actual job sites throughout the community. Recent CATE reform efforts have culminated in training programs with intense independent study research projects that demonstrate students' skills in research, technology utilization, communication, and resource utilization. These research projects help verify that students have mastered the SCANS competencies identified by employers as being critical to successful employment (SCANS, 1991).

Tech Prep articulated college credit is commonly found within CATE courses in all three stages. Four-year high school graduation plans are being utilized by students to effectively plan and maximize their college credits opportunities within CATE/Tech Prep programs. Effective high school guidance programs that develop six-year and eight-year graduation plans provide an even clearer plan for high school students to transition smoothly from their high school training program into postsecondary training programs at technical or community colleges.

The types of CATE programs offered within high schools today should be based on local, regional, state, and national labor market reports and student interests. Obsolete training programs that provide little or no opportunity for employment are a waste of the student's time and effort. Decisions on which training programs to offer should be based on feedback provided by advisory councils, business partnerships, and community needs assessment. Student interest inventory results should be utilized to guide program offerings and target occupations on which to focus. Overall, careful thought and planning should take place annually to ensure CATE programs are relevant based on local needs and interests.

Leadership Opportunities in CATE

CATE student leadership opportunities have not changed much since their inception, even though some of the club names have changed to keep up with politically correct concerns. Still popular are student organizations such as FFA (no longer referred to as Future Farmers of America), Family, Career, and Community Leaders of America (FCCLA previously referred to as Future Homemakers of America-Home Economics Related Occupations or FHA-HERO), Distributive Education Clubs of America (DECA), Business Professionals of America (BPA), Skills USA, VICA (previously referred to as Vocational Industrial Clubs of America), and Health Occupations Students Association (HOSA). These student organizations continue to focus on leadership development and are often integrated into the CATE program curriculum to a point that the student organization is often referred to as the training program and vice versa.

Effective CATE programs often include strong student organizations that involve students in competitive events, community service, and leadership activities. Parental and community support through booster clubs has added strength and support to these student organizations often resulting in major political support systems for program improvement. Law (1994) describes the extent of political support for CATE student organizations as follows:

> The commitment of vocational educators to their student organization is the stuff of legend. Theses, dissertations, and articles abound on the topic. In fact, the belief in these organizations is so ingrained in the ideology of the field that one almost risks professional suicide to raise any questions about them. Governors' proclamation honoring vocational student organizations, individually and collectively, have become a dime a dozen. And in state after state, state boards of education have adopted policies urging local boards to support them as integral parts of instruction (pp. 143–144).

CATE student leadership organizations continue to be strong components of local training programs and the club names continue to be used interchangeably with the course names, such as FFA for Agriculture education.

The Principal's Role

Critical to the success of the Tech Prep reform movement into CATE programs is the school administrator. Craig (1998) believes that the success of Tech Prep programs depends on the involvement of key administrators such as the superintendent, high school principal, and the vocational director. These administrators' responsibilities include the development of a district Tech Prep philosophy and policy, promotion of the Tech Prep concept within the school and community, curriculum restructuring and reform, providing necessary staff training, and development of school planning teams.

Another critical administrative responsibility is the development and support of a clear plan for integrating the Tech Prep reform initiative into existing academic and vocational programs. According to Hull (2000),

> "The old voc-ed courses won't work any more; they were designed to support the work-force of a past generation, which did not require strong academic foundations. Today, these courses won't open minds and doors to lifelong careers with multiple options of achievement and responsibility" (p. 35).

The primary responsibility of reforming existing CATE programs to the Tech Prep system falls mainly on the administrators overseeing these programs, the high school principal and the vocational director. A critical component includes the integration of academic and CATE programs, which requires collaboration between the two disciplines. However, in the age of academic accountability, many principals focus the majority of their time and effort on academic reform and are reluctant to share limited staff development opportunities toward collaborative integrated training among academic and CATE staff.

School principals are challenged to understand the role CATE and Tech Prep play in preparing students for transition into the real world. An effective principal empowers staff members to implement the Tech Prep reform strategies into existing CATE programs and encourages integration activities between academic and CATE staff. The principal also promotes the development of active partnerships with community businesses and postsecondary institutions that result in articulation agreements, internships, and other work-based learning experiences for students and staff.

Applying Your Knowledge

You are the principal of a large urban high school that has offered several different vocational classes for the past three decades without too much variation in the curriculum. These classes usually enroll small numbers of students. Your school graduates only 75% of your seniors each year, and of those seniors, only 20% go on to four-year colleges, and 35% go onto to post-secondary technical training. There is growing pressure from upper administration to reform your vocational program or eliminate it altogether.

QUESTIONS

1. How would you begin to "reform" your vocational program? What data would you gather in order to find the best solution?
2. How could you increase enrollment in your vocational classes?
3. How could you enhance your vocational program to prepare more students for four-year colleges, and for two-year colleges?

4. What would be some advantages and disadvantages of eliminating your vocational program?
5. What would be some advantages and disadvantages of reforming your vocational program?

QUESTIONS FOR THOUGHT

1. How do current career and technology programs differ from vocational programs in the 1960s, 70s and 80s?
2. What is Tech Prep and what are some advantages to belonging to a Tech Prep consortium?
3. What are career clusters and career pathways?
4. How can career and technology education programs help reduce dropout rates and help increase college-going rates?
5. What are some examples of career and technology education extracurricular activities?
6. Explain how career and technology education programs are funded.

References

American Vocational Association. (1992). *The Carl D. Perkins vocational and applied technology education act of 1990: The final regulations.* Alexandria, VA: Author.

Bragg, D. D. (1995). Linking high schools to post-secondary institutions: The role of tech prep. In W. Norton Grubb (Ed.), *Education through occupations in American high schools: The challenges of implementing curriculum integration,* (pp. 235–310), New York: Columbia University, Teachers College.

Bragg, D. D. (2000). Editorial: Reflecting back, looking forward-tech prep and integration of the past, present, and future. *Journal of Vocational Education Research, 25* (3), [On-line], 19-Apr-2001, Available: *http://scholar.lib.vt.edu/e journals/JVER/v25n3/editor.html.*

Brown, C. H. (2000). A comparison of selected outcomes of secondary tech-prep participants and non-participants in Texas. *Journal of Vocational Education Research, 25* (3), [On-line], 24-Apr-2001, Available: *http://scholar.lib.vt.edu/ejournals/JVER/v25n3/ brown.html.*

Commission on the Skills of the American Workforce. (1990). *America's choice: High skills or low wages!* Rochester, NY: National Center on Education and the Economy.

Craig, R. M. (1998). Attitudes of Ohio school administrators toward tech prep. *Dissertation Abstracts International* (Digital Dissertation No. AAT 9842102).

Donelan, C. M. (1999). *The effect of the tech prep program in South Carolina on student success in secondary schools.* Unpublished doctoral dissertation, University of South Carolina, Columbia.

Gray, K. (1991). Vocational education in high school: A modern Phoenix? *Phi Delta Kappan, 71*(6), 437–445.

Hayward, G. C., & Benson, C. S. (1993). *Vocational-technical education: Major reforms and debates 1917–present.* Washington, DC: U.S. Department of Education, Office of Vocational and Adult Education.

Hershey, A., Silverberg, M., & Owens, T. (1995). *The diverse forms of tech-prep: Implementation approaches in ten local consortia.* Princeton, NJ: Mathematical Policy Research.

Hershey, A., Silverberg, M., Owens, T., & Husley, L. (1998). *Focus for the future: The final report of the national tech-prep evaluation.* Princeton, NJ: Mathematical Policy Research, Inc.

Hull, D. M. (2000). *Education and career preparation for the new millennium: A vision for systemic change.* Waco, TX: Center for Occupational Research & Development.

Hull, D. & Grevelle, J. (1998). *Tech Prep: The next generation.* Waco, TX: Center for Occupational Research & Development.

Imel, S. (1993). Vocational education's role in dropout prevention. *ERIC Clearinghouse on Adult, Career, and Vocational Education.* Columbus, OH.

Law, C. J. (1994). *Tech Prep Education: A total quality approach.* Lancaster, PA: Technomic Publishing.

Lynch, R. L. (2000). High school career and technology education for the first decade of the 21th century. *The Journal of Vocational Education Research, 25*(2), [On-line], 4-March-2002, Available: *http://scholar.lib.vt.edu/ejournals/JVER/v25n2/lynch.html.*

National Commission on Secondary Vocational Education. (1984). *The unfinished agenda.* Columbus: National Center for Research in Vocational Education, Ohio State University.

National Commission on Excellence in Education. (1983). *A nation at risk: The imperative for educational reform.* Washington, DC: U.S. Government Printing Office.

Parnell, D. (1993). What is the tech prep/associate degree program? *The Balance Sheet, 75*(2), 6–8.

SCANS. (1992). *Skills and tasks for jobs.* Washington, DC: U.S. Department of Labor.

Secretary's Commission on Achieving Necessary Skills. (SCANS). (1991). *What work requires of schools.* Washington, DC: U.S. Department of Labor.

Silverberg, M. K. & Hershey, A. M. (1995). *The emergence of tech-prep at the state and local levels.* Report submitted to the U.S. Department of Education. Princeton, NJ: Mathematical Policy Research, Inc.

Tech-Prep Texas. (2001). *Closing the gaps: How tech-prep programs have increased participation and success in Texas schools, a five-year study.* Tech-Prep Evaluation, Region 5 Education Service Center, Beaumont, TX.

U.S. Congress. (1994). *Goals 2000: Educate America Act.* Public Law 103–227. Washington, DC: U.S. Government Printing Office.

U.S. Congress. (1994). *School-to-work opportunities act of 1994.* Washington, DC: U.S. Government Printing Office. Public Law 103–239.

U.S. Congress. (1998). *Carl D. Perkins vocational and technical education act of 1998.* Public Law 105–332. Washington, DC: U.S. Government Printing Office.

Warnat, W. I. (1997). Building a school-to-work system in the United States. In L. McFarland (Ed), *New Visions: Education and training for an innovative workforce.* (12–43), Berkley: National Center for Research in Vocational Education, University of California.

Achieving Equity through Enrichment Bilingual Education

7

Leo Gómez

José Agustín Ruiz-Escalante

Language is enchanting, powerful, magical, useful, personal.
Language is our means of discovery of the world
and our response to the world. As teachers
we serve as catalysts for our students to make
the best use of their two or more languages.
Our languages are the most powerful tools we have.

—*C. J. Ovando & V. P. Collier*

Objectives

1. Overview the legal and legislative history of bilingual education
2. Present a theoretical framework for bilingual education
3. Describe the various models of bilingual education

Introduction

As we strive to achieve equity in the education of all students, the need for informed educational leaders is more crucial than ever. Schools across the country are facing growing enrollment of students whose first language is not English. The majority of school leaders lack the necessary preparation for effectively educating this group. Historically, an academic achievement gap has persisted between English speakers and language minority students. Effective leadership requires a comprehensive understanding of the issues affecting this population. The issue of how to effectively educate children who come to school speaking a language other than English has been widely debated in the last 25 years. Bilingual education has become politicized. For instance, in California, Arizona, and Massachusetts the public voted to eliminate bilingual education as an option to educate children who come to school speaking a language other than English. This chapter provides a thorough discussion of legislative, judicial and pedagogical issues impacting the education of second language learners in the American educational system. It emphasizes a paradigm shift from a remedial to an enrichment educational approach for this population (Collier & Thomas, 2004).

The Bilingual Education Debate

The controversy that has surrounded bilingual education since its inception through the Bilingual Education Act of 1968, and the *Lau* decision of 1974, is whether or not it marginalizes the English Language Learner (ELL). No education field has been more widely debated than that of bilingual education (Bake, 2001; Crawford, 2004; Cummins, 1981). However, the debate has centered on the purpose for or extent of ELLs receiving instruction in their native language, versus identifying "best practices" for effectively educating these students. The discussion has focused on short-term language and academic development versus long-term educational reform and equal educational opportunity that address positive educational and social change. Freeman (1998), in her descriptive study of a dual language school, explains that dual language programs are true educational reform that promotes positive social change. The real benefits of bilingualism, that can be delivered through an effective maintenance or dual language bilingual education program, have traditionally not been enjoyed by ELLs due to historical, societal, and political limitations imposed upon them. Much of the debate comes from a lack of understanding of the original purpose and methodology of bilingual education programs as well as the unwillingness among educators to consider alternatives (Rong & Peissle, 1998).

Demographics

The influx of language minority students into the U.S. public school system has steadily increased since the early 1960s. During the 1989–1990 school years alone, there were approximately 2,028,880 limited English proficient (LEP) students in grades K–12. That figure represents 5 percent of the nation's total enrollment in public schools. The LEP population has increased 36 percent in a period of 4 years, while the total K–12 student population has increased only 3 percent (Olsen, 1992).

The controversy has intensified because the number of ELLs continues to increase in public schools. During the 2000–2001 academic year, the number of school age children who speak a language other than English at home was 4,584,946. This figure represents 9.6% of the total school age population. This figure represents a growth of 32.1% from

1997–1998 academic year. The large majority of English Language Learners (ELL), 62.2%, reside in five states. The shift of demographics illustrates that the education of ELLs is not confined to any particular geographic area. It is true that 62.2% of ELLs can be found in 5 states; however, each state in the country and territories has ELLs. For example, Georgia has 64,949 ELLs; New Mexico has more ELLs than Georgia, even though the total state population is much lower than Georgia's. States such as Idaho, Oregon, Washington, North Carolina, Minnesota, and Oklahoma continue to show a growth in the number of ELLs (Kindler, 2002).

According to Kindler (2002), there are over 460 languages represented in the ELL population in the U.S. public schools. More recently, Kindler (2003) reports that 79.2% of ELLs come from Spanish-speaking homes, while the remaining 19.8% come from other languages, the second largest being Vietnamese, which is spoken by 2% of the ELL population.

Defining Bilingual Education

Many educators have provided varied definitions for bilingual education. A comprehensive definition of bilingual education was provided by the U.S. Commission on Civil Rights (1971):

> . . . the use of two languages, one of which is English, as mediums of instruction for the same pupil population in a well organized program which encompasses all or parts of the curriculum and includes the study of the history and culture associated with the mother tongue. A complete program develops and maintains the children's self-esteem and a legitimate pride in both cultures (p. 21).

Bilingual education programs have four common goals: (1) full proficiency and literacy in English and the native language; (2) acquisition of basic and higher order thinking skills for academic achievement and beyond; (3) development of a strong self-concept; and (4) successful transition from completion of school to higher education, work, and community life.

Federal Legislation

The Elementary and Secondary Education Act of 1965 (ESEA) championed by President Lyndon B. Johnson brought national attention to the need to educate children from low income homes, including language minority students. Johnson, the first *"Education President,"* had a special place in his heart for education, especially educating children from poverty backgrounds. He developed this awareness in 1928 when he taught for one year in a segregated school for "Mexicans" in Cotulla, Texas. In many ways Johnson was a typical teacher of the times. He believed in strict discipline, yelling at offenders, occasionally paddling male students, and vigorously enforcing a total ban on speaking Spanish. Although Johnson himself could not speak a second language, he was quoted as saying, "I couldn't quite understand them . . . they couldn't talk English and I couldn't talk Spanish" (Pycior, 1997, p. 19). He was convinced that speaking in Spanish, even at play, would retard a child's academic progress. It is important to note that later, when President Johnson signed bilingual education legislation known as Title VII, an amendment to ESEA of 1965, legitimizing the use of a student's native language as a tool to develop academic achievement.

In 1967, Ralph Yarborough, a strong U. S. senator from Texas, introduced a bill in Congress calling for the establishment of bilingual education programs in the United

States. Senator Yarborough sought to pass a bill specifically to address the needs of Spanish-speaking students (Yarborough, 1994). The bill it was debated because it only addressed the needs of a specific group. To remedy this, the Johnson administration encouraged two members of the House of Representatives to propose a similar bill. Two Mexican-American representatives, one from California and one from Texas, introduced a bill to establish bilingual education programs for all language minority groups. In the end, the House of Representative's bill was adopted. This act appropriated $15 million for bilingual education. This bill was the initiation of the role of the federal government in the education of language minority students. Since then, the Bilingual Education Act has been regularly re-authorized.

The Bilingual Education Act of 1968 did not provide many guidelines for school districts to follow. However, in 1974, the Bilingual Education Act was amended. Congress provided definitions and regulations for the establishment of bilingual education programs. The 1974 amendments gave the first federal definition of bilingual education and program goals, created a network of regional support centers, and encouraged educational institutions to embrace capacity building efforts. In addition, the 1974 amendments also provided funds for teacher training and support for doctoral programs (*Bilingual Education Act,* 1974).

The Bilingual Education Act was once again amended in 1978, and it recognized that the use of the term limited English speaking abilities (LESA) was not appropriate. The term that was adopted was *limited English proficient (LEP).* The LEP term takes into account not only the speaking ability, but the reading and writing ability as well. This amendment also called for the LEP student to be quickly transitioned to an English-speaking environment, and consequently did not fund programs that were designed to maintain the native language of the student (*Bilingual Education Act,* 1978).

In 1984, the Bilingual Education Act was reauthorized. The amended Act created three types of bilingual education programs: 1) *transitional bilingual education,* 2) *developmental bilingual education,* and 3) *special alternative* programs. The federal government provided for increased local control encouraging local school districts to decide what type of program was more adequate for their respective community (*Bilingual Education Act,* 1984).

The amended Bilingual Education Act of 1988 emphasized the development and implementation of *transitional bilingual education* programs. The Act imposed a three-year limit for LEP students to be enrolled in a transitional bilingual program, or in a special language alternative program. Seventy-five percent of the designated funds were distributed to transitional programs and twenty-five to special language alternative programs. Again, the federal government did not approve funds for developmental bilingual education programs designed to maintain the native language (*Bilingual Education Act,* 1988).

Congress once again amended the Bilingual Education Act in 1994. It was by far the most comprehensive bilingual education legislation because it called for bilingualism using the nation's language resources and bilingual education opportunities for all learners. This Act called for educating children through a dual language, enrichment, and additive approach versus a remedial and subtractive instructional program (see section on Models of Bilingual Education) aimed at replacing the child's native language. Another aspect of the Act was that it called for the development of exemplary programs to meet the goal of the Act, and required that non-English-speaking students demonstrate academic success in a number of content areas. This ACT now authorized and funded the establishment of dual language bilingual programs designed to develop and maintain the native language with the goal of biliteracy for ELLs and native English speakers (*Bilingual Education Act,* 1994).

The No Child Left Behind Act (NCLB) of 2001 changed the title and the name of these federal programs from Title VII to Title III, and from Bilingual Education Act to English Language Acquisition, Language Enhancement, and Academic Achievement Act. This is the most drastic change in federal legislation dealing with language minority children. The principle focus of the law is to ensure that children acquire English as soon as possible, and no mention is made about the development of the native language. The other major change in the legislation was funding. Previously, all bilingual education grants were nationally competitive. Under the NCLB Act, funding for bilingual education programs was appropriated to the states using block and formula grants (No Child Left Behind Act of 2002).

Court Cases

Of all the Supreme Court cases, the one that had the greatest impact on bilingual education was undoubtedly *Lau v. Nichols* (1974). This case involved a lawsuit brought against the San Francisco School District by a group of Chinese-speaking parents on behalf of their children. The suit alleged that the San Francisco School District violated their equal rights. The plaintiffs argued that the school denied their children equal protection because they were being instructed in a language they did not understand. The school district argued that they were offering equal education opportunities because the students were attending the same facilities, being taught by the same teachers, following the same curriculum, and being provided the same textbooks. Ruling for the plaintiffs, the Supreme Court stated that it was not enough to provide the same building, teachers, curriculum, and textbooks. This type of education, according to the Court, is not meaningful to students who do not understand English. Judge Douglas wrote:

> Under these state-imposed standards there is no equality of treatment merely by providing students with the same facilities, textbooks, teachers, and curriculum; for students who do not understand English are effectively foreclosed from any meaningful education. Basic English skills are at the very core of what these public schools teach. Imposition of a requirement that, before a child can effectively participate in the educational program, he must already have acquired those basic skills is to make a *mockery of public education* (emphasis authors'). We know that those who do not understand English are certain to find their classroom experiences wholly incomprehensible and in no way meaningful *(Lau v. Nichols, 1974).*

No court case or state/federal legislation had defined specifically the steps or the criteria that school districts needed to use to insure quality educational programs for language minority students until the 5th Circuit issued its decision in *Castañeda v. Pickard* (1981). This Texas case provided the standard for measuring the effectiveness of bilingual programs adopted by the Office of Civil Rights of the United States Department of Education. The Court ordered a three-prong test to measure whether bilingual programs were providing equal education opportunities for language minority students:

1. Are the programs based on some sound education theory?
2. Do the programs devote sufficient resources to reasonably implement the theory?
3. Do the programs assure that they are effective in teaching English and other content areas after implementation for some time?

The rights to bilingual education, the quality of programs, and other issues dealing with educating language minority children have been decided by federal and state courts.

Table 1 Court Cases Impacting Bilingual Education

Case and Court	Result
Serna v. Portales Municipal Schools (1974) 9th Circuit Court of Appeals	Appeal courts ruled that students have a right to bilingual education.
Aspira of New York, Inc. v. Board of Education of the City of New York (1977) Federal Court New York City	No court decision, but parties agreed to a consent decree. The school district agreed to follow *Lau*. The district also agreed not to use submersion to teach non-English-speaking students.
Rios v. Reed (1978) District Court, New York	Non-English-speaking students have a right to quality bilingual education.
Otero v. Mesa County Valley School District No. 51 (1972)	The court rejected the right to a specific bilingual education program.
Keyes v. School District No. 1, Denver, Colorado (1975) 10th Circuit Court of Appeals	The Court ruled that it was not up to the courts to mandate specific programs.
Guadalupe Organization, Inc. v. Tempe Elementary School District No. 3 (1978)	Bureau of Indian Affairs was not required to offer bilingual education programs.
Idaho Migrant Council v. Board of Education (1981) 9th Circuit Court of Appeals	State agencies have the power and responsibility to supervise bilingual education programs in public schools.
Gomez v. Illinois State Board of Education (1987) 7th Circuit Court of Appeals	State boards of education have the responsibility to supervise educational programs for English language learners.
California Teachers Association v. State Board of Education (2001)	Court ruled that Proposition 227 did not have a "chilling effect" on freedom of speech.

A Theoretical Framework for Bilingual Education

Although the term "bilingual education" appears clear in its meaning, it is not. Bilingual education has evolved to mean a number of things. There is considerable controversy regarding the purpose, goals, and effectiveness of bilingual education. As explained by Freeman (1998), due to the variations of educational context, cultural diversity and target populations in the United States, bilingual education continues to be confusing at the policy and instructional levels and in the general population. However, the theoretical basis for bilingual education is quite clear. Research has steadily demonstrated that instruction in a child's first language (L1) facilitates the acquisition of the second language (L2). This fundamental premise is somewhat paradoxical appearing to defy logic and common sense. But this is exactly the linguistic and cognitive premise of all bilingual education models (Gomez, 2000).

LANGUAGES ARE INTERDEPENDENT

The work of Cummins in the late seventies shattered prior naïve theories on the deficit notions regarding bilingualism. Cummins (1981) argued that there was an "intuitively" appealing argument . . . that deficiencies in English should be remedied by intensive instruction in English. In other words, instruction in the native language was time not spent learning in English. He explains that the naïve *Separate Underlying Proficiency*

(SUP) theory of the mid-fifties that suggests that learning in the L1 impedes the acquisition of the L2 has no hard evidence to substantiate it, other than argued on an intuitive basis. In fact, 50 years of research demonstrated that there was either no correlation or a negative correlation between the degree of instruction in the L2 and academic achievement (Crawford, 2004). Cummins (1986) proposes a counter hypothesis to the SUP in his *Common Underlying Proficiency* (CUP) model. He contends that both the L1 and L2 reside in the same part of the brain and development in either is common to both because they reinforce each other at the base. Language is language, and although it may differ at the surface (i.e., speaking, writing), in a person's mind the L1 and L2 clearly support one another. His analogy of a "dual iceberg model" has helped to explain the interaction between languages across the four language abilities: listening, speaking, reading and writing. The analogy of an iceberg in the ocean with two visible peaks above the water, referring to the L1 and L2, may lead one to assume that they are two separate icebergs or two separate languages, when in fact under the water, or at the base of the brain, there is only one iceberg or one language. At the surface level, a bilingual person can separate languages for different linguistic functions such as speaking and writing, but both languages reinforce each other at the base and cognitive and linguistic skills developed in the L1 or L2 are common and support one another.

This leads to the interdependence of the L1 and L2 supported through cognitive and linguistic transfer. As shared by Cummins, the *Interdependent Hypothesis* states that the acquisition of the L2 is largely dependent on the mastery of the L1. That is, a learner who has mastered the cognitive and linguistic basics of the L1 will more readily achieve in the L2. The CUP facilitates the transfer of knowledge and skills from the L1 to the L2. Knowledge and skills are only learned *once* in any language, and once acquired they can easily transfer to the second. This transfer is evident in many language minority children who immigrate well-schooled, and tend to do well in the learning of English, as opposed to those who are less-schooled or illiterate in their L1 and struggle in an English learning environment. Therefore, if a language minority child fails to attain a certain level of literacy in the L1, opportunity for transfer of skills and knowledge from the L1 to the L2 is reduced, and it is likely that he/she will be limited in both languages.

Understanding Language Proficiency

According to the U. S. Commission on Civil Rights (1971), ". . . lack of English proficiency is the major reason for language minority students' academic failure. Bilingual education is intended to ensure that students do not fall behind in subject matter content while they are learning English" (p. 17). Although language minority students in bilingual education programs do learn subject matter in the L1, bilingual education is much more than that. As described by Cummins (1986), bilingual education is the vehicle for communicative proficiency and academic proficiency that underlies both L1 and L2 literacy development. As discussed earlier, literacy development in the L1 is the cognitive and linguistic basis for development of the L2. Transitional bilingual education (TBE) models (see next section) tend to rush language minority students from L1 literacy development to the L2 once these children demonstrate some moderate level skills in English, or communicative proficiency. The result is a child with good conversational skills in both languages, but minimal cognitive or academic skills in either one. An understanding of the distinction between communicative proficiency and academic proficiency has aided many TBE programs in appropriately determining the correct time for transition from the L1 to the L2 mainstream classroom. As explained by Cummins (1986), the first type of language proficiency that language minority children attain in the L2 is referred to as *Basic Interpersonal Communicative Skills (BICS)*. BICS are typically acquired within 2–3 years and are dependent on clues, visual gestures, and physical actions usually associated with conversation and social interactions. BICS are insufficient for the cognitive demands of classroom instruction. Although language minority children may appear fluent in English, they are not linguistically and academically prepared for school success in that language. Children must achieve *Cognitive Academic Linguistic Proficiency (CALP)* in order to succeed in context-reduced and academically demanding school curricula such as English reading, math, science and social studies. CALP in the second language takes approximately 5–7 years to attain, and is best achieved by developing CALP in the L1 and facilitating this knowledge and skill transfer to the L2 or developing both simultaneously.

Models of Bilingual Education

Educators in the United States have used many different models to educate language minority students. Table 2 illustrates different approaches that have been used. There are two major and distinct differences that characterize these approaches: enrichment and additive models, or remedial and subtractive models. Remedial and subtractive models are based on the perspective that the non-English language is a deficit or a problem that must be corrected. Consequently in these models the L1 is not fully developed. Enrichment or additive models assume that the non-English language is an asset that should be fully developed and used as a resource for English acquisition. The table lists these programs according to the degree that the program is remedial and subtractive or enrichment and additive in approach. These approaches also impact the degree of bilingualism and biliteracy of students and the social and cultural assimilation or pluralism developed in classrooms. The most common program models used for educating language minority students in the United States are Late-Exit TBE, Early Exit TBE, Maintenance Bilingual Education, and Dual Language Education.

SUBMERSION

Submersion education is not a bilingual model, and fails to meet the elements defined in the *Lau* decision of 1974. This form of education is often referred to as a "sink or swim" model. This means that the language minority student is submerged in the second language pool (English) with no language assistance, and he or she either sinks or swims on his or her own. Submersion was the only model available prior to the *Lau* decision, and aims for full assimilation that would produce a monolingual child in English, if he swims on his/her own.

LANGUAGE-BASED ESL

English as a Second Language (ESL) programs help language minority child learn the English language. At the elementary level, this model typically focuses on English language development, and is implemented in the form of pull-out lessons. ESL programs use approaches in second language teaching and the focus is on form over function, i.e., these programs are grammar-based, with little, if any, use of the primary language. There is a growing trend to move ESL programs from grammar-based to communicative-based, where the focus is on using the English language in meaningful and purposeful ways. However, there still exists a large number of ESL programs using approaches where students conjugate verbs, memorize vocabulary and translate written passages, and teachers use methods designed to develop second language fluency through repetition. More

Table 2 Remedial versus Enrichment Models for Educating Language Minority Students

Model or Program	Description	Linguistic/Academic and Cultural Goal
Remedial and Subtractive Models of Bilingual Education		
Submersion	Academic instruction in L2 only for language minority students. No instructional support is provided by a trained specialist. This model fails to meet the guidelines set forth in the Supreme Court decision in Lau v. Nichols.	Monolingualism and Full assimilation
Language-Based ESL	Language instruction in L2 only for language minority students. Typically, L2 language instruction, taught by second language specialist, is sequenced and grammatically-based.	Monolingualism and Full assimilation
Content-Based ESL	Academic instruction in L2 only for language minority students. L2 instruction is taught via a content-area by second language specialist. L1 used for concept clarification.	Monolingualism and Full assimilation
Early-Exit Transitional Bilingual Education	Academic instruction in both L1 and L2 for language minority students only, with minimal emphasis on the L1. Typically implemented PK–3rd grade. Continuous emphasis on L2.	Minimal bilingualism and Full assimilation
Late-Exit Transitional Bilingual Education	Academic instruction in both L1 and L2 for language minority students only, with emphasis on the L2. Typically implemented PK–5th grade.	Moderate bilingualism and Assimilation
Enrichment and Additive Models of Bilingual Education		
Immersion Education	Academic instruction through both L1 and L2 for Grades K–12. Originally developed for language majority students in Canada.	Biliteracy Pluralism
Dual Language Education	Academic instruction in both L1 and L2 for either language minority or majority students or both together (two-way). Percentage of language instruction varies in 90–10 and 50–50 models.	Biliteracy Pluralism
Maintenance Bilingual Education	Academic instruction in both L1 and L2 for language minority students only with emphasis on the L1. Typically implemented PK–6th grade.	Biliteracy Pluralism

recently, communicative methods that promote meaningful language interactions focused on function versus form have been growing in popularity. Pull-Out ESL is the most expensive, most common and least effective model for long-term English academic proficiency (Crawford, 1999; Thomas & Collier, 2001).

CONTENT-BASED ESL

Content-Based ESL, also referred to as sheltered English, is based on the premise that academic development of a second language is best achieved by learning content in English in carefully structured and supportive L2 environments. In sheltered English classrooms, the ESL teacher uses the English language in one or more content-areas (e.g., science and social studies). The teacher uses extensive sheltered instruction techniques such as visuals, objects, and gestures designed to make the concepts and language being learned comprehensible. These content-based ESL programs may include all subjects in the curriculum or just one or two content areas (Ovando & Collier, 1998).

TRANSITIONAL BILINGUAL EDUCATION MODELS

Early-Exit TBE

Early-exit TBE transitions language minority students out of L1 instruction early, i.e., typically by second or third grade. At this point in their schooling, students are mainstreamed into all-English classrooms. Early-exit TBE is a subtractive and deficit model. It is subtractive bilingualism in that children are forced to set aside or subtract out their native language and assimilate to the majority language. It is a deficit model in that it operates from a perspective that language minority students are lacking in a skill (English language), and thus in need of remediation. The end result is a student who is typically not fully bilingual and biliterate, but rather monolingual.

As described by Ventrone and Benavides (1998), English-only proponents perceive English as the primary method of assimilation and native language loss as a consequence of English acquisition. Academic success of language minority students is primarily measured through achievement in English, which prompts educators to deliver instruction through the English language. This point is clearly made by Cloud, Genesee, & Hamayan (2000) stating that educators operate on the false assumption that the quickest route to English is to teach in English only, and learning in two languages would only impede this process. Indeed, Cloud et al. (1998) report that research has consistently demonstrated that these assumptions are inaccurate. Furthermore, education that is based on this assumption traditionally results in classroom environments that are remedial and promote low expectations of language minority students. These beliefs fail to consider children's innate ability to learn in two languages and accommodate cultural differences (Cloud, Genesee, & Hamayan, 2000).

Late-Exit TBE

Late-exit TBE typically serves language minority students in pre-kindergarten through fifth grade. Students in these programs receive a minimum of 40% of their instruction in their native language in a number of content-areas (e.g., Spanish language arts, social studies, science and/or mathematics). Although there is greater academic achievement than Early-exit TBE models, these programs tend to promote moderate levels of bilingualism due to the increased time of native language instruction. Language minority students do not achieve full biliteracy due to a continued emphasis on English acquisition and assimilation and a remedial approach to educating language minority students.

For example, the Ramirez, Yuen, and Ramey (1991) study of TBE programs found that early-exit TBE models have certain inherent limitations that impact their effectiveness. Results indicate that language minority students in early-exit TBE programs rarely receive enough instruction in their native language, resulting in low levels of L1 and L2 proficiency as compared to late-exit models. Moreover, instruction provided exclusively in English caused many language minority students to fall further behind their English proficient peers by the end of sixth grade. Traditionally, children are not provided the opportunities they need due to lack of higher academic proficiency in their native language for appropriate and successful transfer into the English curriculum.

There are a number of factors, as explained by Gomez (2000), that continue to negatively influence effective implementation of Late-exit TBE programs. These factors include:

a) The use of standardized testing in English for public school accountability, which in turn prompts educators to *push* for early English acquisition;

b) The lack of educator knowledge regarding the transfer of skills and knowledge from the first language (L1) to the second language (L2) and/or the process of L1 or L2 development;

c) The lack of *consistency* by bilingual teachers in language usage, due to the need for translation and clarification in the child's first language (a consequence of the urgency for early English acquisition);

d) The negative and inferior perceptions of non-English languages and cultures by local, state and national communities; and

e) The inherent belief that equality for these students is achieved as soon as they learn English for it facilitates greater participation in American society.

These limitations, that have greatly and negatively influenced the effectiveness of TBE implementation, have consequently perpetuated an erroneous societal belief that bilingual education in general is not working.

Cummins (1981) and Baker (2001) argue that TBE programs are inherently flawed as educational processes for language minority students. TBE programs are deficit model programs that focus on remediation, and usually push for English acquisition regardless of the child's level of proficiency or validation in the L1. As reported by Lessow-Hurley (2000), there are a number of problems inherent in transitional bilingual programs (a) they are subtractive, rather than additive bilingualism, (b) student exit assessments are routinely based on language skills, versus academic language skills, and (c) mastery of a second language is traditionally unattainable in a three-year period. Educators' urgency for English acquisition, states Baker (2001), is that if language minority students do not rapidly acquire English, they may fall behind their English-speaking peers and not fully participate in society. This line of thinking suggests that TBE programs are grounded on the false notion that equal educational opportunity for ELL students is best served by quickly developing their English proficiency, rather than providing the same educational opportunity for academic success. Freeman (1998) in her analysis of U. S. public schools' requirement to provide *equal educational opportunities* to all students guaranteed by Civil Rights legislation explains the following:

> . . . students who come from other than white middle-class native English-speaking homes and communities are often seen as problems at school. Their differences are labeled as deficits, and they are segregated in special classes (ESL, special education, transitional bilingual programs) for remediation. These segregated programs and classes place strong pressure on minority students to assimilate; the student, and not the educational system, has been required to change. If the individual student does not assimilate, that student (and not the system) is labeled a failure (p. 71).

Transitional models of bilingual education, by their very definition, deny access to an equal educational opportunity for language minority students. These models too often rush language minority students into mainstream all-English classrooms while not preparing them for the demanding cognitive rigor that accompany them. These programs typically ill prepare students in both the L1 and L2. The student cannot academically function in his or her L1, much less the L2. It is through enrichment models, such as dual language education, that students' educational attainments can be supported and equity in learning can be impacted. As described by Thomas and Collier (1997b), not only does dual language education have powerful data that substantiates success for the educational achievement of language minority students, but they are also dynamic models for school reform for *all* students.

MAINTENANCE BILINGUAL EDUCATION

Maintenance bilingual education programs were developed in the early 1970s. The main goal of maintenance bilingual education is to develop full bilingualism and biliteracy. The ideal maintenance program, K–12, has never been fully implemented in the United States. The maintenance model was developed to meet the cognitive and linguistic needs of language minority students.

Proponents of the maintenance program argue that concepts and skills learned in a student's first language transfer to the second language. Another argument is that a strong base in a first language facilitates second language acquisition. One of the most important aspects of the maintenance program identified by advocates is the support it provides for home language and culture and the role it can play in building self-esteem and enhancing achievement (Hakuta & Gold, 1987).

DUAL LANGUAGE EDUCATION

The whole discussion of TBE assumes that the ultimate goal is a child who is academically successful in English. Even if transfer of skills and knowledge into the English curriculum is successful, due to well-implemented TBE programs, the question remains, "Is monolingualism a desired goal?" Freeman (1998) describes a successful dual language school as one in which "practices reflect an ideological assumption that linguistic and cultural diversity is a resource to be developed by all students, and not a problem that minority students must overcome in order to participate and achieve at school" (p. 233).

A dual language bilingual/immersion model, as described by Lindholm (1992) and Lindholm-Leary (2001), includes the following goals for all students: (a) high levels of academic proficiency in two languages for all students; (b) academic success in both languages as determined by conventional measurements; and (c) high levels of cross-cultural understanding and psychosocial competence. Dual language bilingual education models incorporate a strong and positive academic and language enriched environment for all students. Dual language bilingual programs create additive environments. These programs build on what students bring to the classroom, viewing them, their parents, and the community at large as resources in achieving literacy in two languages. Recognizing that the strength in literacy in the L1 provides a strong basis for literacy development in L2, dual language programs emphasize maintenance and development of the L1. This attention to L1 development is not just utilitarian, or a way to more effectively acquire English. By giving the L1 equal status with English, it is valued, validated, and ensures its role in daily living within and outside the school environment. Such an environment is empowering, addressing issues of social justice as well as test scores (Baker, 1996). Brauer (1997) reminds us that dual language models remain true to research in second language acquisition, ensuring that students gain Cognitive Academic Language Proficiency (CALP) and learning strategies in L1 before transfer to L2 is expected of them. Thus, the potential for the cognitive benefits associated with full bilingualism is considerable.

Differentiating the dual language bilingual education models from TBE models is the extent of positive academic and language enrichment received by all students. Recent research findings by Thomas and Collier (1997a, 1997b, 2001) conclude that language minority children schooled in well-implemented dual language bilingual programs attain greater long-term academic and linguistic success in English than their native English peers educated in well-implemented monolingual English programs.

Dual language education is based on additive bilingualism as a form of enrichment where children are given the opportunity to add one or more foreign languages while fully developing their native language. Additive bilingualism is associated with high levels of proficiency in two languages, positive self-esteem and positive cross-cultural attitudes.

As exemplified by the literature (Baker, 1996; Cummins, 1981; Lambert, 1987), TBE models all too often rush ELL's into mainstream classrooms while not preparing them for the cognitive demands of an English curriculum. This model inherently denies an equal educational opportunity for language minority students when compared to native English speakers enjoying consistent instruction in, and validation of, one language (L1). The best hope for effectively educating ELL children, achieving equal educational opportunity, and ultimately changing educational and social policy is through dual language bilingual education practices.

Even though dual language bilingual education programs show great promise for achieving success and equality for ELL students and for the development of biliteracy for all students, they must be well-implemented. According to Thomas and Collier (1997a), the following program elements enhance the academic success of ELL students: (a) content instruction is provided in both the L1 and L2; (b) instructional approaches used in classrooms are authentic and interactive; and (c) changes in the socio-cultural context of schooling exist. These elements are traditionally found in dual language bilingual models. The following common characteristics regarding program structure and instructional strategies are found to enhance program success and maximize student outcomes (Baker, 1996; Brauer, 1997 Lindholm-Leary, 2001; Thomas & Collier, 1997a):

- strong administration/parent support with commitment to implement the program over a 4–6 year period,
- heterogeneous grouping of ELL and non-ELL students learning each others' languages,
- consistent separation of languages for instruction,
- highly qualified staff with high expectations for student achievement,
- equal opportunities for use and validation of the two languages,
- balance of language groups (close to 50–50 is desirable),
- sufficient use of the minority language (at least 50%),
- instructional approaches (i.e. learning centers, resource centers, bilingual pairs/groups, cooperative learning, ESL/SSL, discovery learning, vocabulary enrichment in L1 & L2),
- close home-school collaboration with active parent involvement.

Although dual language programs share certain characteristics and are based on the same orientation, they vary in many ways. For instance, they are called by different names and involve different languages and different student populations. In addition, there are different program models, and these models are implemented in a variety of ways. While the literature steadily points to the success of dual language education, these programs are referred to in a variety of ways: a) dual language education (DLE), b) developmental bilingual education (DBE), c) two-way bilingual education (TWBE), d) two-way immersion (TWI), e) dual immersion (DI), and f) enriched education. Educators use the general term, dual language education, because this term captures the essential attribute, the use of two languages for instruction, and it serves as an umbrella for several program models.

There is also variation in the languages included in the programs. Dual language programs have been implemented in the United States for native English speakers and speakers of Spanish, Cantonese, Korean, French, Portuguese, Haitian-Creole, Tagalog, Arabic, and Japanese. Districts have also considered implementing programs in Hmong and Vietnamese. The Center for Applied Linguistics maintains a data base of dual language programs. New programs are frequently added and the list of non-English languages continues to expand. However, the overwhelming majority of dual language programs are Spanish and English.

TWO TYPES OF DUAL LANGUAGE EDUCATION

Dual language education (DLE) programs vary in both languages of instruction and student characteristics. There are two basic types of DLE programs based on student characteristics: Two-way and One-way. Two-way programs are defined as having a student population where a minimum of two-thirds of the students are of one language group. This situation creates a greater balance of both groups, and students come together in two ways: 1) both language groups are present, and 2) both language groups learn in two languages. In one-way programs, well over two-thirds of the students come from the same linguistic and ethnic background. In this situation students come together in only one way, i.e., one language group learning in two languages.

Dual language programs also vary in how time is allocated for instruction in each language. The two basic models, the 90/10 model and the 50/50 model, vary in how the programs divide the time each language is used for instruction. In the 90/10 model the non-English language is used 90% of the time in the early grades, with gradual introduction of English instruction. At about the third or fourth grade, the program achieves 50/50 instruction and this balanced instruction continues through sixth grade. Many schools have adopted this model with the early emphasis on the non-English language to help compensate for the dominance of English outside the school context. One variation within the 90/10 model involves literacy instruction. In most 90/10 programs, all ELL students learn to read and write in the non-English language. However, in some programs all students receive initial literacy instruction in their native language, and the rest of the day is divided with 90% of the instructional time in the non-English language and 10% in English. In the 50/50 model, students learn in each language 50% of the time throughout the program. In many programs, all students learn to read in their primary language and then add the second language. Time for the two languages may be divided in various ways—half day, alternate day, or even alternate week. This model is often used in areas with limited numbers of bilingual teachers. Teachers can team-teach, and the bilingual teacher can provide the non-English language to one group in the morning and the other group in the afternoon (or on alternate days or weeks). As this brief review indicates, despite the common characteristics among dual language programs, considerable variation exists in the languages used for instruction, the student population, and the time each language is used. Schools planning to implement a dual language program should choose the model that fits their student population and also is responsive to community perceptions and needs.

Conclusion

According to Berliner and Biddle (1995), by the year 2030, approximately 40% of school-age population will be non-English speaking. Can we afford not to close the equity and achievement gap between these two groups? An effective educational leader must have a complete understanding of the historical, socio-political, and theoretical factors affecting the education of second language learners. Particularly, educational leaders should understand the transition the field has made from a remedial to an enrichment paradigm. Informed decisions are critical for effectively educating all students and closing the academic achievement gap in this age of accountability. The changing demographics of America's public schools demand that educational leaders have cutting-edge knowledge of pedagogical practices that effectively meet the needs of the students they serve.

Thomas and Collier (2001), in their study of effective bilingual/ESL programs for language minority students, conclude that dual language education models hold the greatest promise for effectively educating ELL students. With the rapid increase of culturally and linguistically diverse students populating today's schools, changes in policies, programs and practices that positively address the changing demographics make quality programs for ELLs not only necessary, but inevitable. A dual language model is the best hope for effectively educating and empowering the growing numbers of ELL students in today's schools. For both ELL and non-ELL students, dual language bilingual approaches appear to challenge and stimulate their learning with positive cognitive advantages for those achieving biliteracy.

Applying Your Knowledge

The following passage is from *Bless me Ultima,* a novel written by Rudolfo Anaya (1972). This passage describes the mental anguish that a non-English speaking child may face when attending school for the first time. This negative experience can be more harmful if the school does not offer instruction in the child's native language. In addition it can have a long lasting effect on the child's academic and social development.

> *Miss Maestas was a kind woman. She thanked the boy whose name was Red for bringing me in, then asked my name. I told her I did not speak English.*
>
> *"¿Cómo te llamas?" She asked.*
>
> *"Antonio Márez," I replied. I told her my mother said I should see her, and that my mother sends her regards.*
>
> *She smiled. "Anthony Márez," she wrote in a book. I drew closer to look at the letters formed by her pen. "Do you want to learn to write?" she asked.*
>
> *"Yes," I answered.*
>
> *"Good," she smiled . . .*
>
> *She took me to the front of the room and spoke to the other boys and girls. She pointed at me but I did not understand her. Then the other boys and girls laughed and pointed at me. I did not feel so good. Thereafter I kept away from the groups as much as I could and worked alone (Anaya, 1972; p. 54).*

QUESTIONS

1. From an academic and social point of view, what educational approach would have prevented Antonio's negative experience?
2. As an educational leader, what type of professional development would you recommend for this teacher to ensure that all students have a positive educational experience?
3. What should Ms. Maestas have done differently to ensure that Antonio's first day of school was a meaningful experience?

4. Effective educational leaders provide equitable academic, linguistic, and social opportunities where non-English-speaking and English-speaking students learn together. Explain the different ways that this can be accomplished.
5. Discuss similar experiences that you have had or have witnessed in your educational career.

QUESTIONS FOR THOUGHT

1. If you were asked to provide a 15-minute presentation to the local board of education regarding programs to be offered to English Language Learners, what would you include in and exclude from your presentation? Why?
2. How do the values and beliefs of the school leadership affect programming decisions for English Language Learners?
3. Do you perceive dual language programs to be an option for ALL children? Why or why not?
4. How do decisions regarding ELL programming affect other programs that might be in the school such as Migrant Education, Gifted and Talented Education, and Special Education? Conversely, do these programs have an impact on ELL programming? Explain.

For Additional Information Online

Bilingual Education Resources on the Net *www.estrellita.com/bil/html*

Office of English Language Acquisition, U.S. Department of Education *www.ed.gov/about/offices/list/oela/index.html?src-mr*

The National Association for Bilingual Education *www.NABE.org*

References

Anaya, R. (1972). *Bless me, Ultima.* Berkeley: TQS Publications.

Aspira of New York, Inc. v. Board of Education of the City of New York, 394 F. Supp. 1161 (S.D. N.Y 1973).

Baker, C. (2001). *Foundations of bilingual education and bilingualism* (3rd ed.). Philadelphia: Multilingual Matters Ltd.

Berliner, D. C., & Biddle, B. J. (1995). *The manufactured crisis: Myths, fraud, and the attack on America's public schools.* Reading, MA: Addison-Wesley.

Bilingual Education Act of 1968, Pub. L. No. 90–247, § 81 Stat. 783 (1968).

Bilingual Education Act of 1974, Pub. L. No. 93–380, § 81 Stat. 816 (1974).

Bilingual Education Act of 1978, Pub. L. No. 95–561, § 92 Stat. 2268 (1978).

Bilingual Education Act of 1984, Pub. L. No. 98–511, § 98 Stat. 2379 (1984).

Bilingual Education Act of 1988, Pub. L. No. 100–297, § 102 Stat. 274 (1988).

Bilingual Education Act of 1994, Pub. L. No. 103–382, (1994).

Brauer, J. Z. (1997). *Learning strategies of native English-speaking fourth grade students in a dual language bilingual education program.* Unpublished manuscript, Boston University School of Education.

California Teachers Association v. State Board of Education, 263 F. 3rd 888 (9th Cir 2001).

Castañeda v. Pickard, 648 F. 2d (5th Cir. 1981).

Clound, W., Genesee, F., & Hamayan, E. (2000). *Dual language instruction: A handbook for enriched education.* Boston: Heinle & Heinle.

Collier, V. P., & Thomas, W. P. (2004, Winter). The astounding effectiveness of dual language education for all. *NABE Journal of Research and Practice, 2*(1). 1–20.

Crawford, J. (2004). *Educating English language learners: Language diversity in the classroom* (5th ed.). Los Angeles, CA: Bilingual Education Services.

Cummins, J. (1981). The role of primary language development in promoting educational success for language minority students. In J. Cummins (Ed.) *Schooling and language minority students: A theoretical framework* (pp. 3–49). Los Angeles: Evaluation, Dissemination, and Assessment Center, California State University.

Cummins, J. (1986). Empowering minority students: A framework for intervention, *Harvard Education Review 56*(1), 18–36.

Freeman, R. D. (1998). *Bilingual education and social change.* Philadelphia: Multilingual Matters, Ltd.

Gómez, L. (2000). Two-way bilingual education: Promoting educational and social change. *The Journal of the Texas Association for Bilingual Education, 5*(1), 43–54.

Gomez v. Illinois Board of Education, 811 F. 2nd 1030 (7th Cir. 1987).

Guadalupe Organization, Inc. v. Tempe, 587 F. 2d 1022 (Circuit, 1978).

Hakuta, K. & Gould, L. J. (1987). Synthesis of research on bilingual education. *Educational Leadership, 44*(6), 39–45.

Idaho Migrant Council v. Board of Education, 647 F. 2d 69 (10th Cir. 1981).

Idaho Migrant Council v. Board of Education (1981) 9th Circuit Court of Appeals.

Keyes v. School District No. 1, Denver, Colorado, 521 F. 2d 465 (10th Cir. 1975).

Kindler, A. L. (2002). *Survey of the states' limited English proficient students and available educational programs and services 1999–2000.* Washington: National Clearinghouse for English Language Acquisition and Language Instructional Education Program, The George Washington University.

Kindler, A. L. (2003). *Survey of the states' limited English proficient students and available educational programs and services 2000–2001.* Washington: National Clearinghouse for English Language Acquisition and Language Instructional Education Program, The George Washington University.

Lambert, W. E. (1987). An overview of issues in immersion education. In *Studies in immersion education: A collection for U. S. educators* (pp. 8–30). Sacramento: California State Department of Education.

Lau v. Nichols, 414 U.S. 563 (1974).

Lessow-Hurley, J. (2000). *The foundations of dual language instruction.* New York, NY: Addison Wesley.

Lindholm, K. J. (1992). Dual language bilingual/immersion education: Theory, conceptual issues, and pedagogical implications. In R. V. Padilla, & A. H. Benavides (Eds.), *Critical perspectives on bilingual education research* (pp. 195–220) Tempe, AZ: Bilingual Press.

Lindholm-Leary, K. J. (2001). *Dual language education.* Buffalo, NY: Multilingual Matters, Ltd.

No Child Left Behind Act of 2002, Pub. L. No. 107–110. § 115 Stat. 1429 (2002).

Olsen, L. (1991). *California Perspectives.* San Francisco: California Tomorrow.

Otero v. Mesa County Valley School District No. 51, 408 F. Supp. 162 (D.C. Colo. 1972).

Ovando, C. J., & Collier, V. P. (1998). *Bilingual and ESL classrooms: Teaching in a multicultural contexts* (2nd ed.). Boston: McGraw-Hill.

Pycior, J. L. (1977). *LBJ & Mexican Americans: The paradox of power.* Austin: University of Texas Press.

Ramirez, J. D., Yuen, S. D., & Ramey, D. R. (1991). *Final Report: Longitudinal study of structured immersion strategy, Early-exit and Late-exit transitional bilingual education programs for language-minority children.* San Mateo, CA: Aguirre International.

Rios v. Reed, 480 F. Supp. 14 (U.S. D.C. E.D.N.Y. 1978).

Rong, S. L. & Peissle, J. (1998). *Educating immigrant students: What we need to know to meet the challenges.* Thousand Oaks, CA: Corwin Press.

Serna v. Portales Municipal Schools, 351 G. Supp. 1279 (N.D. N. Mex. 1972).

Thomas, W. P., & Collier, V. (1997a). *School effectiveness for language minority students.* Washington, DC: George Washington University, National Clearinghouse for Bilingual Education (NCBE)-Resource Collection Series.

Thomas, W. P., & Collier, V. (1997b). Two languages are better than one. *Educational Leadership, 55*(4), 23–26.

Thomas, W. P., & Collier, V. P. (2001). *A national study of school effectiveness for language minority students' long-term academic achievement.* Retrieved September 4, 2002, from *www.crede.ucsc.edu/research/llaa/1.1_es.html.*

U.S. Commission on Civil Rights. (1971) *A better chance to learn.* Washington, DC: U.S. Printing Press.

Ventrone, N. A., & Benavides, A. H. (1998). Bilingual education and the English-only movement: Public attitudes through mass media. *The Journal of the Texas Association for Bilingual Education, 4*(2), 2–13.

Yarborough, R. (1994). Perspectives on the first national bilingual education act. In R. Rodriguez, N. Ramos, & J. A. Ruiz-Escalante. (Eds.). *Compendium of readings in bilingual education Issues and practices* (pp. 291–293). San Antonio: Texas Association for Bilingual Education.

Early Childhood/Early Childhood Special Education

8

Mary Kay Zabel

Since the National Association for the Education of
Young Children (NAEYC) defines "early childhood"
as the ages of birth through eight years *(www.naeyc.org)*,
it is clear that any elementary school contains
a number of ECE programs and classrooms.

—Mary Kay Zabel

Objectives

1. Understand the principles of developmentally appropriate practice and their application to programs for all young children
2. Discuss the principles and methods of appropriate assessment for young children with disabilities and their typical peers
3. Identify the continuum of programs and intervention practices that should be available for infants and young children with and without disabilities, and the role of families in these programs
4. Apply this knowledge by assessing programs for young children in a particular school or district

Historical/Legislative Background

National and legislative interest in the care and education of young children began to surface in the United States in the early 1900s. At this time, day care centers were operated selectively and were a part of the social welfare system, designed for "pathological" families (Howard, 2001). The Great Depression and the WPA (Works Progress Administration) furthered the notion that young children could benefit from group care by establishing 1,900 WPA day care centers serving 40,000 children by 1937 (Howard, 2001). As World War II took its toll on the families of the world, Europe and the United States increased the numbers and types of childcare available to parents and children.

In the 1950s, investigations into the effect of poverty on children and families became a policy initiative, culminating in the passage of the Economic Opportunity Act of 1964. This legislation eventually resulted in the creation of the Head Start program—a program which "recognized the linkage between children's health and development, the importance of local community-based control, the emphasis on supporting parents in their decision making, and the need to be able to thoughtfully coordinate the many needed services from different domains . . . "(Guralnick, 1997, p. 4). Very soon after the establishment of Project Head Start (1965), the Handicapped Children's Early Education Program was created (1968) to fund model preschool programs for children with disabilities. The continued progress and development of both these strands of early childhood education have been closely linked from that point. In 1972, Congress required Head Start to reserve 10% of its enrollment for children with disabilities, and in 1975, PL 94–142, the Education for All Handicapped Children Act (EAHCA) provided incentive funding for programs serving children 3–5 years of age who had disabilities. Each subsequent amendment of EAHCA has provided for more services for young children with disabilities, and programs serving these children are now required of all schools by the Individuals with Disabilities Education (IDEA).

Many states now endorse or certify teachers of young children with a "blended" or "integrated" license. Such an endorsement credential often combines early childhood education and early childhood special education in one license, rather than having separate licensure for each. In addition, programs for infants and toddlers (birth to age three) are often a part of this mix. While programs for children three years of age and older are clearly a part of the school district responsibility, the supervision of programs for infants and toddlers varies from state to state. Each state identifies a lead agency to oversee these programs, and that can vary with the decision of the state agencies. Approximately equal numbers of states selected their Department of Education or their Department of Health to administer this part of IDEA, while remaining states and territories designated other agencies such as Mental Health, Mental Retardation, or Human Resources as their lead agencies (Howard, 2001).

Program Description

Two of the major themes in early childhood education and early childhood special education are developmentally appropriate practice, and natural environments. Developmentally appropriate practice (DAP) is the title given to the widely researched and accepted outline of factors necessary for high quality care and education of young children. It is promoted and disseminated by the National Association for the Education of Young Children (NAEYC) and forms the bedrock for many of the decisions made by teachers and administrators every day. According to Bredekamp and Copple (1997), 12 principles delineate DAP:

1. Domains of children's development—physical, social, emotional, and cognitive—are closely related. Development in one domain influences and is influenced by development in other domains.
2. Development occurs in a relatively orderly sequence, with later abilities, skills, and knowledge building on those already acquired.
3. Development proceeds at varying rates from child to child as well as unevenly within different areas of each child's functioning.
4. Early experiences have both cumulative and delayed effects on individual children's development; optimal periods exist for certain types of development and learning.
5. Development proceeds in predictable directions toward greater complexity, organization, and internalization.
6. Development and learning occur in, and are influenced by, multiple social and cultural contexts.
7. Children are active learners, drawing on direct physical and social experience as well as culturally transmitted knowledge to construct their own understandings of the world around them.
8. Development and learning result from interaction of biological maturation and the environment, which includes both the physical and social worlds that children live in.
9. Play is an important vehicle for children's social, emotional, and cognitive development, as well as a reflection of their development.
10. Development advances when children have opportunities to practice newly acquired skills as well as when they experience a challenge just beyond the level of their present mastery.
11. Children demonstrate different modes of knowing and learning, and different ways of representing what they know.
12. Children develop and learn best in the context of a community where they are safe and valued, their physical needs are met and they feel psychologically secure (pp. 10–15; also available on NAEYC website, *www.naeyc.org*).

While all of these principles are important for administrators and school leaders in constructing quality programs for young children, one of the most critical is number nine—the importance of play. In this era of high stakes testing, quality performance assessments, and outcomes-based learning, it is critical for school leaders to understand the vital nature of play in the development of cognitive, social, motor, and language skills in the young child. As Lamb stated (2001), "Creating a learning environment based on play activities requires considerable time, commitment, and resources" (p. 100). Both children with disabilities and their typically developing peers learn and expand their horizons through play activities. Their interactions with each other, their observation of peers using materials in various ways, and their exposure to various play environments are crucial to the acquisition of skills that will allow them to be successful students in the upper grades.

Identification and Assessment

Children under the age of five are identified for inclusion in early childhood education (ECE) and early childhood special education (ECSE) programs in a variety of ways. Children entering Head Start programs must meet income guidelines based on the Department of Health and Human Services poverty level delineations for the current year. As stated previously, 10% of the enrollment of Head Start classes is reserved for students with disabilities; these disabilities can be in any area of development, including speech and language. Young children who might need services provided in ECSE programs for three to five year olds can be referred in a variety of ways. Referrals may come from parents who have concerns about the development of their children, from physicians who have similar concerns, or the children may be identified in a district-wide screening open to all families residing in the district. These screenings, usually staffed by district personnel, have as their sole purpose the identification of children who might benefit from further assessment. No diagnostic, programmatic, or referral decisions should be made on the basis of a screening test, as these are only designed to note the need for further information.

Once children in the 3–5 age range have been referred by a parent or other interested party, or have been identified as needing further assessment by a screening, assessment procedures similar to those for older children with disabilities are considered. All the procedural safeguards, notification requirements, and parental permissions required for any child under IDEA are also required for young children (see Chapter 1, Special Education). In addition, the Division for Early Childhood, a division of the Council for Exceptional Children, suggested the following recommended practices designed to fully include families in the assessment procedure, to see that assessment is individualized and appropriate, and to ensure that assessment provides useful information for intervention. These practices are for families with children in the infant toddler range as well as the three to five group (Sandall, McLean, & Smith; 2000). Some of the recommended practices for including families are:

1. Professionals provide families with easy access by phone or other means for arranging initial screening and other activities.
2. Professionals ensure a single point of contact for families throughout the assessment process.
3. Families receive a written statement of program philosophy regarding family participation in assessment planning and activities (p. 23).

Recommended practices for ensuring individualized and appropriate assessment for the child and family include:

1. Professionals use multiple measures to assess child status, progress, and program impact and outcomes (e.g. developmental observations, criterion/curriculum-based interviews, informed clinical opinion and curriculum-compatible norm-referenced scales).
2. Professionals choose materials and procedures that accommodate the child's sensory, physical, responsive, and temperamental differences.
3. Professionals rely on materials that capture the child's authentic behaviors in routine circumstances.
4. Professionals seek information directly from families and other regular caregivers, using materials and procedures that the families themselves can manage, to design—Individual Family Service Plan/Individual Education Plan (IFSP/IEP) goals and activities.
5. Professionals assess children in contexts that are familiar to the child (p. 24).

Practices assuring that assessment provides useful information for intervention include:

1. Families and professionals assess the presence and extent of atypical child behavior that may be a barrier to intervention and progress.
2. Professionals use functional behavioral analysis of behavior to assess the form and function of challenging behaviors.

3. Program supervisors, in concert with the ECE/ECSE team, use only those measures that have high treatment validity (i.e., that link assessment, individual program planning, and progress evaluation).
4. Professionals appraise the level of support that a child requires in order to perform a task.
5. Professionals report assessment results in a manner that is immediately useful for planning program goals and objectives (p. 25).

While even these abbreviated lists (for full lists see Sandall, McLean, & Smith, 2000) seem daunting in their length and detail, such attention to the procedure and content of assessment practices is necessary when working with children where diagnostic labels may be difficult or impossible to apply, and where the full participation of the family is critical.

Most programs for children three to five years of age who have disabilities also include typically developing peers. This program model has become the most popular way of serving the educational needs of young children with disabilities because of its emphasis on the development of typical behaviors and skills. Deciding on the method of choosing typical peers is an important part of the ECE/ECSE team's (including the principal or other designated school leader) program design. Some school districts accept applications and place typical peers on a first come, first served basis, while others review the applications and try to balance the class in terms of age and gender. An approach used by some school districts gives the preschool-aged children of teachers in the district first chance at these typical peer slots. That procedure often increases the likelihood that the typical peers will have good language, cognitive, and social skills—in addition to providing a nice perk to teachers. Whatever the method chosen, care should be taken to ensure that the typical peers do, in fact, exhibit development appropriate to their age. It is tempting to utilize peer spaces to serve children who do not meet the requirements for special education service, but would nonetheless benefit from such help. While this is a laudable intention, it does defeat the purpose of having typical peers for the children with disabilities and can substantially add to the ECE/ECSE teacher's actual caseload, without increasing resources.

Program Models

There are many different models of service provision in this area of education/special education. For the purposes of clarity, they will be discussed under three broad headings: infant/toddler programs (children with disabilities only); early childhood/early childhood special education integrated programs; and separate early childhood and early childhood special education programs.

INFANT/TODDLER PROGRAMS

As discussed earlier in this chapter, these programs may come under the lead of many different state agencies, but no matter which lead agency is chosen (education, health, mental retardation, developmental disabilities), the school district is inevitably part of the plan. Schools are frequently the first point of contact for parents who are seeking services for their infant or toddler whom they suspect may have developmental delays. It is critical, therefore, that a first contact person be clearly designated by the school district, and such information publicized where parents can find it. Information on screening, referral processes, and information sources should be provided to physicians' offices, public health departments, social services offices, churches, schools, and other places where parents of young children might be found. Once families in need of services have been identified, the above assessment practices should be put into place and assessment conducted in the areas of specific needs.

After the assessment process has been concluded, an Individual Family Service Plan (IFSP) is written for the child and his or her family. This plan is similar to an IEP, but has some important differences. First of all, the inclusion of the word "family" in the title is no accident. While the IEP focuses on the needs of the child, the IFSP focuses on family needs. The infant or toddler is always viewed in the context of his or her family. IFSPs seek to strengthen the family's ability to enhance the child's development, and this is done through a series of outcomes and activities, not the goals and objectives and/or benchmarks found in the IEP. The IFSP resembles the IEP, however, in that it is written in full collaboration with parents and team members; that the team sees all outcomes and activities as essential to the child's optimal development; and that transitions to other levels of service (center-based programs, for example) are a part of the plan.

If the infant or toddler qualifies for services, the next decision centers on services to be provided. The recommended practice is that infant/toddler services—whether provided by a speech/language therapist, an occupational/physical therapist, an early intervention teacher (ECSE) or by a combination of these and other professionals—should be in the "natural environment" where "natural routines" can be a part of the process (Raver, 1999). The natural environment for most infants is, of course, the home. Services may be provided in the child's home, the home of another caregiver (e.g. relative, day care provider), or some other environment that is a part of the child's natural routine. Clearly, the purpose of such placement of services is designed to help parents integrate exercises, activities, learning strategies, and language experiences into the daily fabric of their lives with their children. Activities and experiences that can be integrated into meal times, bath times, diaper changing times—any aspect of the family's routine—is the goal for interventionists at this level. Learning experiences integrated in this way are much more likely to be repeated, reinforced and made a part of what happens in this family on a daily basis.

EARLY CHILDHOOD EDUCATION/EARLY CHILDHOOD SPECIAL EDUCATION INTEGRATED PROGRAM

Programs for 3–5 year olds with and without disabilities are based on two models. They may be *inclusive* (the main focus of the program is on typically developing young children, but children who have disabilities are welcomed, included, and curriculum and activities are adapted for their needs—Head Start is an example); or *integrated* (class sizes are smaller, program focus is on both children with disabilities and typically developing peers, and the ratio of children with disabilities to typical peers tends to be larger than in inclusive programs). In both types of programs, early childhood special education teachers, speech/language therapists, occupational/physical therapists, and other specialists may provide services in the classroom or other appropriate places.

Curriculum areas in the EC/ECSE classroom may include many different types of learning and exploration. Major goals for this age group include helping children learn problem-solving skills, making choices, and engaging in active exploration of the environment and materials. Teachers strive to provide engaging and stimulating settings, to promote a supportive classroom environment, and—perhaps most importantly—to create a language-rich environment (Dunlap, 1997). Acquiring a useful language system, whether it is spoken word, sign language, a picture exchange program, or a language system supported by assistive technology, is a critical task for the preschool years. Teachers of students with special needs as well as those of typically developing children emphasize, elaborate, generate, modify, and support all types of language use in the EC/ECSE classroom.

Teachers also provide dramatic play areas, where socialization skills may be learned and practiced, and children have an opportunity to work through areas in their lives where such play may help them sort out feelings and behavior. A reading or library center is an essential part of the EC/ECSE classroom where a comfortable environment and a wealth of interesting, engaging books encourage children to explore literature alone or with peers and teachers. An area with blocks for building, supporting math concepts, fine motor abilities, cooperative play and problem solving is also an integral part of such a program (Lamb, 2001). Science and math materials, puzzles and games, an art activity center, and tables for sensory exploration, perhaps containing sand, water, or other materials, also aid in learning for all children (Lamb, 2001).

Classroom assessment is a large part of any program serving young children, although such assessment may not resemble techniques used by teachers of children in upper grades. Children who have IEPs are, of course, continually assessed based on the goals, objectives, and benchmarks written by the IEP team to guide and evaluate their progress. Assessment in this area will largely rely on daily teacher observation and recording of data, and a clipboard or file system for each child is often utilized for this purpose. Other assessment systems, such as the Work Sampling System, are available for assessing progress for all children (Dichtelmiller, Jablon, Marsden, & Meisels, 2001). This system, available for preschool (age three) through fifth grade, provides specific, measurable developmentally appropriate guidelines to "enhance the process of observation and to ensure the reliability and consistency of teachers' observations" (Dichtelmiller et al, 2001, p. vii). The guidelines are drawn from many local, state, and national standards supporting curriculum development. While this system incorporates standards from these various agencies, they do not form an external template designed to fit every child. As Meisels says, "[The Work Sampling System] does not stand on its own: it comes to life only in the hands of a teacher. Like a car it needs a driver, like a book it requires a reader, like a musical composition it calls for a performer" (Dichtelmiller, Jablon, Dorfman, Marsden, & Meisels, 2001, p. xiv). There are also curriculum planning programs, such as the Activity-Based Approach to Early Intervention that integrate assessment, planning, and evaluation from the beginning, providing a linked system that supports positive outcomes for children (Bricker, Pretti-Frontczak & McComas, 1998).

EARLY CHILDHOOD SPECIAL EDUCATION PROGRAMS

While the majority of school or center-based programs serving young children with special needs follow the integrated or inclusive models discussed above, there are programs where all the children enrolled have specific disabilities. These programs are sometimes associated with schools for older children serving that disability (e.g., state schools for the blind or for the deaf), programs that serve low-incidence disabilities (e.g., deaf/blind) or programs that may be associated with public or private facilities (psychiatric centers or hospitals) (Handleman & Harris, 2001). These programs often make efforts to see that the children spend time in some way with typically developing peers. Peer interaction at any age, but particularly as children are acquiring and refining group social interaction skills, should be an essential part of any program.

EARLY CHILDHOOD PROGRAMS

Since the National Association for the Education of Young Children (NAEYC) defines "early childhood" as the ages of birth through eight years *(www.naeyc.org)*, it is clear that any elementary school contains a number of ECE programs and classrooms. Reconciling the growing demands for high stakes content testing at younger ages with the demonstrated and research-based needs for developmentally appropriate learning environments for young children is a major task for teachers and administrators. The goals of both are similar—at least in intent: to provide the best possible educational experience for children. Many teachers, however, focus on this task from an input perspective. They are most concerned with how the children acquire knowledge and skills, many employing a constructivist approach (leaning heavily on the work of Piaget) that emphasizes children being involved in authentic tasks, and working on projects that require active learning. The teachers' skills are utilized to integrate such learning into themes, set up opportunities for the learning to take place, and guide children on their own process of discovery (Branscombe, Castle, Dorsey, Surbeck, & Taylor, 2003). The focus of many governing bodies is on outcomes. The only questions being asked involve how well children have learned specific concepts and mastered specific skills.

While this may be something of an oversimplification of the issues, this is a debate that is going on in literally every state and locale in the nation. Our ability to resolve these competing agendae will be critical in the effort to provide a truly appropriate education to all children over the coming years. Issues such as content testing in Head Start, prekindergarten programs in all schools, and full day kindergarten are some of the points where these camps are engaging one another. Such dialogue is good if it eventually results in compromise that is beneficial. As Lamb (2001) points out, "Some communities feel the need for full-day rather than half-day kindergarten. Research has not shown that academic test scores increase when kindergarten is conducted for a full day; however, test scores in these early years are not accurate indicators of the long-term effects of early education on academic achievement, particularly if individual needs are met the first years of school" (p.105). She goes on to point out that it *is* clear that for many children (particularly ELL—English Language Learners—students), kindergarten does provide a language-rich environment and that provides a great opportunity for growth. She concludes, "The real question is whether or not a truly rich kindergarten program can be achieved in a 3–4 hour program. In kindergarten if children spend time in each learning center, engage in outdoor play, enjoy music and art, and are involved in large group activities, a half-day program may not suffice" (p. 106). This illustrates the task that is really before early childhood educators and administrators. The key is in asking the right questions—what constitutes a rich and responsive learning environment for young children? And how can we use and devise appropriate measures to demonstrate that it is effective? Our decisions must be based on what we know and what we continue to learn about quality programs for young children, and our commitment must be to see that they are implemented for all.

Assessing the Situation

Using the Administrator's Essentials Checklist for EC/ECSE, evaluate an early childhood program with which you are familiar. Are there aspects of the program that need immediate attention? Whose responsibility is it to see that these recommendations for appropriate practice are in place? Do you see areas where knowledge and skills may be at an awareness level, but need more resources? More focus? More administrative attention? What would the next steps be?

Administrator's Essentials Checklist for EC/ECSE

I. **Administrators, other professionals, and families shape policy at the national, state, and local levels that promote the use of recommended practices in EC/ECSE.**
Examples/Notes:

Is this practice evident in policy/procedure?   ❏ *Yes*   ❏ *Emerging*   ❏ *No*

II. **Administrators ensure that they and their staff have the knowledge, training, and credentials necessary to implement the recommended practices in EC/ECSE.**

A. Program coordinators/supervisors have training in EC/ECSE, intervention and supervision.
Examples/Notes:

Is this practice evident in policy/procedure?   ❏ *Yes*   ❏ *Emerging*   ❏ *No*

B. Administrators are affiliated with professional EC/ECSE organizations and encourage staff to maintain their affiliations. Continuing education such as attendance at meetings and conferences to enhance professional growth is supported.
Examples/Notes:

Is this practice evident in policy/procedure?   ❏ *Yes*   ❏ *Emerging*   ❏ *No*

1. Program policies provide clear job descriptions and provide for personnel competencies and on-going staff development, technical assistance, supervision, and evaluation to inform and improve the skills of practitioners and administrators.
Examples/Notes:

Is this practice evident in policy/procedure?   ❏ *Yes*   ❏ *Emerging*   ❏ *No*

III. Program policies and administration promote families as partners in the planning and delivery of services, supports, and resources.

A. When creating program policies and procedures, strategies are employed to capture family and community voices and to support the active and meaningful participation of families and community groups including those that are traditionally underrepresented.
Examples/Notes:

Is this practice evident in policy/procedure?   ❑ *Yes*   ❑ *Emerging*   ❑ *No*

B. Program policies create a participatory decision-making process of all stakeholders including individuals with disabilities. Training in teaming is provided as needed.
Examples/Notes:

Is this practice evident in policy/procedure?   ❑ *Yes*   ❑ *Emerging*   ❑ *No*

C. Program policies ensure that families understand their rights including conflict resolution, confidentiality, and other matters.
Examples/Notes:

Is this practice evident in policy/procedure?   ❑ *Yes*   ❑ *Emerging*   ❑ *No*

D. Program policies are examined and revised as needed to ensure that they reflect and respect the diversity of children, families, and personnel.
Examples/Notes:

Is this practice evident in policy/procedure?   ❑ *Yes*   ❑ *Emerging*   ❑ *No*

E. Program policies are provided in sufficient detail and formats so that all stakeholders understand what the policy means.
Examples/Notes:

Is this practice evident in policy/procedure?   ❑ *Yes*   ❑ *Emerging*   ❑ *No*

F. Program policies require a family-centered approach in all decisions and phases of service delivery (system entry, assessment procedures, IFSP/IEP, intervention, transition, etc.) including presenting families with flexible and individualized options for the location, timing, and types of services, supports, and resources that are not disruptive of family life.
Examples/Notes:

Is this practice evident in policy/procedure?   ❏ *Yes*   ❏ *Emerging*   ❏ *No*

G. Program policies provide for the dissemination of information about program initiative and outcomes to stakeholders.
Examples/Notes:

Is this practice evident in policy/procedure?   ❏ *Yes*   ❏ *Emerging*   ❏ *No*

IV. **Program policies and administration promote the use of recommended practices.**

A. Program policies reflect recommended practices including personnel standards, child-staff ratios, group size, caseloads, safety, assistive technology and EC/ECSE service and practices. Incentives, training, and technical assistance to promote the use of recommended practices in all settings are provided.
Examples/Notes:

Is this practice evident in policy/procedure?   ❏ *Yes*   ❏ *Emerging*   ❏ *No*

B. Program policies establish accountability systems that provide resources, supports, and clear action steps to ensure compliance with regulations and ensure that recommended practices are adopted, utilized, maintained, and evaluated resulting in high quality services.
Examples/Notes:

Is this practice evident in policy/procedure?   ❏ *Yes*   ❏ *Emerging*   ❏ *No*

C. Program policies support the provision of services in inclusive or natural learning environments (places in which typical children participate such as the home or community settings, public and private preschools, child care, recreation groups, etc.). Strategies are used to overcome challenges to inclusion.
Examples/Notes:

Is this practice evident in policy/procedure? ❑ *Yes* ❑ *Emerging* ❑ *No*

D. Program policies ensure that the IFSP/IEP is used on a regular and frequent basis to determine the type and amounts of services, the location of services and desired outcomes.
Examples/Notes:

Is this practice evident in policy/procedure? ❑ *Yes* ❑ *Emerging* ❑ *No*

E. Program policies ensure that family supports, service coordination, transitions, and other practices occur in response to the child and family needs rather than being determined by the age of the child.
Examples/Notes:

Is this practice evident in policy/procedure? ❑ *Yes* ❑ *Emerging* ❑ *No*

F. Program policies ensure that multiple instructional models are available to meet the individual needs of children (e.g., less structure-more structure; child-driven to teacher-driven; peer-mediated to teacher mediated, etc.).
Examples/Notes:

Is this practice evident in policy/procedure? ❑ *Yes* ❑ *Emerging* ❑ *No*

G. Administrators provide for a supportive work environment (e.g., hiring and retention policies, compensation and benefits, safety, workspace, etc.).
Examples/Notes:

Is this practice evident in policy/procedure? ❑ *Yes* ❑ *Emerging* ❑ *No*

V. Program policies and administration promote interagency and interdisciplinary collaboration.

A. Program policies include structures and mechanisms such as job descriptions, planning time, training, and resources for teaming resulting in meaningful participation for on-going coordination among professionals, families, and programs related to service delivery including transition.
Examples/Notes:

Is this practice evident in policy/procedure?   ❑ *Yes*   ❑ *Emerging*   ❑ *No*

B. Program policies facilitate and provide for comprehensive and coordinated systems of services through interagency collaboration by clearly delineating the components, activities, and responsibilities of all agencies.
Examples/Notes:

Is this practice evident in policy/procedure?   ❑ *Yes*   ❑ *Emerging*   ❑ *No*

C. Program policies result in families and professionals from different disciplines working as a team developing and implementing IFSPs/IEPS that integrate their expertise into common goals.
Examples/Notes:

Is this practice evident in policy/procedure?   ❑ *Yes*   ❑ *Emerging*   ❑ *No*

VI. Program policies, administration, and leadership promote program evaluation and systems change efforts at the community level.

A. A shared vision (of all stakeholders), clear values/beliefs, and an understanding of the culture and context to be changed guide efforts to restructure and reform systems. Decisions about what to change result from regular analysis and evaluation of discrepancies among the vision, beliefs, knowledge, and current practices.
Examples/Notes:

Is this practice evident in policy/procedure?   ❑ *Yes*   ❑ *Emerging*   ❑ *No*

B. Assessment of the interests, issues, and priorities of constituent groups guides the selection and direction of leadership and systems change strategies.
Examples/Notes:

Is this practice evident in policy/procedure? ❏ *Yes* ❏ *Emerging* ❏ *No*

C. Leadership and systems change efforts produce positive outcomes for children, families, and communities that are responsive to their needs. Evaluation data are used to ensure: (a) service utilization, (b) more efficient and effective supports for children, families, and staff, and (c) appropriate systems change leadership and strategies.
Examples/Notes:

Is this practice evident in policy/procedure? ❏ *Yes* ❏ *Emerging* ❏ *No*

D. Leadership capacity, risk taking, and shared decision-making among professionals and families at all levels of the organization are cultivated.
Examples/Notes:

Is this practice evident in policy/procedure? ❏ *Yes* ❏ *Emerging* ❏ *No*

E. Leadership and systems change efforts include attention to: timely job-embedded professional development, funding, program evaluation, accountability, governance, program accreditation, curriculum and naturalistic instruction/supports.
Examples/Notes:

Is this practice evident in policy/procedure? ❏ *Yes* ❏ *Emerging* ❏ *No*

F. Leadership and systems change efforts rely on strong relationships and collaboration within and across systems: between consumer and system, across systems that deal with children and families, among components within a system, and among professionals from diverse disciplines.
Examples/Notes:

Is this practice evident in policy/procedure?   ❏ *Yes*   ❏ *Emerging*   ❏ *No*

G. Leadership is committed and willing to change organizational structures (staffing, schedules, teaming) to be responsive to individual needs.
Examples/Notes:

Is this practice evident in policy/procedure?   ❏ *Yes*   ❏ *Emerging*   ❏ *No*

H. Change is institutionalized through the development of coordinated management and accountability systems.
Examples/Notes:

Is this practice evident in policy/procedure?   ❏ *Yes*   ❏ *Emerging*   ❏ *No*

I. Resources are provided for program evaluation that occurs along established time points, incorporating appropriate measurable indicators of progress including child and family outcomes and preferences.
Examples/Notes:

Is this practice evident in policy/procedure?   ❏ *Yes*   ❏ *Emerging*   ❏ *No*

J. Program evaluation is comprehensive, is multi-dimensional, and incorporates a variety of methods for assessing the progress and outcomes of change. Evaluation efforts take into account differing cultural, contextual, demographic, and experiential perspectives including those of parents and of individuals with disabilities.
Examples/Notes:

Is this practice evident in policy/procedure?   ❏ *Yes*   ❏ *Emerging*   ❏ *No*

K. Program policies delineate all components of service delivery and provide for tracking and evaluation of all components, including child and family outcomes, to ensure that recommended practices are implemented as intended.
Examples/Notes:

Is this practice evident in policy/procedure?   ❏ *Yes*   ❏ *Emerging*   ❏ *No*

(adapted from Smith, B. J. (2000). Administrator's essentials: Creating policies and procedures that support recommended practices in early intervention/early childhood special education. In Sandall, S., McLean, M. E., & Smith, B. J. (Eds.) *DEC recommended practices in early intervention/early childhood special education.* Reston, VA: Division for Early Childhood, Council for Exceptional Children.)

Applying Your Knowledge

In Monday morning's mail, you find this letter from the parent of one of the children in the ECSE classroom. The teacher in this classroom is experienced and skilled as an ECSE teacher and uses play as the major method of instruction for students in her classroom. Mrs. Smith has exhibited concern on a previous occasion, stating that Anwar is not 'catching up' to the other children she knows. Since Anwar has Down syndrome and a fairly substantial hearing loss, 'catching up' is probably an appropriate goal at this time.

Dear Ms. Alessjandro;

I am writing this letter to you because I am afraid if I come to talk to you after school, I will not remember all the things I want to say. I am really concerned about Anwar's learning and I am considering asking that he be placed in another ECSE classroom.

Please do not think that I dislike his teacher, or that Anwar is unhappy...that is not the problem. He loves to go to school and he loves being in the class and playing with the other children. I guess that is part of the problem. I am afraid that Anwar needs more than playing, and that is all he does in Ms. Finch's room.

As you know, Anwar's Down syndrome and hearing problems make it very difficult for him to learn, and I am afraid that without some very specific learning, he will not be able to succeed in the world at all. I know that he has disabilities, but he is almost four and a half years old, and most people still cannot understand him when he talks to them. He does know several signs, and that is helpful at home, but I think he needs to have more specific time in learning to speak and learning to do the things other children his age do.

This last weekend, my sister and her family were at our house, and I was amazed to see all the things her three year old could do! She listened to stories and said some of the words with her mother, she built things with blocks, she counted 'one, two' and she could sit for a long time to play with her toys. Anwar does none of these things.

Like I said, he really likes to come to his program, but I am afraid he is falling farther and farther behind the other children, because all he does is play. I know you and Ms. Finch have told us parents that you teach through play, but I don't see that Anwar is learning much. Soon he will be in school with bigger children, and he won't be able to do any of the things that are required in the classroom. I don't feel that I can let this situation continue. I am sorry to have to say these things, because I know you are a caring person and you have been very kind to Anwar. But I must look out for his future.

Thank you for your time.

Sincerely,

Mrs. Antelia Smith (Anwar's mother)

QUESTIONS

1. How will you structure your discussion with Mrs. Smith—what questions will you ask? Who will you ask to be present?
2. Assuming that you believe this program to be the most appropriate one for Anwar, how will you help Mrs. Smith to see that his needs are being met?
3. What actions, other than your conversation with Mrs. Smith, will you suggest to address her concerns?

QUESTIONS FOR THOUGHT

1. What would be some questions that you would ask of applicants for an early childhood teaching position in your school to assure that the individual understands and advocate Developmentally Appropriate Practice (DAP)?
2. If you were charged with organizing a workshop for principals on understanding and supporting quality early childhood/early childhood special education programs, what would your content be and what are some activities you might use in delivering the identified content?
3. Are you an advocate of using standardized achievement tests with your children? Explain your position.
4. How do program issues in EC/ECSE link to other special instructional programs, e.g., migrant education, bilingual education, gifted/talented, etc.?
5. How do IEPs and IFSPs differ? Why are IFSPs especially important for work with young children?
6. How would you go about organizing a quality child find effort? Explain what you would do, who you would involve and why?

For Additional Information Online

National Association for the Education of Young Children *www.naeyc.org*

The Children's Defense Fund *www.childrensdefense.org*

Council for Exceptional Children (link to Division of Early Childhood) *www.cec.org*

Early Childhood Research Institute *www.clas.uiuc.edu*

Assistive Technology and Communication for Early Childhood *www.uchsc.edu/library*

References

Bredekamp, S., & Copple, C. (Eds.). (1997). *Developmentally appropriate practice in early childhood programs.* Washington, D.C.: National Association for the Education of Young Children.

Branscombe, N. A., Castle, K., Dorsey, A. G., Surbeck, E., & Taylor, J. B. (2003). *Early childhood curriculum: A constructivist perspective.* Boston: Houghton Mifflin.

Bricker, D., Pretti-Frontczak, K., & McComas, N. (1998). *An activity-based approach to early intervention* (2nd edition). Baltimore, MD: Paul H. Brookes.

Dichtelmiller, M. L., Jablon, J. R., Dorfman, A. B., Marsden, D. B., & Meisels, S. (2001). *Work sampling in the classroom: A teacher's manual* (3rd edition). NY: Pearson Education.

Dichtelmiller, M. L., Jablon, J. R., Marsden, D. B., & Meisels, S. (2001). *The work sampling system: Preschool through third grade, omnibus guidelines* (4th edition). NY: Pearson.

Dunlap, L. L. (1997). *An introduction to early childhood special education.* Boston: Allyn and Bacon.

Guralnick, M. J. (1997). *The effectiveness of early intervention.* Baltimore, MD: Paul H. Brookes.

Handleman, J. S., & Harris, S. L. (Eds.). (2001). *Preschool education programs for children with autism.* Austin, TX: ProEd.

Howard, V. F., Williams, B. F., Port, P. D.& Lepper, C. (2001). *Very young children with special needs: A formative approach for the 21st century* (2nd edition). Upper Saddle River, NJ: Merrill/Prentice-Hall.

Lamb, H. (2001). Early childhood education. In G. Schroth and M. Littleton (Eds.) *The administration and supervision of special programs in education.* Dubuque, IA: Kendall/Hunt.

Raver, S. A. (1999). *Intervention strategies for infants and toddlers with special needs: A team approach* (2nd edition). Upper Saddle River, NJ: Merrill/Prentice-Hall.

Sandall, S. M., McLean, M. E., & Smith, B. J. (Eds.). (2000). *DEC recommended practices in early intervention/early childhood special education.* Reston, VA: Council for Exceptional Children.

Programs for Gifted and Talented Students

9

Robert Dunbar

Gwen Schroth

Although gifted students can and do emerge from all varieties of home environments, many parents of gifted students require a high level of involvement in the education of their child. In most cases, the principal's job is to support and facilitate this involvement.

—Robert Dunbar & Gwen Schroth

Objectives

1. Define gifted and talented
2. Discuss identification processes
3. Overview various program approaches for providing services
4. Discuss G/T parent involvement

Introduction

Every campus works with students possessing various kinds of exceptional abilities. These students may be doing work in one or more subjects far beyond what is considered normal for their age. They may be involved in their own independent projects, allowing them to explore and advance their skills, or they may lack the necessary direction or resources to do this. One child might be doing research on electricity while another simply sits bored in a science class. In English class, one may be writing a novel in the style of her favorite author while another fails to complete assignments that seem unimportant to her. Some excel; some do not. Some seize opportunities; some fail to recognize them. All are gifted, and each will benefit from instruction and adult relationships that address and nurture their unique educational needs.

Gifted students receive services in a variety of educational settings; the range of delivery designs is almost as great as that among the children themselves. There are gifted and talented magnet schools serving hundreds of high performing children and small, rural schools providing special services to only a few gifted students at a time. In either case, and in all the possible cases in between, it will ultimately fall to the principal to see that students identified as gifted receive instruction that is appropriate to their abilities. The principal must ensure that gifted and talented students are appropriately identified and that their teachers have the necessary skills and knowledge to work with them.

Unlike Special Education or Title I, there is no federal safety net to guarantee that schools provide services to gifted and talented students. The vast majority of legislation related to these students comes from the states. All but four of the fifty states have a definition for high ability children. Over half of these are defined in legislation while the others were created by state education agencies (Bathon, 2004). In both cases, minimal and essentially unmeasurable standards are often set and accountability for schools in their delivery of services to gifted and talented students is negligible. If the principal fails to make services to gifted students a priority, the most likely outcome is that these students will simply fail to receive services, and they and society will suffer for that loss. The last thirty years has seen significant growth in research on the needs and characteristics of gifted learners. Still, there is evidence that in many schools, gifted students fail to receive even the attention that common sense would warrant (Vanderkam, 2003).

Gifted or Talented?

The terms "gifted" and "talented" don't always serve to clarify discussion of high ability students. Different sources often use them to describe different kinds of abilities. State definitions slightly favor "gifted and talented" over "gifted" (Bathon, 2004). The National Association for Gifted Children (2004) uses the terms to describe the breadth of students' abilities. In their nomenclature, "gifted" students possess a broad range of exceptional abilities, and "talented" students possess a more narrow set of abilities or even an exceptional ability in a single area. In the United Kingdom, the Qualifications and Curriculum Authority (2001) uses the term "gifted" to describe high ability in an academic area and "talented" to describe similar ability in a non-academic area. Most sources simply don't bother to make a distinction and use terms like "gifted and talented," TAG, and GT as if they were single descriptors.

GIFTED CHILDREN

As with special education, there is great variation among gifted children. Each child seems to possess a unique combination of skills and needs. Tannenbaum (1983) attributes giftedness to a combination of general ability, special ability, non-intellective factors (like ego, strength, and dedication), environmental factors, and chance factors. Each child is a unique combination of these five components, and, consequently, each brings a unique set of needs and abilities to the educational setting.

Many gifted children present unevenly socially. They may at one moment discuss an academic subject with the perception and acuity of an informed adult and at the next moment exhibit a childish response to something else. Adults and other children often do not know how to respond to them. They may react with fear or confusion to the behaviors of gifted children. As these feelings are reflected back on the children, they become part of the information that they use to develop understandings of themselves and strategies for dealing with other people. This can sometimes lead to dysfunctional behaviors. Roedell (1984) describes a number of social and emotional vulnerabilities to which gifted children may be prone. Each of these is, a least partly, a response to environmental pressures:

Uneven development. This term describes the gap between intellectual and emotional age. In a setting where it is understood by adults, this condition has few consequences. It mainly becomes a problem when adults expect the child's emotional responses to correspond with their intellectual abilities. Instead, adults should expect and promote age appropriate emotional behaviors.

Perfectionism. When a parent calls the school concerned that his or her gifted child is spending hours on homework each night and has time to do nothing else, perfectionism is usually a component of the problem. Perfectionism sounds benign, but this can become destructive to gifted children and their families. Perfectionist students benefit from having teachers indicate the amount of time each assignment should require and by getting specific directions when work is assigned. When perfectionism is the result of an underlying emotional issue, counseling may also be necessary.

Underachievement. One of the classic manifestations of a gifted student is underachievement. This is most often seen in students who are placed in inappropriate educational settings or who have problems at home. Gifted students may begin to underperform in any grade, but this is most likely to begin in the middle grades (Peterson & Colangelo, 1996). Once a pattern of underachievement has begun, student performance is likely to decline in all subjects. Underachieving students can become re-engaged in academic work as late as grades 11 and 12 when provided with appropriate instruction and support.

Identification

The identification of gifted students is largely left to local standards. State legislation refers only to identified students without specifying how that identification is to take place. This means that standards may vary from district to district.

The most common method of identifying gifted students is through the use of standardized aptitude tests, like the Cognitive Abilities Test, and norm-based achievement tests, like the Iowa Test of Basic Skills. Districts may determine that student performance at or beyond a certain level qualifies that student for services. A comprehensive identification process should include information from a variety of sources. A rubric that assigns points based on test scores from multiple measures, academic performance, and teacher recommendations may provide a more complete picture of a student's abilities. On such a rubric, students would need to earn a predetermined number of points to qualify for services. Even this kind of selection process can be problematic, as gifted students, for various reasons, are not always high performing students.

Some demographic characteristics that can impact identification include:

Age. Identification of students as young as six is done through individual assessments. Tests to assess younger students usually are scored based on reading readiness and the sophistication and elaboration of student responses to tasks completed during the testing. Early readers and students inclined to embellish a story or picture in detail will score high on these aptitude tests.

Ethnicity. Minority students remain underrepresented among gifted students. One of the chief reasons for this may be bias in the testing materials. To overcome this, some researchers have begun to experiment with other types of assessments. In one study, African-American and economically disadvantaged students were given a performance-based assessment. This instrument identified a number of high ability students who would have otherwise been overlooked (VanTassel-Baska, Johnson, & Avery, 2002). This study also showed that simply lowering the screening criteria on existing standardized assessments had a similar effect. In another study, researchers administered a nonverbal ability test to a sample of 20,270 K–12 students (Naglieri & Ford, 2003). On this nonverbal test, 5.6% of white students, 5.1% of African-American students, and 4.4% of Hispanic students scored at or above the 95th percentile. These results were more inclusive of African-American and Hispanic students than those of more traditionally written assessments. This reemphasizes the need for a variety of assessments in a district's identification process.

Language. Limited English proficiency also limits student performance. Multilingual students tend to advance more slowly than their English-only peers through the first few years of school and then catch up afterward. Standard measures fail to account for this. One way to compensate would be to assign points on a district's identification rubric differently for young multilingual students.

Designing Instruction

What constitutes "gifted" instruction also varies. There are numerous models and formulas for gifted instruction (Renzulli, 1986). Models currently used by schools include the Autonomous Learner Model, Integrative Education Model, the Enrichment Triad and Secondary Triad Models, the Enrichment Matrix Model, and the Cognitive-Affective Interaction Model. Each contains varying proportions of strategy instruction, depth of content instruction, independent study, and interdisciplinary work.

One recent example of a highly evolved model for curriculum for gifted students is the "parallel curriculum" (Tomlinson, Kaplan, Renzulli, Purcell, Leppien, & Burns, 2002). In this model, the study of each of the core disciplines (English, science, math, social studies, etc.) includes a core curriculum and three additional curricula (connections, practice, and identity) designed to draw students into that discipline in a meaningful way. The core curriculum consists of all of the key facts, concepts, generalizations, and so forth that students need to understand the discipline. This emphasizes understanding over rote and must be presented in a careful and coherent manner. The curriculum of connections explores the range of instances throughout and beyond the discipline. It asks students to consider how similar events will vary in different contexts or how they will be viewed from different perspectives. The curriculum of practice emphasizes real world applications. This curriculum challenges students to think like historians, mathematicians, chemists, and other discipline-based people. Finally, the curriculum of identity requires students to examine their own abilities and interests and then determine what contributions they are prepared to make in the disciplines they are studying. In the parallel curriculum, all four of these curricula must be present in each discipline of study. Over time, each would be visited and revisited like four strands intertwined across the time period of study.

Teachers without experience teaching gifted children may be apprehensive and unsure about what types of enrichment are appropriate. Resources are available both in print and online that provide many examples of activities that are appropriate for use with gifted students. Many of these would easily lend themselves to use with gifted students in a regular education classroom. The best of these activities are those that allow students to pursue an interest in depth and with the support of multiple resources (VanTassel-Baska, 1998). Archambault, Westberg, Brown, Hallmark, Emmons, and Zhang (1993) list ten opportunities gifted children need as part of their instructional program. These include the opportunity to:

1. Pursue advanced level work.
2. Be exposed to higher level thinking skills.
3. Use enrichment centers.
4. Pursue a self-selected interest.
5. Work in groups with students having common interests.
6. Move to a higher grade for specific subject area instruction.
7. Work with students of comparable ability across classrooms at the same grade level.
8. Work on an advanced curriculum unit on a teacher-selected topic.
9. Participate in competitive programs focusing on thinking skills/problem solving.
10. Receive concentrated instruction in critical thinking and creative problem solving.

Depending on the individual interests and needs of the students, a teacher may have a student working with various resources about the same subject or from the same source. Analyzing and imitating the work of accomplished artists and professionals can be a key component of enrichment. A student may read several works by the same author, identify the key attributes of that writer's style, and then imitate that in his or her own writing.

The common element running through all of these ideas is that gifted students learn best when they have regular contact with other gifted students and adults and where this contact allows them to analyze the thinking processes and strategies of these individuals. Tutoring non-gifted peers does not meet this requirement. Nor does running errands for the teacher (Kearney, 1996). One occasionally finds schools who argue that they treat all students like gifted students and therefore no differentiation is necessary. This philosophy is ill advised.

Acceleration can be a viable instructional option for high-performing gifted students. Decisions about acceleration are best done on a case by case basis and with the full participation of parents (Smith, 2003). Immediate benefits must be weighed against possible future consequences. A good decision about acceleration usually requires a clear view of a child's academic options through high school and beyond. Acceleration can be one of the more contentious issues in gifted education. There are people with strong opinions both for and against. One advocate of acceleration goes so far as to say that advanced students who are not accelerated have been "decelerated" (Elkind, 1988) or that this is in effect "age discrimination" (Kearney, 1996).

Staffing

Preparing teachers to work with gifted students requires careful and comprehensive planning. Teachers who are sent to a workshop or receive a day of training at school are unlikely to make significant changes in instruction. Instead, there must be application-focused training with equally strong follow-up training. The principal needs to support this training by providing ongoing leadership, modeling and discussing the strategies with teachers, and provide material resources where necessary. Collaboration among teachers is also an essential element in integrating new instructional techniques (Johnsen, Haensly, Ryser, & Ford, 2002). Gallagher (1989) advises supervisors to closely monitor and evaluate implementation of new curriculum at seven levels:

1. Selection of the curriculum.
2. Evaluate teacher preparation.
3. Provide feedback on organization and lesson planning.
4. Evaluate classroom presentation.
5. Evaluate teacher/student interaction.
6. Review teacher perception of impact.
7. Review measurable impact on student learning.

There is some evidence that teachers with certain personality traits may be more effective in working with gifted students. A study of 1,247 gifted students and 63 teachers reported that the teachers who showed a preference for intuition and thinking on the Myers-Briggs Personality Type Inventory were more likely to be rated highly by high ability students (Mills, 2003). These would be teachers who tend to prefer to work with abstract themes and concepts, are open and flexible, and value logical analysis and objectivity. Another study found that teachers who modeled and valued creativity were more likely to be effective with gifted students (Rejskind, 2000). This study suggests that teachers ask questions that stimulate creativity, reward students' creativity, model creativity, and teach creative problem solving. Identifying teachers for work with gifted students and providing those teachers with on-going support are important leadership contributions principals can make to assure quality programming.

Service Models

The methods of delivering gifted instruction vary greatly, especially from district to district. In larger districts that may have gifted coordinators or lead teachers, program organization may be the element of instruction the principal controls least. For reasons often more related to issues of finance, personnel, and facilities, than to instruction, districts try to adopt types of services best suited to their particular circumstances.

The most common way students receive services is from a regular classroom teacher. In these cases, the teacher receives training to prepare him or her to organize supplemental instruction that addresses the characteristics and needs of gifted students. Teachers then provide this in regular classes (honors or upper level where these are available), supplementing or replacing the regular instruction as appropriate. The biggest advantage of this arrangement is that the alignment between regular class assignments and the enriched instruction is more likely to be good. The main disadvantage is that it may provide a gifted student only limited contact with other gifted students.

Another way districts serve gifted students is through pull-out programs. In this program model, students identified as gifted/talented are pulled out of their regular classes on a daily or weekly basis to receive enriched instruction. The content of this instruction may or may not be related to the curriculum of the student's regular academic classes. School administrators are responsible for providing classroom space (often a rare commodity) for this instruction during these times. This can also be problematic when the pull-out causes the students to miss key class activities or when the pull-out content and class content are not aligned.

Occasionally, districts choose to serve gifted students through a campus designated for gifted students. Typically, this is a magnet school serving both gifted students from throughout the districts and general education students living in proximity to the campus. At the high school level, it might be a campus with a large number of Advanced Placement course offerings or one that offers an International Baccalaureate program. This can be a win-win arrangement when a district needs to serve a large population of gifted students and where it may have a campus that is struggling to maintain enrollment or high academic standards. In this type of arrangement, magnet students may comprise 50% or more of the total campus enrollment.

Concurrent enrollment allows a student to take coursework from one school while enrolled in another. This can occur in a variety of ways. One type of concurrent enrollment is when a student at one school takes coursework from another campus in the district. An example of this would be middle school students taking a high school geometry class in the morning and then returning to their campus for the remainder of their coursework. In the same manner, an elementary student might take a class at the middle school. High school students may take classes at the local university or junior college. All of these cases require careful planning by administrators at both campuses to ensure that issues of timing, grading, and transportation have been addressed and that students and parents have a clear understanding of these processes. Many schools require parents to sign an agreement specifying how each of these will be handled and by whom.

The correspondence course is another type of concurrent enrollment, although online and video courses are quickly overtaking these. Online curricula, email, message boards, and live video feed have made these courses more like traditional ones. Students can interact in real time with teachers and classmates. With online coursework, students in small, rural schools can take advanced coursework for gifted students offered by prestigious universities. For school administrators, this also requires careful planning, specific agreements with parents, and systems for monitoring student progress during the course.

In a recent survey of students scoring at or above the 95th percentile, 67% of students reported that they received multiple accommodations, the most prevalent of these being pull-out programs, academic competitions, after school and summer enrichment, and working at a higher grade level in their regular classrooms (Swiatek & Lupkowski-Shoplik, 2003). Schools seem to be using a variety of models to address gifted students' needs. However, of concern in this report was that 12% of the students indicated that they received no accommodations whatsoever.

Student Grouping

In the course of designing and planning a program for gifted students, discussion will inevitably lead to the subject of ability grouping. There is some confusion among educators and parents as to the effectiveness of ability grouping. An effective campus administrator should understand what the research has to say on this subject. Some researchers (Slavin, 1987) have suggested that homogeneous grouping of students is harmful. This is true in cases where students are grouped, but instruction remains the same for all groups. No one is advocating this for gifted students. Rather, homogeneous grouping of gifted students is done so that students may receive instruction that is different and more appropriate to their needs than what is done in the general classroom. There is evidence that this type of grouping which includes instruction specialized for the needs of each group is helpful for students of all abilities (Kulik & Kulik, 1990).

Assessment and Accountability

ASSESSMENT

Gifted education defies current notions of assessment and accountability. Measuring the degree to which an instructional program has impacted the performance of a gifted student is extremely difficult. The current assessment movement in education has emphasized the use of criterion referenced tests to determine the mastery of minimum skill levels. On these tests, a "ceiling effect" conceals the total learning of most gifted students. In other words, they tend to get nearly everything right on these tests, and, because of that, the tests don't let them demonstrate all that they know. In fact, many non-gifted students have equal or similar scores.

Norm-referenced tests provide more information about the actual abilities of gifted students. A norm-referenced test assigns students to a position on a nationally normed bell curve based on their performance. Data from these tests is better suited to the identification, comparison, and ranking of gifted students. Above level tests, most commonly college admissions tests used with students at the middle grades or lower, are also used to measure the learning of gifted students. The most common tests for this are the SAT and ACT, but scores from AP tests, CLEP, and IB tests can also be useful (Hansen, 1992).

ACCOUNTABILITY

In this age of statewide testing and school report cards, the performance of gifted students is barely considered, if at all. The main reason for this is the difficulty in measuring the effect of instruction on gifted learners. Did a highly gifted student do well on a math exam because she learned it in school or because she enjoys working on math in her spare time? Only extensive pre-testing and post-testing could determine this.

The Texas Legislature recently required the Texas Education Agency (TEA) to develop a measure that would demonstrate the effectiveness of funds allocated to gifted education. In response, TEA created a pilot program to develop a set of projects gifted students could complete at their schools to be scored and used to determine the degree to which they had benefited from their enriched instruction. This included a detailed rubric for evaluating student work.

For all of this effort, it is likely that, other than the development of some new assessment materials, this project will do little to answer the question the legislature originally asked: How is current funding impacting learning for gifted students? While it can show in great detail where students are in their learning, it cannot show how instruction has affected this. For gifted students, school is just one of many sources of learning that might include summer camps, private tutoring, individual study, peers, siblings, parents, or the internet. Controlling for all of these variables to find the effect of school is problematic in the study of any student, but it is even more difficult with gifted students who are much more likely to receive learning from multiple sources.

Despite the difficulty of measuring learning for gifted students, advocates of gifted education are quick to point out that the current emphasis on proficiency does little to provide appropriate instruction for our nations' most gifted learners, leaving these students with little attention and few resources.

At present, the No Child Left Behind Act aims the nation's attention and resources at ensuring that nonproficient students move systematically toward proficiency. There is no incentive for schools to attend to the growth of students once they attain proficiency, or to spur students who are already proficient to greater achievement, and certainly not to inspire those who far exceed proficiency. To provide encouragement—even the impetus—to ensure that schools plan for the growth of every child, thus attending to both equity and excellence, would not require a great deal (Tomlinson, 2002).

Documentation

Along with ensuring that services are delivered, principals must also oversee the documentation of those services so that the campus is prepared for any audit by the district or state that might require these. This includes documentation of specific instructional modifications such as curriculum enrichment, acceleration, or supplemental services as well as documentation of teacher training, particularly that which is required by the district or state.

When a teacher is hired or reassigned to a classroom that will include gifted students, that teacher is often required to complete initial training on the needs and characteristics of gifted learners. (In Texas, this requires 30 clock hours of training.) After this, there may be an annual training requirement of 3–6 clock hours. The principal is responsible for maintaining current records of teacher training.

Parental Involvement

Although gifted students can and do emerge from all varieties of home environments, many parents of gifted students require a high level of involvement in the education of their child. In most cases, the principal's job is to support and facilitate this involvement.

One of the first things parents will want to see is a detailed description of the school's plan for enrichment. It is important that such a plan exist and that it be available in a form which is useful to parents. If a gifted student is being served in a regular education classroom, this plan should describe the curricular modifications that will occur throughout the semester. Concurrently, when parents raise concerns about their child or that child's classes, administrators should be responsive and prepared to spend time listening and developing solutions.

Collaboration of parents and school personnel as advocates for the educational needs of gifted students is common, and this can occur in the form of an informal group lobbying a superintendent or school board or a more organized group working with a state legislature. Regardless of the magnitude of the effort, the most effective advocacy tends to come from groups and individuals who,

1. Make continuous efforts.
2. Settle for acceptance . . . at first.
3. Possess at least one "champion," a member with exceptional motivational skills and leadership ability.
4. Are prepared when an opportunity arises.

5. Are non-adversarial in their approach.
6. Accept intermediate goals in pursuit of larger ones (Robinson & Moon, 2003).

Organizational Components for School Enrichment

Joseph Renzulli (1994), reflecting on extensive experience working with schools on improving services to gifted learners, suggests six school components necessary for what he calls the Schoolwide Enrichment Model. These six components are as follows:

1. A Specialist: Renzulli advocates that a school staff include a full time non-teaching enrichment specialist who is responsible for providing instructional support for teachers and managing the overall enrichmnet program. For most schools, this may be an unrealistic requirement. But most schools do have the ability to utilize one staff member, teacher, counselor, or administrator, to act in this capacity. Assigning direction of the enrichment program to one individual increases the likelihood that there will be consistency and coherency in the program, and it ensures that teachers will know where to go for help in working with gifted students.

2. A Team: An enrichment team, not unlike the more common campus improvement team, consists of teachers, parents, and an administrator who meet periodically with the specialist to review and modify the enrichment program. In a school where a number of committees already exist, this could become the responsibility of one of those existing committees.

3. A Plan for Professional Development: Haphazard attempts at teacher training do little to elevate the quality of enrichment. Training is best where it specifically targets the goals of the enrichment team and when it includes opportunities for follow-up and reflection.

4. Connection to Professional Organizations: Renzulli, here, advocates that schools participate in a particular organization developed by him. An equally useful alternative might include active participation in a state affiliate of the National Association for Gifted Children or similar group. These state affiliates often have annual conventions and produce regular newsletters. They are also often active in monitoring and lobbying state legislatures as advocates for gifted learners.

5. Parent Inclusion: Many parents of gifted students are already active participants in the education of their children. Renzulli proposes that schools provide structured training for parents to both orient them with the enriched curriculum and equip them to facilitate the learning of their child.

6. A Democratic School Management Plan: Renzulli advocates that schools have open management with groups like campus improvement teams comprised of teachers, administrators, support personnel, and parents. Through these democratic structures, Renzulli argues, "policies should be enacted only after considered study, dialogue, and debate, and final policy should be adopted only following experimental or pilot periods during which changes in practice are field tested and evaluated" (p. 291).

Renzulli's model shows how important the principal's role is in creating an environment where gifted students can flourish. All of the components described above require direct action and support by the principal. Without this support, none of these could sustain themselves more than a short period of time.

Looking Ahead

The prospective principal must understand that everything described here represents only the current state of education for gifted and talented students. There is growing evidence that our understanding of issues related to these students is rudimentary at best. New research suggests that schools may soon be required to reconsider the nature of giftedness and provide increasingly individualized instruction to a larger and more diverse group of gifted learners.

The most prevalent forms of intelligence testing and the current nomenclature with which we describe gifted education suggest that students can be arranged along a linear continuum of intelligence and be accurately termed "gifted" at and above a certain point. However, emerging understandings of intelligence indicate that the nature of ability may be more complex than our current interventions can effectively address.

Howard Gardner (1983) suggests that our current understanding of intelligence is flawed because it describes only a singular intelligence when there are actually a number of distinct abilities or intelligences possessed by each person. Gardner's theory of multiple intelligences proposes seven separate areas of ability including linguistic, musical, logical-mathematical, spatial, bodily-kinesthetic, interpersonal, and intrapersonal.

The implications of this theory for educators are significant. It questions our notions of both assessment and intervention for gifted students. In each case, it calls upon educators to increase the diversity of options and individualize the delivery of services in a manner not unlike what is currently done in special education.

Applying Your Knowledge

Mrs. Smith enrolls her twins, Jeff and Joy, in Greenwood Middle School in January. In a conference with the new principal, Mrs. Smith says that Jeff and Joy were both in the gifted program in their former school and expects that they will both be placed in GMS's middle school gifted program immediately. The principal notices that Joy's scores on the tests administered in her former school are slightly lower than her brother's and is not certain Joy will qualify for GMS's program. Noticing the principal's hesitancy, Mrs. Smith becomes insistent that Joy be included in the gifted program saying, "Joy will be crushed if Jeff makes it and she doesn't. I don't know if she can take it." The principal is aware that the mother is going to be persistent in her request but also knows that the school's gifted program is far from satisfactory. The curriculum is not challenging and the teacher lacks creativity in her teaching practices.

QUESTIONS

1. What will be the impact on the twins if Joy does not qualify for the gifted program at GMS and should that be a consideration in the placement decision?
2. How does this situation mirror what the authors of this chapter presented regarding the services available for gifted students?
3. As the principal what will be your response to this parent? Explain.
4. What programmatic and community relations consequences may occur if Joy is admitted to the gifted program? What about if she is not admitted?

QUESTIONS FOR THOUGHT

1. How do students qualify for a gifted program in your school district?
2. What is your district's policy for admitting gifted transfer students at the beginning of the year? Do mid-year transfers differ from that?
3. What strategies can a principal use when dealing with parents whose child does not qualify for the gifted program? Should exceptions be made?
4. Should alternatives to a gifted program be made available for students who come close to qualifying but do not?
5. What can this principal do to improve the gifted program in the scenario above?
6. What steps would you take to establish a system that determines the effectiveness of the gifted program in your school?

For Additional Information Online

Council for Exceptional Children *www.cec.sped.org*

Johns Hopkins University Center for Talented Youth *www.jhu.edu/~gifted/*

National Association for Gifted Children *www.nagc.org*

The National Foundation for Gifted and Creative Children *www.nfgcc.org*

References

Archambault, F. A., Jr., Westberg, K. L., Brown, S. W., Hallmark, B. W., Emmons, C. L., & Zhang, W. (1993). *Regular classroom practices with gifted students: Results of a national survey of classroom teachers* (Research Monograph 93102). Storrs, CT: The National Research Center on the Gifted and Talented, University of Connecticut.

Bathon, J. M. (2004, June). *State gifted and talented definitions,* Education Commission of the States. Retrieved September 11, 2004 from *http://www.ecs.org/clearinghouse/52/28/5228.htm.*

Elkind, D. (1988). Acceleration. *Young Children, 43*(4).

Gallager, J. J. (1989). Curriculum Development and evaluation in school programs for gifted students in VanTassel-Baska, J. L. & Olszewski-Kubilius, P. (eds.) *Patterns of influence on gifted learners: The home, the self, and the school.* (pp. 178–191) New York: Teachers College Press.

Gardner, H. (1983). *Frames of mind.* New York: Basic Books.

Hansen, J. (1992). Discovering highly gifted students. *Understanding our Gifted, Open Space Communications, 4*(4).

Johnsen, S. K., Haensly, P. A., Ryser, G. R., & Ford, R. F. (2002). Changing general education classroom practices to adapt for gifted students. *Gifted Child Quarterly 46*(1), 45–63.

Kearney, K. (1996). Highly gifted children in full inclusion classrooms. *Highly Gifted Children, 12*(4).

Kulik, J. A. & Kulik, C. C. (1990). Ability grouping and gifted students. In N. Colangelo & G. A. Davis (Eds.), *Handbook of Gifted Education.* Boston: Allyn & Bacon.

Mills, C. J. (2003). Characteristics of effective teachers of gifted students: Teacher background and personality styles of students. *Gifted Child Quarterly 47*(4), 272–281.

Naglieri, J. A. & Ford, D. Y. (2003). Addressing underrepresentation of gifted minority children using the Naglieri Nonverbal Ability Test (NNAT). *Gifted Child Quarterly 47*(2), 155–169.

National Association for Gifted Children. (2004). *Parent information. Retrieved 11, 2004 from* http://www.nagc.org/ParentInfo/index.html#who.

Peterson, J. S. & Colangelo, N. (1996). Gifted achievers and underachievers: A comparison of patterns found in school files. *Journal of Counseling and Development, 74,* pp. 39–407.

Qualifications and Curriculum Authority. (2001). *Guidance on teaching the gifted and talented.* Retrieved September 11, 2004 from *http://www.nc.uk.net/gt/general/index.htm.*

Rejskind, G. (2000). TAG teachers: Only the creative need apply. *Roeper Review* 22(3), 153–157.

Renzulli, J. S. (1986). *Systems and models for developing programs for the gifted and talented.* Mansfield Center, Connecticut: Creative Learning Press.

Renzulli, J. S. (1994). *Schools for talent development: A practical plan for total school improvement.* Mansfield Center, Connecticut: Creative Learning Press.

Robinson, A. & Moon, S. M. (2003). A national study of local and state advocacy in gifted education. *Gifted Child Quarterly 47*(1), 8–25.

Roedell, W. (1984). Vulnerabilities of highly gifted children. *Roeper Review, 6*(3), 127–130.

Rogers, K. (1993). Grouping the gifted and talented: Questions and answers. *Roeper Review, 16*(1).

Slavin, R. E. (1987). Ability grouping: A best-evidence synthesis. *Review of Educational Research,* 57, pp. 293–336.

Smith, D. (2003). Acceleration: Is moving ahead the right step? *Monitor on Psychology, 34*(5), 63.

Swiatek, M. A. & Lupkowski-Shoplik, A. (2003). Elementary and middle school student participation in gifted programs: Are gifted students underserved? *Gifted Child Quarterly 47*(2).

Tannenbaum, A. J. (1983). *Gifted Children: Psychological and educational perspectives.* New York: MacMillan.

Tomlinson, C. A. (2002), Proficiency is not enough: The No Child Left Behind Act fails to balance equity and excellence. *Education Week,* November 2002, pp. 36, 38.

Tomlinson, C. A., Kaplan, S. N., Renzulli, J. S., Purcell, J., Leppien, J., & Burns, D. 2002). *The parallel curriculum: A design to develop high potential and challenge high-ability learners.* Thousand Oaks, California: Corwin Press.

Vanderkam, L. (2003). SAT talent searches lead nowhere for many. *USA Today,* January 20, 2003.

Van Tassel-Baska, J. (1998). *Excellence in educating gifted and talented learners.* Denver: Love.

VanTassel-Baska, J., Johnson, D., & Avery, L. D. (2002). Using performance tasks in identification of economically disadvantaged and minority gifted learners: Findings from Project STAR. *Gifted Child Quarterly 46*(2), 110–123.

Counseling 10 Programs

Richard Lampe
Jerry Trusty
Reba Criswell

Responsibilities of school counselors vary, based on the needs of constituencies served and the understandings and expectations of principals who are ultimately responsible for guidance operations in their schools.

R. Lampe, J. Trusty, and R. Criswell

Objectives

1. Describe the historical and the contemporary scope of school counseling services and the appropriate responsibilities of the school counselor and others in the delivery of up-to-date services.
2. Explain current models for the organization, development, implementation, and evaluation of school counseling programs
3. Present legal and ethical considerations of which administrators should be aware that are related to school counseling
4. Provide outcome research evidence of the effectiveness of comprehensive school counseling programs and suggestions as to how administrators and counselors can promote counseling program effectiveness

Introduction

Of the various services and programs for which educational administrators have responsibility, counseling programs may be one of the least well defined. Some states provide models for organized, comprehensive counseling programs with specified services (Sink & McDonald, 1998), and recently, a national model has been published by the American School Counselor Association (ASCA) (2003). In addition, a framework for school counseling programs has been presented by the Education Trust (2003). Models notwithstanding, local administrators have varying dominion over how programs are implemented (Përusse, Goodenough, Donegan, & Jones, 2004). Whereas this may at first glance seem desirable for administrators, without research-based guidelines and administrative understanding of how counseling services can be effectively organized and orchestrated, students are less likely to receive the services they need.

Ponec and Brock (2000) described the relationships between school counselors and principals as crucial, yet principals and counselors sometimes see things differently. Summarizing the perspectives of students in counseling and in educational leadership departments at their university, Shoffner and Williamson (2000) wrote that principals-in-training focus on tasks, results, and legal liabilities, while counselors-in-training focus on process, dealing with the dilemma, and the importance of confidentiality. Shoffner and Williamson also described 14 points of conflict between counselors and principals including, for example, formal authority versus shared leadership, discipline, and evaluation of the counselor. Përusse et al. (2004) pointed out that the three counselor tasks that were most highly supported by school principals were the same three tasks that were most frequently performed by school counselors. Further, these tasks were listed as *inappropriate* for school counselors in ASCA's National Standards, which the authors reported were endorsed by the National Association of Secondary School Principals and the National Association of Elementary School Principals. Përusse et al. expounded that "most school principals continue to believe that appropriate tasks for school counselors include clerical tasks such as registration and scheduling of all new students; administering cognitive, aptitude, and achievement tests; and maintaining student records" (p. 159). Points of conflict such as these may be due to insufficient reciprocal understanding of roles of counselors and principals and the lack of opportunities for each to learn about the responsibilities of the other. Therefore this chapter includes a brief history of school counseling, definitions of related terms, and descriptions of appropriate roles of school counselors. Also presented are contemporary views on how counselors' services can be integrated into an organized guidance program as well as several ethical and legal guidelines related to school counselors. Finally, suggestions are offered regarding administrators' and counselors' responsibilities for enhancing the counseling program's contributions to overall school effectiveness.

History of School Counseling

Although many pertinent events and conditions occurred earlier, the beginnings of the school counseling movement (or school guidance, as the concept has commonly been called) are often said to have taken place in the early 1900s (Gysbers & Henderson, 2000; Picchioni & Bonk, 1983). Societal changes during and following the Industrial Revolution, such as immigration to urban areas, resulted in concentrations of populations in urban industrial centers and negative by-products such as slums, ghettos, inattention to individual rights, and masses of unskilled laborers (Schmidt, 2003; Picchioni & Bonk, 1983). With the increasing availability of public education to students from varying economic backgrounds, the resulting student population's needs expanded well beyond preparation for professional positions in areas such as law, medicine, and the ministry (Smith & Gideon, 1929). Subsequently, several schools began to provide guidance in areas of concern such as moral development and vocational choice.

Because of the expanding needs of students and the broadening expectations placed on public schools, guidance outgrew its vocational focus to include a broader range of services such as interpreting standardized tests and counseling students with personal/social and educational problems. Today, counselors provide an even wider range of services. For example, these include consultation with parents and teachers, coordination of various activities, referral for specialized assistance, and teaching age-appropriate guidance curriculum to foster the personal/social, educational, and career development of all students. Ideally, counselors operate as part of the educational team in an early childhood through twelfth-grade counseling program that is planned and organized to meet the needs of all students.

Recent developments and initiatives in school counseling such as the American School Counselor Association (ASCA) National Model (ASCA, 2003) and the National Center for Transforming School Counseling (NCTSC) of the Education Trust (Education Trust, 2003) support this new vision of school counseling and school counselor roles. These endeavors are committed to the educational development of all students from early-childhood through college and to closing achievement gaps among socioeconomic and racial-ethnic groups. These efforts promote school counselors' involvement in the process of raising standards and implementing accountability systems. Both the ASCA National Model and the Education Trust focus on leadership, advocacy, and collaboration roles of school counselors. In short, the frameworks offered by these new efforts seek to align school counselors more closely with the academic missions of schools. Historically, school counselors have often been perceived by school administrators, parents, and laypersons as providing services that are ancillary to the academic missions of schools; and school counselors are often relegated to these ancillary roles. School counselors themselves have experienced role confusion over the last few decades (see Baker & Gerler, 2004; Brown & Trusty, 2005), and school counselors themselves may seek ancillary responsibilities.

Definitions of Related Terms

Guidance is sometimes used as the "umbrella" term that encompasses all of the services that counselors and others provide to promote student development. These services collectively are organized into *guidance programs* (albeit, some more organized than others). In current terminology, *counseling program* is sometimes used instead of *guidance program* (cf. ASCA, 2003; Gysbers & Henderson, 2000). It is also popular to use the term *guidance curriculum* to refer to age-appropriate and planned goals, objectives, and activities related to personal/social, educational, and career development that counselors (and sometimes teachers) provide, often in the classroom. *Counseling* in schools historically has denoted a process involving a special relationship in which a trained professional (the counselor) directly assists students with personal problems and concerns. *Therapy* (also *psychotherapy*) is usually differentiated from school counseling in that therapy is more often associated with treatment of deep-rooted, long-standing psychological problems of clients or patients in clinical or medical settings (Myrick, 2003). In non-school settings (in community agencies and hospitals, for example), distinctions between counseling and psychotherapy are less delineated.

Counselor Responsibilities

Duties of school counselors vary according to grade level assignment, student and community needs, expectations of school administrators, and governmental regulations; however, there are several broad categories of activities and services that describe appropriate counselor responsibilities. These characteristically include, but are not limited to, counseling, consultation, coordination, assessment, large-group guidance, and program management—each of which will be summarized in this section. How these different yet interdependent roles can be incorporated into an organized program will be presented in the subsequent section.

COUNSELING

When used in school settings to describe a specific activity (as opposed to a "counseling" program or to the "counseling" profession) *counseling* refers to a process that involves helping students deal with problems of a personal/social, academic, or career development nature (Starr, 1996; ASCA, 2003). Counseling is provided to students on an individual or small group basis. If provided on a small group basis, the group is small enough to allow the counselor to monitor and incorporate the interactions of the group members. Whether on an individual or group basis, counseling usually relates to each student's problems and goals. Involving a relationship between the student and the counselor and theory-based techniques, counseling is not equated with advising or providing information.

Definitions of counseling vary, sometimes extending the domain of counseling beyond developmental and situational concerns into the area of addressing pathology as well. For school children, treatment of pathology, if necessary, is preferably provided by specialists other than the school counselor, possibly through a referral to a resource such as a psychologist, psychiatrist, or community mental health agency counselor (see ASCA, 2003).

CONSULTATION

Although school counselors sometimes use consultants to secure information or to discuss options for dealing with certain situations (perhaps the counselor needs the assistance of a qualified professional regarding how to proceed in an unusual case, how to address an ethical or legal concern, etc.), counselors also provide consultation as a service. In the role of consultant (as opposed to using a consultant), the school counselor provides service to the student indirectly—usually through direct contact with teachers, parents, and/or school administrators (Starr, 1996). For example, a teacher (called the consultee) who is having difficulty with a student might contact the school counselor (the consultant) for assistance. In their interactions, the counselor and teacher share information, discuss options, and perhaps jointly generate a plan of action for the teacher to implement (Myrick, 2003).

In consultation, although the direct contact interaction is between the counselor and the consultee, the focus of their interaction is on the student—on how the consultee might interact directly with the student for the benefit of the student. In providing consultation, the counselor should guard against focusing on resolution of a personal problem the consultee might introduce. For example, the parent may seek assistance from the counselor for his/her alcoholism. Although this parent would probably benefit from personal counseling, provision of such for the parent is generally not within the role of the school counselor (American School Counselor Association, 1998).

The counselor sometimes provides consultation on a group basis. For example, the counselor could work with a group of parents regarding parenting techniques, or the counselor could conduct professional development activities for teachers regarding interpretation of test results. In both examples, the ultimate beneficiaries are the students.

COORDINATION

As a counselor intervention, Myrick (2003) defined coordination as "the process of managing different indirect guidance services to students, including special events and general procedures" (p. 345). In providing this service, counselors are called upon to collect and disseminate information and to develop and maintain positive working relationships with other school professionals and outside resources in the community (Texas Counseling Association, 2004). As a coordinator, the counselor may also plan and arrange meetings, develop and operate special programs, supervise others, and provide leadership (ASCA, 2003; Myrick, 2003). Examples of specific activities that counselors sometimes coordinate include career day, financial aid workshops, referrals of students to outside community agencies or practitioners, peer helper programs, orientation, scholarships, and so forth.

It is possible for coordination to become a "catch-all" for quasi-administrative duties that are assigned to the counselor, leaving insufficient time and resources for the counselor to adequately serve students in ways more aligned with the counselor's professional qualifications. Coordination of the school's testing program is one example. Although often done by a school counselor, coordinating testing involves a large amount of time securing, counting, packaging, and administering tests—activities not requiring the qualifications of a professional counselor yet limiting the counselor's availability to provide more direct services (Burnham & Jackson, 2000).

ASSESSMENT

Assessment (sometimes called appraisal) refers to collecting and interpreting data to facilitate more-informed decisions. Assessment of students is accomplished by using standardized instruments (usually measuring achievement, aptitude, interest, or personality) and by less standardized techniques such as interviews, surveys, and observations. School counselors may also participate in the assessment of various environments affecting students such as school climate, home environment, and peer groups (Drummond, 2004).

In schools, assessment results are commonly used for purposes of student description (achievement level, educational diagnosis), placement (courses, special programs), prediction (educational or career planning), or to provide information for the school (curriculum planning, program effectiveness). To serve these purposes, school counselors interpret assessment results as needed to students, parents, teachers, and school administrators. Administration and interpretation of specialized assessments may require the services of the school diagnostician, school psychologist, or school psychometrist.

LARGE GROUP GUIDANCE

Counselors can provide information for and lead discussions with large groups of students. Often referred to as classroom guidance, the focus of this activity is involving students as a group with information designed to meet their developmental needs. Commonly, large group guidance has instructional objectives related to personal and social skills, educational development, and career planning. Although instructional in nature, delivery of large group guidance is not restricted to a lecture format; discussions, multi-media, panels, guest speakers, and other means of involving students in learning are frequently involved. As described, large group guidance is differentiated from group counseling, wherein a smaller and more cohesive group of students interact with each other and a counselor "for more intense and private assistance" (Myrick, 2003, p. 253).

A planned sequence of large group guidance objectives is often outlined in a *guidance curriculum,* with content and delivery methods that are age-appropriate. A school's guidance curriculum should be planned with the overall needs of the students in mind. Some states provide guidance curriculum guidelines that can be useful in forming an individual school's (or district's) plan. Sink and MacDonald (1998) reported that 11 of 41 states reviewed provided guidance curriculum models, with more states having models being developed. At the national level, the ASCA National Model (ASCA, 2003) offers tools for gauging the scope and sequence of the guidance curriculum. In the National Model, the guidance curriculum is organized around *student competencies and indicators* from which learning objectives for guidance lessons and units can be developed.

Large group guidance is often delivered by the school counselor, although classroom teachers also teach guidance-related curriculum. In such cases, counselors can assist teachers with planning and resource materials (TCA, 2004). Counselors and teachers also work together to evaluate students' meeting of the guidance learning objectives (Brown & Trusty, 2005). For example, a school counselor and teacher may work together in delivering guidance lessons on time-management skills to fourth-graders; and the teacher evaluates students' time-management competencies in academic classes. According to Starr (1996), the guidance curriculum and guidance program should not be seen as ancillary to the school curriculum and school activities. Rather, it should be viewed as an integral component of the total curriculum and school.

PROGRAM MANAGEMENT

Whether viewed from the perspective of a lone counselor trying to serve all students in a rural area, or of a group of counselors serving a particular school, or of a central-office director of guidance for an entire district in a large city, the counselor should be involved at some level in management of the guidance program. Program management responsibilities include planning, implementing, evaluating, and advocating for a comprehensive guidance program. Program management involves organizing personnel, resources, and activities (related to assessed needs and in accordance with carefully developed goals and objectives) in order to better serve students (TCA, 2004). The ASCA National Model (ASCA, 2003) provides valuable direction and tools in developing and managing comprehensive school counseling programs.

Organization of Services

Although the responsibilities described in the preceding section include many of the services provided by counselors, an effective guidance program is more than a loosely connected, unplanned, or hit-or-miss collection of counselors' efforts. Gysbers, Lapan, and Jones (2000) described a contemporary approach to guidance programming as involving the counselor in an "organized, sequential, structured, district-wide program of guidance and counseling K–12" (p. 349). Several resources (e.g., ASCA, 2003; Gysbers & Henderson, 2000; Myrick, 2003; Starr, 1996) have included a description of how effective programs could be organized.

This section summarizes the Gysbers and Henderson (2000) comprehensive program model. This model is largely the basis for the ASCA National Model (ASCA, 2003). The Gysbers and Henderson model interrelates three broad elements: (a) content, which outlines what students should be able to do, or competencies, as a result of experiencing the guidance program; (b) organizational framework, that addresses the what, why, and assumptions underlying the program as well as the program's major components; and (c) the resources needed to effectuate the program.

CONTENT

According to Gysbers and Henderson (2000), an organized comprehensive guidance program specifies student competencies that are distinct and developmentally appropriate for different grade levels. These age-appropriate competencies are grouped into domains such as academic development, interpersonal skills, responsible choices, and knowledge of self and others; and it is common to use the same list of domains for all grade levels. Several resources are available for administrators and counselors to assist with the identification of age-appropriate competencies and with grouping these into domains, including models from the American School Counselor Association (ASCA, 2003), the state of Missouri (Gysbers, Starr, & Magnuson, 1998), the state of Texas (Texas Education Agency, 2004), and the state of New Hampshire (Carr & Hayslip, 1989).

ORGANIZATIONAL FRAMEWORK

Gysbers and Henderson (2000) delineated the organizational framework of a guidance program through identification of four major program components. These components, briefly introduced in the paragraphs below, include guidance curriculum, responsive services, individual planning, and system support.

Guidance Curriculum. Earlier in this chapter, guidance curriculum was described as referring to age-appropriate and planned goals, objectives, and activities related to personal/social, educational, and career development. The guidance curriculum, one of the four guidance program components, is often implemented through classroom units taught by counselors, by counselors and teachers on a team basis, or by teachers with counselor support and consultation. Other vehicles for implementing the guidance curriculum involve larger group activities such as career days, college/technical school nights, financial aid workshops, and orientations of students to a new school level. Through the guidance curriculum, many desired student competencies are addressed. Examples of age-appropriate curricular goals, objectives, and activities related to guidance are available in the literature (e.g., ASCA, 2003; Gysbers & Henderson, 2000), but these are samples only—to provide a starting place for the evolution of a locally appropriate guidance curriculum.

Responsive Services. Whereas the guidance curriculum component provides guidance-related content to all students for everyday life skills, the responsive services component is designed to provide prevention and/or intervention related to immediate concerns of a smaller number of students (TEA, 1998). That is, this component targets students' immediate needs (ASCA, 2003). According to Starr (1996), these services should be available to (but not needed by) all students, and students often initiate services in this component. These students are in situations where (a) preventive action is called for because of threats to healthy development or (b) remedial intervention is necessary to resolve a problem that is already interfering in a student's life. Counselors' responses to either of these situations often involve the earlier described roles of consultation, counseling (including crisis counseling), and/or referral (Brown & Trusty, 2005).

Individual Planning. A third component of a comprehensive guidance program is individual planning (Gysbers & Henderson, 2000). This component focuses on helping each individual understand self-development and formulate and monitor plans that are goal oriented. Planning courses to be taken in high school to reach one's goals is an example (see Trusty & Niles, 2003). In assisting students with their individual planning, counselors attempt to help students understand and maneuver through viable alternatives and to help students avoid premature and irrevocable decisions. Although plans regarding personal/social development are included, much of the individual planning component is related to educational and career domains. Even though titled *individual planning,* a portion of this component is accomplished through group guidance—particularly with regard to awareness and exploration of educational and career opportunities (Niles, Trusty, & Mitchell, 2004). An individual's plan that is made in secondary school is grounded in developmental guidance curriculum activities carried out in elementary school.

System Support. The fourth guidance program component, system support, is necessary to sustain the other three. System support activities include, for example, conducting research regarding program effectiveness, providing for continuing professional development of counselors, promoting the program through public relations, organizing and managing the program, educating parents, and consulting with teachers (Gysbers & Henderson, 2000). Because the guidance program is an integral part of the larger school program, counselor activities that support the school as a system, such as serving on academic curriculum committees, serving on community committees and boards, and assessing student needs also provide relevant system support (ASCA, 2004). Many system support activities are carried out through the earlier mentioned counselor roles of consultation and program management.

Component Balance. The four guidance components described above are integrated in different proportions based on the needs of the students. This is particularly evident as one compares and contrasts time spent in each component at elementary, middle, and high school levels. In general, counselors and administrators should expect more emphasis on guidance curriculum than other components at the elementary level, and this focus usually decreases at the upper grade levels. On the other hand, individual planning usually involves less time in the program at the elementary level, but it increases significantly in high-school programs. Responsive services maintain a steady and significant portion of the time balance at all three levels. The fourth component, system support, also maintains a fairly steady emphasis through all levels, generally involving less time than the other components throughout (e.g., Gysbers & Henderson, 2000; TEA, 2004). These typical component ratios are not rigid, however, and should be adjusted as student needs change.

RESOURCES NEEDED

An organized counseling program requires a commitment to providing adequate resources. Some of these resources include adequate counseling department staff, involved parents, staff development opportunities, community resources, materials, supplies, equipment, and facilities. If these are not already in place, funds need to be earmarked for required resources (TEA, 2004).

Outcome Research Supporting School Counseling Programs

School counselors are increasingly required to provide evidence that school counseling programs make a difference in student achievement (e.g., Brigman & Campbell, 2003;

House & Martin, 1998; Lapan, 2001; Paisley & Hayes, 2003). In this section several outcome research studies are presented that support organized school counseling programs' contributions to student development. For instance, Lapan, Gysbers, and Petroski (2001) found middle school students who attended schools with more fully implemented guidance and counseling programs reported better relationships with teachers, more satisfaction with the quality of education received, feeling safer in school, perceiving their education to be important to their future, earning higher grades, and experiencing fewer problems associated with the physical and interpersonal school environment. These results are consistent with previous comprehensive school counseling program research involving high school students (e.g., Lapan, Gysbers, & Sun, 1997). Similar findings by Nelson and Gardner (1998) revealed high school students in schools with more fully implemented guidance programs achieved higher grades on the ACT examination, took more advanced science and mathematics courses, and perceived a better overall educational experience than students in less implemented programs. In a causal-comparative study, Sink and Stroh (2003) concluded that regardless of socioeconomic status, elementary-age children (grades 3 and 4) who remained in schools with well-established comprehensive school counseling programs performed better on academic achievement tests than their peers in schools without programs in place. These results echo the efforts of the ASCA National Model (ASCA, 2003) and the Education Trust (2003) regarding closing the achievement gap among socioeconomic groups. Lapan et al. (1997) pointed out that spending time with students to devote to implementation of comprehensive school counseling programs did not detract from student academic progress. Instead, these efforts appeared to play a positive role in the enhancement of student academic achievement. Other reviews involving school counseling outcome research support the findings of these studies (see Whiston, 2003; Whiston & Sexton, 1998, for summaries).

In a survey of school counselors, Gysbers, Lapan, and Blair (1999) found those school counselors who rated their programs as more fully implemented reported higher levels of engagement with students, teachers, and parents; more visibility in the school and community; and more time delivering counseling services and less time on clerical duties. Sink and Yillik-Downer (2001) suggested that perhaps the more highly invested school counselors are in the development and implementation of the counseling program, the greater the likelihood that they will assume an increased "ownership" of the program and recognize its value in relation to overall student success.

Developing, Implementing and Evaluating the Program

School counseling literature provides several models for developing a program (e.g., ASCA, 2003; Gysbers & Henderson, 2000; Schmidt, 2003; TEA, 2004). Among these, various authors have chosen different labels for the steps in the program development process, and some variations exist in the order of proposed actions to be taken. However, similarities are more common than differences, and in many program development models: an assessment is made of the current program, organizing for change occurs, needs are assessed, planning and designing the new or revised program is done, the program is implemented, and the implemented program is evaluated. Also, using a committee (steering committee, guidance committee, advisory committee) is commonly recommended to facilitate the process throughout its steps (e.g., Gysbers & Henderson, 2000; Myrick, 2003; Schmidt, 2003).

ASSESSING THE CURRENT PROGRAM

Assuming that some form of counseling or guidance activities exist, an informal determination that the current counseling program is not as effective as it could or should be is often the spur for change. Once change is being considered, a more formalized assessment of the current program is in order. This assessment might begin with a review of the current written program plan with regard to adequacy and extent of implementation. Potential indicators of the level of program adequacy could include reviews of counselor logs; program budgets; student records; job descriptions and actual involvement of counselors and other personnel; feedback from students, parents, teachers, and administrators; and adequacy of facilities, materials, and equipment (Schmidt, 2003; TEA, 2004).

ORGANIZING THE SUPPORT NEEDED FOR CHANGE

Moving a school from the situation of having guidance as a bare collection of services to having a comprehensive and organized counseling program involves a level of change that often raises anxiety and sometimes evokes resistance. Having commitment from all staff, including administrators, is important. The process of change itself should not overwhelm staff, and time and budget must be set aside for assessing, organizing, planning, implementing, and evaluating the program. Mitchell and Gysbers (as cited in Gysbers & Henderson, 2000) emphasized that an effective organized change process is incremental rather than abrupt.

Appropriate leadership for the change process should be identified. Gysbers and Henderson (2000) proposed (a) that a steering committee be formed to manage the overall change process and (b) that a school-community advisory committee be formed to provide recommendations and advice as a liaison between the school and community. The advisory committee does not form policy or make decisions. The steering committee must be small enough to manage its charge and large enough to be representative of counselors, administrators, teachers, parents, special school personnel (such as the special education coordinator and the school nurse), and perhaps community leaders. The steering committee in this stage would work with the administration and meet with the school board to inform and to seek support and authorization to proceed with the change process.

ASSESSING NEEDS

Gibson, Mitchell, and Higgins (1983) and Niles et al. (2004) described needs assessment as the foundation of program development. They describe processes for assessing the needs of the community, the school, and the target populations (primarily students, but also teachers and parents). A variety of techniques is available ranging from surveys, interviews, focus groups, and Delphi studies to examination of school and public records. Russo and Kassera (1989) described a comprehensive needs-assessment package effectively used in a large high school. In addition to providing a useful needs-assessment model, they pointed out that needs may vary depending on sub-groupings in the student population (such as grade level, gender, ability group, racial, and ethnic differences), and that this lack of homogeneity suggests that needs particular to certain groups must not fall victim to pressures to identify only overall needs.

DESIGNING THE PROGRAM

A general program model (such as the model described above consisting of guidance curriculum, responsive services, individual planning, and system support) is adopted and studied thoroughly by the steering committee. The content areas to be infused in the comprehensive guidance curriculum are determined. In designing the program, the assessed needs should be considered on the bases of both frequency and intensity before they are prioritized to form the basis for overall program goals, particular curriculum content areas, program balance, and specific program objectives. Gysbers and Henderson (2000) have suggested an alternative that the formal needs assessment (see preceding section) be conducted *after* the program is designed in order to use desired student competencies established in the program designing stage as items in the formal needs assessment.

IMPLEMENTING THE PROGRAM

Implementing the program involves carrying out the designed improvements and using the school counselors in accordance with job descriptions that properly utilize counselors' competencies. Carefully designed and prioritized activities, provision of staff development for counselors and others involved in the program, and acceptance of a fitting model for the evaluation of school counselor performance facilitate implementation (TEA, 2004).

EVALUATING THE PROGRAM

Broadly defined, evaluating the counseling program involves gathering data about the program and using the data to draw conclusions about the value of the program. As such, evaluation forms the basis for changing a program to increase its effectiveness, for demonstrating accountability (i.e., responsiveness) to needs, and for counselors' professional development and growth. Proper program evaluation requires clearly stated goals that are agreed upon by those involved in the evaluation procedure. As one would find in many fields, program evaluation is a continuous process, not an outcome goal itself. Subsequent to evaluation, requirements for change are recognized, and the cycle of organizing, assessing, designing, and implementing becomes continual.

Evaluating the counseling program entails using data about the (a) *delivery of ser-vices* and (b) the *outcomes* related to those served. Schmidt (2003) clarified that *delivery of services* can be evaluated by reporting how many times the services were provided, how many people received the services, and how much time was spent delivering the services. Services-oriented evaluations may also focus, for example, on the balance of time allocated to the different program components, availability of the counselors, timely delivery of services, and relationships between counselors and other school personnel. Program evaluation may also be approached by assessing *outcomes*. This aspect of evaluation centers on assessing the development and/or improvement of competencies in areas such as study skills, decision-making strategies, academic grades, career awareness, and school attendance—either on a school-wide basis or as needed on an individual student basis. For example, if the counseling program is patterned after the ASCA Competencies and Indicators (ASCA, 2003), the degree to which students meet the Competencies and Indicators are salient evaluation data. If such assessments are limited to school-wide data, the program runs the risk of not addressing the needs of individual students or of small groups of students (Schmidt, 2003). Also, using school-wide achievement or behavior data for evaluation purposes can be problematic because so many variables are related to students' achievement and behavior (Brown & Trusty, 2005).

Inherent in program effectiveness is the effectiveness of the counselors in performing their roles. Therefore, an effective means of evaluating individual counselor performance should be incorporated into program evaluation (TEA, 2004). Regardless of the evaluative procedures or databases used, evaluation of individual counselor performance should be based on the job description that the counselor is expected to follow. The procedures should be understood by the evaluator and counselor in advance, and the model should be flexible enough to reflect variations agreed upon by the counselor and evaluator. Schmidt (2003), ASCA (2003), and the Texas Counseling Association (2004) provided models for counselor performance evaluation. Evaluations were based on data gathered through a variety of means such as observations (live or taped), interviews, self-reports, input from those receiving services, products developed by counselors, records of activities, and outside expert review. If observations of counselors performing activities are being used as a database, guidelines regarding such observations should be agreed upon. Several resources (e.g., Gysbers & Henderson, 2000; Henderson & Lampe, 1992; TCA, 2004) are available to assist with developing guidelines for using observation as a database in counselor performance evaluation.

Ethical and Legal Guidelines

Ethical and legal considerations affect principals and counselors daily. School counselors have two major sources of ethical guidelines: (a) the *Ethical Standards for School Counselors* (ASCA, 2004) and (b) the *ACA Code of Ethics and Standards of Practice* (American Counseling Association, 1995). In order for the administrator to better understand the counselor's role and decisions, it is important for school administrators to be aware of several ethical issues addressed in these codes. Although ethical standards are not in themselves laws, they often relate to legal issues. Administrators must be familiar with federal and state laws that affect education and counseling in particular. These issues include the release of records, discrimination, documentation, academic requirements, testing, staffing, reporting child abuse, credentials, and special populations. Two general ethical issues drawn from the *Ethical Standards for School Counselors,* both with possible legal ramifications, are presented in the following paragraphs.

Ethically, the school counselor's primary obligation is to the counselee, and information obtained by the counselor is kept confidential unless there is clear and imminent danger to the counselee or others or legal requirements for disclosure. In clear and imminent danger situations, the counselor is ethically called upon to inform appropriate authorities. An ethical dilemma is presented to the counselor when an administrator demands confidential information that does not fall into the above categories. Confidentiality also applies to counseling records, which are to be released only according to prescribed laws and school policies (ASCA, 2004).

Another ethical issue that school counselors and administrators sometimes see differently involves dual relationships, wherein the counselor and the client have a relationship outside of counseling that might impair the counselor's impartiality and/or the willingness of the student to participate in counseling. Obvious examples include sexual contact with clients, counseling family members, and counseling one's own students if the counselor is also a teacher of record. A dual relationship problem occurs when the counselor is called upon to administer or witness punishment or is placed in a potentially disciplinary "spotlight" such as hall monitor. In small communities, some dual relationships are impossible to avoid (e.g., children of family, children of friends, or members of the same church), and the ethical standards provide guidelines for reducing the potential for harm if dual relationships are unavoidable (ASCA, 2004).

Counselor Roles in Promoting Counseling Program Effectiveness

In addition to effectively carrying out the counselor roles described earlier in this chapter, the counselor has responsibility for doing so in a professional manner (ASCA, 2003; TCA, 2004). This requires a commitment to following ethical standards, carrying one's load, being timely and available, maintaining collegiality, advocating for students, and modeling service. The counselor should demonstrate and promote teamwork among school professionals and keep administrators informed (within ethical limits of confidentiality). The school counselor also is obligated to engage in professional development to stay knowledgeable of current social conditions, techniques, ethical standards, and laws.

Administrator Roles in Promoting Counseling Program Effectiveness

Administrators' roles in promoting the formation and effectiveness of a comprehensive counseling program are varied. These may differ some by administrative level (e.g., principal and superintendent), but regardless of the level, the roles at different levels often parallel each other.

For example, at all levels, the administrator plays an important role of supporting program development/improvement efforts in house (among faculty and staff) and in the community. Formal and informal (and frequent) public relations activities, whether spoken or written, can have substantial impact. The administrator must promote a budget that allows for the necessary resources, clerical assistance, facilities, information resources, assessment tools, equipment, and supplies. Also in the budget, the administrator must address funding for professional development activities to better meet the needs of the district by improving the competencies of the counselors (Gysbers & Henderson, 2000).

The administrator plays an important role in hiring an adequate number of properly qualified professional counselors. This is particularly crucial given the shortages of counselors in some locations and the calls for lowering the ratio of school counselors to students, both of which could force administrators to hire less than qualified counselors (Towner-Larsen, Granello, & Sears, 2000).

Assuming properly qualified counselors are hired, the administrator, particularly the building principal, exercises a central role in determining whether or not counselors are involved in non-guidance activities. Burnam and Jackson (2000) reported that although counselors do perform the functions described in contemporary program models, there are discrepancies and wide variations. They further suggest that assignment of non-guidance duties to counselors remains a most troublesome practice and that involvement of administrators is vital in determining who best should carry out these non-guidance tasks. Gysbers and Henderson (2000) echoed this problem, arguing that it is necessary to streamline counselor involvement in non-guidance activities. Myrick (2003) pointed out that coordination, an appropriate role of counselors, can become a "catch all" source of overload, and that coordination of activities should be shared with other personnel to give counselors time for more direct services.

If a lead counselor in a school is not available to do so, the principal is often responsible for evaluating the effectiveness of individual counselors. This requires an understanding of the proper roles of counselors, a commitment to using counselors fittingly, and knowledge of suitable standards and databases upon which to base the evaluations (TCA, 2004). Closely related to evaluation is supervision, or overseeing the work of others to improve performance and professional development (Borders & Leddick, 1987).

Henderson and Lampe (1992) described an effective model of supervision of counselors in a large school district, with particular emphasis on clinical supervision involving feedback regarding counselor activities observed in progress.

Summary

Responsibilities of school counselors vary, based on the needs of constituencies served and the understandings and expectations of principals who are ultimately responsible for guidance operations in their schools. This chapter described varying responsibilities of counselors, defined commonly used counselor-related terms, and explained how counseling and guidance services can be organized, improved, and evaluated. Several outcome research studies supporting the implementation of organized school counseling programs were presented, and some of the ethical situations that counselors and principals might see from different perspectives were addressed. Also, the importance of the counselor and the principal working as a corps for the benefit of students was emphasized. The following case study and questions were constructed to help pull together the information and ideas presented in this chapter.

Applying Your Knowledge

As principal of a school in an urban area, you believe you have a good working relationship with the three counselors employed. There are 2,100 students in your school, and budget constraints will not allow the employment of an additional counselor. However, funding has been approved for the hiring of a clerical assistant.

The school counselors appear to be working together as a team by dividing the workload equally among them. In order to meet students' needs, they assume full responsibility for conducting classroom guidance activities. They also provide academic planning for all students and in-service training for teachers. In addition, they coordinate the school's standardized testing program (without much complaint) as well as actively coordinate other programs and special projects. Even though the school counselors work hard and are extremely busy, you would like to see more individual and group counseling being conducted. Another area of concern is that very little has been done regarding providing data to prove the effectiveness of the counseling program.

Recently, you attended a seminar concerning current issues in school counseling. This seminar addressed the development of a comprehensive school counseling program. As a result of information gained, you have identified ways in which you think the counseling program in your school could be strengthened. You have scheduled a meeting with the school counselors as a team to develop a plan to work toward improving the counseling program.

QUESTIONS

1. What strengths do you identify in the existing school counseling program? What are some of the weaknesses?
2. What would be the first step toward initiating change in the counseling program?
3. What contributions could students, parents, and community members make toward the operation of a comprehensive counseling program? What could be done to elicit their support?
4. What role could teachers in the school play in changing the counseling program?

5. Do you anticipate a counselor-student ratio of 1:700 students a barrier to the effective implementation of a comprehensive counseling program? If so, what are some suggestions for dealing with these challenges?
6. What could be done to provide data to assess the effectiveness of the counseling program?

QUESTIONS FOR THOUGHT

1. What are the major advantages of a comprehensive counseling program? What might be some disadvantages?
2. When implementing change, what are the benefits of a master plan of action?
3. What is the importance of program evaluation? What is the importance of individual counselor evaluation? How often should these processes occur, and what might be done to lessen the overwhelming task?
4. In what ethical and legal aspects of counselor functioning should an administrator seek professional development?

For Additional Information Online

For Additional Information Online

American Counseling Association *http://www.counseling.org.*

American School Counselor Association *http://www.schoolcounselor.org.*

References

American Counseling Association. (1995). *ACA code of ethics and standards of practice.* Alexandria, VA: Author. Retrieved April 13, 2004, from *http://www.counseling.org/site/PageServer?pagename=resources_ethics.*

American School Counselor Association. (2004). *Ethical standards for school counselors.* Alexandria, VA: Author.

American School Counselor Association. (2003). *The ASCA national model: A framework for school counseling programs.* Alexandria, VA: Author.

Baker, S. B., & Gerler, E. R., Jr. (2004). *School counseling for the Twenty-First Century* (4th ed.). Upper Saddle River, NJ: Pearson Education.

Borders, L. D., & Leddick, G. R. (1987). *Handbook of counseling supervision.* Alexandria, VA: American Association for Counseling and Development.

Brigman, G., & Campbell, C. (2003). Helping students improve academic achievement and school success behavior. *Professional School Counseling, 7,* 91–98.

Brown, D., & Trusty, J. (2005). *Designing and implementing comprehensive school counseling programs: Promoting student competence and meeting students' needs.* Pacific Grove, CA: Brooks/Cole.

Burnham, J. J., & Jackson, C. M. (2000). School counselor roles: Discrepancies between actual practice and existing models. *Professional School Counseling, 4,* 41–49.

Carr, J. V., & Hayslip, J. B. (1989). Getting unstuck from the 1970s: New Hampshire style. *The School Counselor, 37,* 41–46.

Drummond, R. J. (2004). *Appraisal procedures for counselors and helping professionals* (5th ed.). Upper Saddle River, NJ: Merrill.

Education Trust. (2003). Homepage. Retrieved March 3, 2004, from *http://www2.edtrust.org/edtrust/default.* Author.

Gibson, R. L., Mitchell, M. H., & Higgins, R. E. (1983). *Development and management of counseling programs and guidance services.* New York: Macmillan.

Gysbers, N. C., & Henderson, P. (2000). *Developing and managing your school guidance program* (3rd ed.). Alexandria, VA: American Counseling Association.

Gysbers, N. C., Lapan, R. T., & Blair, M. (1999). Closing in on the statewide implementation of a comprehensive guidance program model. *Professional School Counseling, 2,* 357–366.

Gysbers, N. C., Lapan, R. T., & Jones. B. A. (2000). School board policies for guidance and counseling: A call to action. *Professional School Counseling, 3, 349–355.*

Gysbers, N. C., Starr, M., & Magnuson, C. (1998). *Missouri comprehensive guidance: A model for program development, implementation, and evaluation.* Jefferson City, MO: Missouri Department of Elementary and Secondary Education.

Henderson, P., & Lampe, R. E. (1992). Clinical supervision of school counselors. *The School Counselor, 39,* 151–157.

House, R. M., & Martin, P. J. (1998). Advocating for better futures for all students: A new vision for school counselors. *Education, 119,* 284–291.

Lapan, R. T. (2001). Results-based comprehensive guidance and counseling programs: A framework for planning and evaluation. *Professional School Counseling, 4,* 289–299.

Lapan, R. T., Gysbers, N. C., & Petroski, G. F. (2001). Helping seventh graders be safe and successful: A statewide study of the impact of comprehensive guidance and counseling programs. *Journal of Counseling & Development, 79,* 320–330.

Lapan, R. T., Gysbers, N. C., & Sun, Y. (1997). The impact of more fully implemented guidance programs on the school experiences of high school students: A statewide evaluation study. *Journal of Counseling & Development, 75,* 292–302.

Myrick, R. D. (2003). *Developmental guidance and counseling: A practical approach* (4th ed.). Minneapolis, MN: Educational Media Corporation.

Nelson, D. E., & Gardner, J. L. (1998). *An evaluation of the comprehensive guidance program in Utah public schools.* Salt Lake City, UT: The Utah State Office of Education.

Niles, S. G., Trusty, J., & Mitchell, N. (2004). Fostering positive career development in children and adolescents. In R. Përusse & G. E. Goodnough (Eds.), *Leadership, advocacy, and direct services strategies for professional school counselors* (pp. 102–124). Pacific Grove, CA: Brooks/Cole.

Paisley, P. O., & Hayes, R. L. (2003). School counseling in the academic domain: Transformations in preparation and practice. *Professional School Counseling, 6,* 198–204.

Përusse, R., Goodenough, G. E., Donegan, J., & Jones, C. (2004). Perceptions of school counselors and school principals about the National Standards for School Counseling Programs and the Transforming School Counseling Initiative. *Professional School Counseling, 7,* 152–161.

Picchioni, A. P., & Bonk, E. C. (1983). *A comprehensive history of guidance in the United States.* Austin, TX: Texas Personnel and Guidance Association.

Ponec, D. L., & Brock, B. L. (2000). Relationships among elementary school counselors and principals: A unique bond. *Professional School Counseling, 3,* 208–217.

Russo, T. J., & Kassera, W. (1989). A comprehensive needs-assessment package for secondary school guidance programs. *The School Counselor, 36,* 265–269.

Schmidt, J. J. (2003). *Counseling in schools: Essential services and comprehensive programs* (4th ed.). Boston: Allyn & Bacon.

Shoffner, M. F., & Williamson, R. D. (2000). Engaging preservice school counselors and principals in dialogue and collaboration. *Counselor Education and Supervision, 40,* 128–140.

Sink, C. A., & MacDonald, G. (1998). The status of comprehensive guidance and counseling in the United States. *Professional School Counseling, 2,* 88–94.

Sink, C. A., & Stroh, H. R. (2003). Raising achievement test scores of early elementary school students through comprehensive school counseling programs. *Professional School Counseling, 6,* 350–364.

Sink, C. A., & Yillik-Downer, A. (2001). School counselors' perceptions of comprehensive guidance and counseling programs: A national survey. *Professional School Counseling, 4,* 278–288.

Smith, L. W., & Gideon, L. B. (1929). *Planning a career. New York: American Book Company.*

Starr, M. F. (1996). *Comprehensive guidance and systematic educational and career planning: Why a K–12 approach?* Journal of Career Development, 23, 9–22.

Texas Counseling Association (TCA). (2004). *Texas evaluation model for professional school counselors* (2nd ed.). Austin, TX: Author.

Texas Education Agency. (2004). *A model comprehensive developmental guidance and counseling program for Texas public schools: A guide for program development pre-K–12th grade.* Austin, TX: Author.

Towner-Larsen, R., Granello, D. H., & Sears, S. J. (2000). Supply and demand for school counselors: Perceptions of public school administrators. *Professional School Counseling, 3,* 270–276.

Trusty, J., & Niles, S. G. (2003). High-school math courses and completion of the bachelor's degree. *Professional School Counseling, 7,* 99–107.

Whiston, S. C. (2003). Outcomes research on school counseling services. In B. T. Erford (Ed.), *Transforming the school counseling profession* (pp. 435–447). Upper Saddle River, NJ: Merrill.

Whiston, S. C., & Sexton, T. L. (1998). A review of school counseling outcome research: Implications for practice. *Journal of Counseling & Development, 76,* 412–426.

Alternative Education Programs 11

Diana K. Freeman

An alternative program is an educational program
designed to meet the needs of a targeted
population of students who do not
experience success in the
traditional school setting.

—Diana K. Freeman

Objectives

1. To learn the history of the modern alternative education
   movement
2. To learn the most common characteristics of the modern
   alternative education movement
3. To develop an understanding of the administrator's role in
   an alternative program

Introduction

Alternative programs within the school setting address a wide variety of educational offerings. Any program that differs from the mainstream traditional school is often dubbed an alternative program. This wide array creates great difficulty when trying to define exactly what comprises an alternative program or what falls under the umbrella of alternative education. Perhaps the most concise definition of an alternative program, and the one used for the purposes of this chapter, is "an educational program that embraces subject matter and/or methodology that is not generally offered to students of the same age or grade level in traditional school settings, which offers a range of educational options and includes the students as an integral part of the planning team" (New Jersey Department of Education as quoted in Katsiyannis & Williams, 1998, p. 276).

Alternative programs can be found as freestanding independent schools operating as a part of a local education unit, a private school, or a charter school. An alternative program may also function as a school-within-a-school. Still other alternative programs are offered as support programs for certain qualifying students within the traditional school setting (Knight & Kneese, 1999). An alternative program may include non-educational support services such as health services or social services.

As indicated in the definition above, method of instructional delivery is one definitive factor of alternative education. Alternative programs embrace non-traditional teaching techniques. The strict time frame associated with course work in the traditional school is either expanded or compressed to meet the need of the student. Traditional pencil and paper work is exchanged for project-driven assignments. Vocational experience is honored as progress toward completion of graduation requirements. Business and community members act as teachers and mentors. While any of these methodologies can be found in traditional schools, their existence there is considered innovative; however, such methods are considered commonplace in the alternative program (Guerin & Denti, 1999; Knight & Kneese, 1999).

Another common determinant of what is considered an alternative program is the target population. Generally, alternative education is designed to benefit students who are not successful in a traditional school setting, students who are considered at risk (Lange & Sletten, 2002). A sub-group of at risk students is those who have committed some type of rule violation or crime that places them within a class of students who are removed from the traditional campus. A third group of students identified as candidates for alternative programs are those students qualified for special education services according to IDEA (Individual with Disabilities Education Act). Some alternative programs are designed specifically to address juvenile offenders while other programs address at risk students in general. Some programs exclude students with a qualifying condition under IDEA while others include them and still others are offered exclusively to students with an Individual Education Plan (IEP) as defined by IDEA (Lange & Sletten, 2002). Each alternative program defines for itself the target population.

This lack of a cohesive, common definition has made the process of studying alternative programs difficult. The number of studies concerning alternative education is limited, and those that do exist generally are limited to describing the characteristics of the program. Even fewer studies have been conducted concerning the effectiveness of the alternative program. The bulk of the articles addressing alternative education give information about a single program and tout the specific design of that particular program. If an individual is interested in an overarching view of alternative programs, he/she must gather and synthesize the material him/herself. Authors and sources for this information will be given at the end of this chapter.

History of Alternative Education

Educational opportunities designed to meet the needs of differing groups of students have been a part of the American educational system since the beginning. However, the alternative education movement now present in this country began in the Civil Rights movement of the 1960s (Lange & Sletten, 2002). The Elementary and Secondary Education Act (ESEA) of 1965 focused attention on the public schools as a major weapon in the war on poverty. Education was also considered key in the fight against social injustice. The ESEA provided funding from the federal government to support new educational programs designed to battle these enemies (Lange & Sletten, 2002).

The alternative programs of the 1960s focused on equity. The public schools were viewed as discriminatory institutions organized in such a way that the individuality of the learner was ignored. Success was measured by academic progress in terms that failed to recognize the growth and advancement of many students. The alternative school provided a different school structure tailored to meet the needs of the students who were not successful in the traditional school (Raywid, 1998). These newly structured schools were commonly called alternative schools by the end of the 1960s (Neumann, 1994).

The alternative education movement had split into two distinct categories by the end of the sixties: those inside public education and those outside public education. The alternative programs outside public education had two forms. The Freedom Schools developed to provide minority students access to a high quality education that was not perceived as available in the public schools. The Freedom Schools had a community base and focus and appeared in settings ranging from storefronts to church basements (Lange & Sletten, 2002). In a different vein, the Free School Movement focused on the fulfillment and achievement of the individual; the traditional school was seen as confining and limiting. Students were free to define what they would or would not learn. The only rule taught was that each individual had the right to determine what was correct for him/herself (Lange & Sletten, 2002).

The alternative programs available outside public schools influenced public school educators to develop similar options within the public school system. One broad category of public school alternative programs was the Open School. "These schools were characterized by parent, student and teacher choice; autonomy in learning and pace, non-competitive evaluation; and a child-centered approach" (Lange & Sletten, 2002, p. 4). The Open School movement is credited with instigating the many different alternative programs that grew within the public schools during the 1970s. Raywid (1998) classified the alternative programs of this era according to the school's focus for change: the student, the school, or the educational setting.

The back to basics emphasis of the 1980s and the increasing number of students identified as functioning below average achievement levels also influenced alternative schools. Options available to students began to narrow and the focus was remedial. The organization of these schools was formal and hierarchical; the curriculum was conventional and featured drill and practice (Neumann, 1994). Student and teacher choice was no longer a defining characteristic of alternative programs. Another focus of this decade was the development of alternative programs to educate disruptive students (Lange & Sletten, 2002).

The decade of the 1990s saw a growth in the number of alternative schools. Once again, student and teacher choice returned as a key characteristic of alternative programs. The rise in reports of violent acts committed on school campuses supported the continuation and growth of alternative programs designed to house disruptive and adjudicated youth (Kleiner, Porch, & Farris, 2002). Raywid (1994) also classified the schools of this era into three types. The Type I alternative schools were schools of choice designed to create a fulfilling environment for the students and adults associated with the program. Type II alternative schools were last-chance programs designed to provide students one final chance before expulsion; the students in Type II schools did not attend by choice. Type III alternative schools had a remedial focus. The students were viewed as needing either academic or social/emotional rehabilitation or both. The presumption was that with the remediation, the student would be able to return to a traditional school environment. Any single alternative school could include characteristics of any or all of the three pure types.

The current emphasis on accountability and the use of standardized tests as measures of student achievement will undoubtedly influence alternative programs as they do traditional programs. The direction the alternative programs will take is as yet unclear. The alternative schools in existence now, in the early part of the 21st Century, continue the patterns begun in the 1990s. Raywid's classification of Type I, II, and III alternative schools is still applicable.

Characteristics of Alternative Programs

As noted earlier, ambiguity surrounds alternative programs. No single factor applies to all alternative programs. A survey conducted in 2002 by Kleiner, Porch, and Farris for the National Center for Educational Statistics Fast Response Survey System entitled *Public Alternative Schools and Programs for Students At Risk of Education Failure: 2000–01* provides the most recent compilation of characteristics of alternative programs. Prior to that effort, Raywid led a national survey published in 1982 with a more narrow focus. She identified and questioned secondary alternative schools of choice, schools she had identified as Type I. Other prominent alternative education researchers, Fashola and Slavin (1997; 1998), have completed descriptions and evaluations of various commercial programs designed to benefit at risk students. Various other practicing educators and researchers have developed lists of common characteristics found among alternative programs. (For example, see: Knight & Kneese, 1999; Rutter & Margelofsky, 1997.) The following is a compilation of the characteristics identified in these works.

CHOICE

Choice is identified as one of the key factors present in alternative programs. Choice in this instance indicates the student's freedom to choose whether or not to become a member of that particular alternative program or school. This freedom of choice is considered critical to the student's commitment to the program ("Alternative Schools for Disruptive Youth," 1991; Neumann, 1994; Raywid, 1982, 1994). A sense of commitment or community is linked to school and student success (Leone & Drakeford, 1999).

The school must create an environment to make and maintain the sense of community. This allows the students and the staff to work together to create meaningful and personal goals for learning. The change in the learning structure fosters the continuation of the sense of community that in turn maintains the cooperative spirit of the program. The cycle is a prominent feature in alternative programs of choice (Leone & Drakeford, 1999; Raywid, 1994).

Raywid (1994) finds that Type I schools, alternative schools of choice, have demonstrated greater and longer lasting positive effects than either Type II or Type III schools. The students create a connection with the program and achieve more than they had at any point in their enrollment in a traditional school. "Students who had never engaged with school, or rarely succeeded at it, are sometimes transformed as to attitude, behavior, and accomplishment" (Raywid, 1994, p. 28). Anecdotal evidence from these schools supports this position, but very little empirical evidence exists concerning the effectiveness of alternative schools ("Alternative Schools for Disruptive Youth," 1991; Lange & Sletten, 2002).

The concept of choice also applies to the faculty of the alternative school or program. The true sense of community will not develop if the teachers do not also form a personal commitment to the program. Murdock (1999) identified the student's perception of the teacher's long-term expectation as the greatest influence over student engagement and discipline. Knight and Kneese (1999) also identified a respectful, trusting student-teacher relationship as a common strategy among alternative programs. Gold (1995) states that "giving students warm, interpersonal support" (p. 8) is one of two key components for successful schools.

SIZE

Closely related to the ability to create a sense of community and belonging for both students and teachers is the size of the alternative program. In fact, a decreased school size is identified quite frequently as a defining factor of an alternative program (Duke & Griesdorn, 1999; Neumann, 1994). Size in this case does not refer to the square footage of the facility but to the number of students and teachers served by the program. When students were asked to identify the factors of a traditional school most inhibitive to success, they listed large group instruction as one of the two most inhibiting factors (Rutter & Margelofsky, 1997). The alternative program strives to overcome this by limiting class size. This particular restriction has caused some alternative programs to turn away prospective students or to place these students on a waiting list (Kleiner, Porch, & Farris, 2002).

Method of Instructional Delivery

Instructional practices considered innovative in the traditional school have long been practiced in the alternative setting. The underlying premise of the flexibility in teaching methodology is that students must be provided the opportunity to succeed. The alternative school is rooted in the idea that the structure of the traditional school does not fit or benefit all learners; therefore, the school must change to more closely match the student. Some traditional school attempts to address the varied needs of the learner such as tracking, ability grouping, or labeling are noticeably missing in the alternative program (Neumann, 1994).

Common instructional practices within the alternative program include thematic units, high-interest topics, portfolios and other alternative assessments, technology, affective education, and transition skills (Guerin & Denti, 1999). Secondary level alternative programs frequently include a vocational component so that a student can earn credit toward graduation and a wage at the same time (Fashola & Slavin, 1998). Clear, concise goals developed by teacher and student collaboration are also prominent characteristics (Knight & Kneese, 1999). The students who attend alternative programs generally have a background of academic failure; so the structure of the program itself must include added academic supports and the opportunity to learn how to learn ("Alternative Schools for Disruptive Youth," 1991). Tutors and mentors are frequent support systems put in place along with frequent recognition for academic improvement and social gains (Fashola & Slavin, 1998; Knight & Kneese, 1999). Slavin (1996) goes so far as to state that no improvement in student achievement will be realized until the day-to-day instructional practices change to support that improvement.

TARGET POPULATION

The most frequently identified population targeted by alternative programs is students at risk of educational failure. Generally, an at risk student is a student who is not expected to complete the traditional course of public school education, grades kindergarten through 12, in 13 years. Individual state or local agencies may include more specific criteria in the definition of at risk. Many factors contribute to a student being at risk, and no single factor or group of factors is an absolute predictor of a student's tendency to not succeed in school. Some of the more commonly identified at risk factors include performing below standard on standardized and local assessments, repeating a grade level, having an original language different from the language of instruction, and engaging in criminal activity (Freeman, 2002).

Guerin and Denti (1999) identified an extensive list of characteristics common among students in alternative settings. This list includes low socio-economic status, limited English proficiency, ethnic minority, poor literary and academic skills, inadequate social-emotional-behavioral skill, impulsivity and poor judgment, limited or unavailable family support, and lack of positive adult role models. One criticism of alternative schools is that they serve as a dumping ground for unwanted students from minority cultures and low socio-economic situations (Sagor, 1999). Studies of alternative schools have not indicated this to be entirely true. The ethnic percentages within the alternative programs basically mirror the surrounding community and schools. These same studies do indicate an overrepresentation of economically disadvantaged students (Freeman, 2002; Kleiner, Porch, & Farris, 2002).

One target population receiving more attention in the current alternative education environment is the disruptive or adjudicated youth. Many articles cite an increase in juvenile crime and violent acts reported on school campuses (Ferrara, 1993; Sprague & Walker, 2000; Vann, Schubert, & Rogers, 2000). One response has been the creation of alternative schools designed specifically to address that group of students. Raywid (1994) identified these schools as Type II alternative schools or last chance schools. The schools received this designation because they are quite often the student's last chance to avoid expulsion. Interestingly, one of the most effective behavioral intervention strategies available to schools is an engaging academic program. Some last chance schools have recorded instances of student achievement and behavioral improvement; however, to do so the schools have usually incorporated many of the structures more common to the Type I schools or alternative schools of choice (Raywid, 1994; Vann, Schubert, & Rogers, 2000).

STUDENT FAMILY

Because students in alternative programs and at risk students in general have limited or unavailable family support and lack positive adult role models, the alternative program often includes a component designed to bolster the student's family. Fashola and Slavin (1998) identify recognition of family importance as a common theme of effective alternative programs. Parent involvement is linked to student improvement and success particularly for the at risk student, the potential dropout, and those with poor social skills. Quite often, schools find themselves unable to create behavioral changes in the students without parent improvement (Buroker, Messner, & Leonard, 1993).

Parents of at risk students who participated in a parent education program in the Lima City School District of Lima, Ohio indicated several positive outcomes. The parents were pleased with their participation in the program and found it to be both important and necessary for parents of students in an alternative education program. The parents also indicated an increased ability to use positive parenting behaviors and extinguish negative parenting behaviors. The parents were also able to increase their involvement with their child's education. Another benefit of the parenting program was the formation of a support group of parents with students facing similar issues (Buroker, Messner, & Leonard, 1993). Based on this study, a parent education component is recommended for parents of at risk students. Other studies have also reported positive student gains from mandatory parent and student counseling ("Alternative Schools for Disruptive Youth," 1991).

COMMUNITY AGENCIES

Quite often the alternative program student's needs are greater than the scope of the actual program. Walker and Hackman (1999) advocate collaboration between the school and various community agencies to most effectively meet these needs. Many alternative schools do cooperate with various social and community agencies. The alternative schools most often work in conjunction with the juvenile justice system. A clear majority of alternative schools and programs also collaborate with community mental health agencies, police or sheriff's departments, child protective service, health and human services, drug and/or alcohol clinics, community organizations, and family organizations. A lesser percentage of alternative programs report collaboration with crisis intervention centers, family planning/child care/child placement agencies, job placement centers, and park and recreation departments (Kleiner, Porch, & Farris, 2002). A policy statement from the American Academy of Pediatrics entitled *Out-of-School Suspension and Expulsion* (November 2003) makes another plea for cooperation between schools and health agencies. This particular statement argues that schools should provide services to rule out a mental or physical impairment or illness as the cause of the misbehavior. In order to do this, a school has to collaborate with a physician or health clinic.

Alternative Programs in the United States

The number of alternative programs available to students within the United States continues to increase (Katsiyannis & Williams, 1998; Kleiner, Porch, & Farris, 2002; Raywid, 1982). Raywid (1982) located 2500 secondary alternative schools of choice; Katsiyannis and Williams (1998) reported that 20 states had a state-adopted definition of alternative education and 22 states had legislation that addressed alternative education. Technical assistance to alternative schools was provided by 30 states, and state funding for alternative schools was available in 23 states. Alternative programs were endorsed by 37 states. In the latest survey of alternative schools and programs, Kleiner, Porch, and Farris (2002) indicated that 39 percent of the public school districts in the country offered at least one alternative school or program, and overall 10,900 public alternative schools or programs were in existence during the 2000–01 school year.

Alternative programs for secondary students outnumber those offered for elementary students. Slightly more than half of the districts that provided an alternative program indicated that at some point demand for enrollment exceeded the capacity. The enrollment size and metropolitan status of the district also correlated with the provision of alternative schools or programs. Urban districts were more likely to provide an alternative school or program than suburban districts that in turn were more likely to offer an alternative program than rural districts. Large districts, 10,000 students or more, were more likely to administer an alternative program than mid-size districts, 2,500–9,999 students, that were more likely to administer an alternative program than small districts, less than 2,500 students. Interestingly, districts in the southeast region of the country were more likely than those in the Northeast, Central, and Western regions to provide an alternative school or program (Kleiner, Porch, & Farris, 2002).

The provision of alternative schools was also investigated in relation to the percent of minority enrollment and poverty concentration within the school district. Districts with greater than 50 percent minority enrollment were more likely to provide an alternative program. The percentage of districts offering an alternative program decreased as the percentage of minority enrollment decreased. Additionally districts with a poverty concentration greater than 20 percent were slightly more likely to administer an alternative program than districts with a poverty concentration of 11 to 20 percent, and those districts were more likely to offer an alternative program than districts with a poverty concentration of 10 percent or less (Kleiner, Porch, & Farris, 2002).

These statistics pose no surprises when the target population and purpose of alternative schools and programs are considered. At risk students have a greater tendency to be from a minority culture and a low socio-economic status. Urban areas by virtue of the size of the population house larger school districts and have a greater number of minority citizens and citizens living in poverty concentration.

Administrator's Role in Alternative Programs

The flexible and non-traditional structure associated with alternative programs does create some differences in the role of the administrator. Quite often in an alternative program, the teachers take on additional responsibilities traditionally relegated to the administrator. The small size of many alternative programs does limit the number of administrators assigned. Some small alternative programs do not have an administrator but are managed exclusively by the teaching staff (Neumann, 1994).

The repertoire of instructional strategies required of teachers in alternative schools demands a highly supportive staff development program. The administrator does not have to be the individual that teaches all the staff development, but the administrator must support the provision of the continuous learning opportunities. The administrator is also the faculty member with the greatest responsibility for locating and evaluating programs and methods that will benefit the students and the alternative program in general (Fashola & Slavin, 1997; Griffin, 1993; Slavin, 1996).

Wong (1994) believes that the principal must create a climate of participation within the school. The alternative school works to include the family of the students with the teachers and the administrator; the principal's responsibility is to create a culture in which all stakeholders work together for the betterment of the students. Wong continues to say that the teachers are responsible for creating innovative classrooms, and parents are responsible for providing input and securing the financial resources necessary for the school to offer a quality program.

Griffin (1993) used the secondary level School Attitudinal Survey to determine current alternative students' feelings regarding their traditional campus and their alternative campus. Each student responded to the survey twice, once in September in regard to the traditional campus and once in January in regard to the alternative campus. The results of the survey were then used to provide guidance to administrators.

Griffin (1993) discovered that the students viewed the teachers in the alternative school as more genuinely concerned about students and less authoritarian in nature and less likely to show favoritism. The students also felt that they had more input in decision-making. The students also viewed the alternative teachers as more enthusiastic about their job. Overall, the students were more satisfied with the alternative school than the traditional school.

From these findings, Griffin (1993) concluded that the administrator should model and advance equitable treatment of all students. The principal needs to develop a caring, non-threatening school environment. The administrator can also demonstrate enthusiasm for her job and promote a culture that embraces enthusiasm. Finally, the administrator needs to provide an opportunity for students to express their desires and opinions. The principal sets the tone of the program and the standard to be met by all participants.

Existing alternative school principals gave the following advice to administrators beginning an alternative program (Freeman, 2002, p. 65):

- decide what the mission and philosophy of the school should be. This should align with the vision of the district. Visiting other alternative campuses can help develop a discussion of core values,
- pick your faculty well,
- they're still kids and need to be taken care of. You need to treat them with respect before they will respect you. Love and respect,
- be flexible and patient,
- work with the traditional school principals to find out their needs.

Very few formal programs of study or individual classes exist to prepare educators to work in alternative programs although the structure of the alternative programs demand a more robust knowledge of teaching methodologies and behavior management strategies (Prater & Sileo, 2000). Teachers and administrators are quite often left on their own to develop the expanded body of knowledge and intrapersonal skills needed to function successfully in an alternative program. The administrator is the member of the school team that sets the standard for the teachers, students, and parents (Griffin, 1993; Wong, 1994).

Summary

An alternative program is an educational program designed to meet the needs of a targeted population of students who do not experience success in the traditional school setting. The alternative program is generally smaller in size than the traditional school and provides a non-traditional method of instructional delivery. The civil rights movement of the 1960s gave rise to the current educational alternative programs, and the number of such programs continues to increase. Alternative programs are available in all geographic areas of the United States and in local school districts of varying sizes and characteristics. However, large, urban districts with a high percentage of minority cultures and poverty class students have a greater tendency to offer an alternative program. Quite often the teachers in the alternative program have an expanded role in the administration of the program. Administrators of alternative programs must establish a caring, supportive environment of which all students take ownership.

Applying Your Knowledge

You are the principal of a high school (grades 9–12) in a suburban school district of 25,000 students. The demographics of the district are changing. The minority population is growing and the number of second language learners is increasing. The superintendent has asked you to chair a committee to create a plan for your school district to meet the needs of the growing population of at risk students and to increase the number of students who graduate with a high school diploma.

QUESTIONS

1. Who do you want to serve with you on this committee?
2. What are the first five decisions that must be made by the committee?
3. Describe the type of program you create.
4. Change the demographics of the district to be a) an urban district of 100,000 students, b) a rural district of 1,000 students. How does this change your answers to the first three questions?

QUESTIONS FOR THOUGHT

1. How have the political and social events of history influenced alternative education?
2. Which of the general characteristics of alternative programs do you feel is most important? Why?
3. Develop a proposal for an alternative program to meet the needs of your student population.
4. What alternative programs do you have in your district or community? What purpose(s) do they serve? Are the programs successful in achieving their purpose(s)? How do you know?
5. Are the administrative responsibilities in an alternative program different from those in a regular program? How? Why?
6. If you could design a preparation program for teachers in alternative programs, what topics would you include and what skills would you emphasize? Be ready to justify your choices.

For Additional Information

Three authors stand out as critical references and authorities on the subject of alternative education: Robert Slavin, Gary Wehlage, and Mary Anne Raywid. Slavin has focused his efforts on evaluation and creation of programs designed specifically for students placed at risk. Wehlage and Raywid have both studied the structures of alternative schools and programs and their defining characteristics. Raywid has been particularly helpful with her classification of alternative schools. She has also worked diligently to identify existing alternative schools.

When one undertakes a study of alternative education, the process itself can become daunting. The body of work pertaining to alternative education can be found in three broad categories: at risk students, alternative education, and special education. All three areas must be investigated to find a complete picture. Even then, little information is available. Many of the works published concerning alternative education are simply commercials for a particular existing program. The information in these articles can be useful; however, one must take care to not accept everything said as applicable across all settings.

Opportunities for research abound in the field of alternative education. The information currently available is only the groundwork for future studies. The student population is continuing to diversify, and schools must adapt to meet the needs of the variety of learners. The alternative program is designed to meet those needs. Reliable data will be needed so decisions can be made to benefit the students.

References

Alternative schools for disruptive youth. (1991). *School Safety,* 8–11.

American Academy of Pediatrics. (2003). Out-of-school suspension and expulsion. *Pediatrics, 112*(5), 1206–1209.

Buroker, C. D., Messner, P. E., & Leonard, B. C. (1993). Parent education: Key to successful alternative education programs. *Journal of School Leadership,* 3, 635–645.

Duke, D. & Griesdorn, J. (1999). Consideration in the design of alternative schools. *The Clearing House, 73*(2), 89–92.

Fashola, O. & Slavin, R. (1997). Promising programs for elementary and middle schools: Evidence of effectiveness and replicability. *Journal of Education for Students Placed At Risk, 2*(3), 251–307.

Fashola, O. & Slavin, R. (1998). Effective dropout prevention and college attendance programs for students placed at risk. *Journal of Education for Students Places At Risk, 3*(2), 159–183.

Ferrara, M. M. (1993). Strategies and solutions: Alternative campuses for disruptive students. *Schools in the Middle, 2*(3), 14–17.

Freeman, D. K. (2002). A descriptive study of elementary alternative schools for at risk students in Texas (Doctoral Dissertation, Texas A&M University-Commerce, 2002).

Gold, M. (1995). Charting a course: Promise and prospects for alternative schools. *Journal of Emotional and Behavioral Problems, 3*(4), 8–11.

Griffin, B. L. (1993). Administrators can use alternative schools to meet student needs. *Journal of School Leadership, 3*(4), 416–420.

Guerin, G. & Denti, L. (1999). Alternative education support for youth at risk. *The Clearing House, 73*(2), 76–78.

Katsiyannis, A. & Williams, B. (1998). A national survey of state initiatives on alternative education. *Remedial and Special Education, 19*(5), 276–284.

Kleiner, B., Porch, R., & Farris, E. (2002). *Public alternative schools and programs for students at risk of education failure: 2000–01* (NCES 2002–004). U.S. Department of Education. Washington, DC: National Center for Education Statistics.

Knight, S. & Kneese, C. (1999). Examining student perceptions in four instructional programs for students at risk. *Teaching and Change, 7*(1), 17–32.

Lange, C. M. & Sletten, S. J. (2002). *Alternative education: A brief history and research synthesis.* Alexandria, VA: National Association of State Directors of Special Education.

Leone, P. E. & Drakeford, W. (1999). Alternative education: From a "last chance" to a proactive model. *The Clearing House, 73*(2), 86–88.

Murdock, T. (1999). The social context of risk: Status and motivational predictors of alienation in middle school. *Journal of Educational Psychology, 9*(1), 62–75.

Neumann, R. (1994) A report from the 2nd annual conference on alternative education. *Phi Delta Kappan, 75,* 547–549.

Prater, M. A. & Sileo, T. W. (2000). Preparing educators and related school personnel to work with at-risk students. *Teacher Education and Special Education, 23*(1), 51–64.

Raywid, M. A. (1982). The current status of schools of choice in public secondary education: Alternatives, options, magnets. Washington DC, National Institute of Education. (ERIC Document Reproduction Service No. ED 242055)

Raywid, M. A. (1994). Alternative schools: The state of the art. *Educational Leadership, 52*(1), 26–31.

Raywid, M. A. (1998). The journey of the alternative school movement: Where it's been and where it's going. *High School Magazine, 6*(2), 10–14.

Rutter, R. & Margelofsky, M. (1997). How school structures inhibit students at risk. *The Journal of At Risk Issues, 3*(2), 3–12.

Sagor, R. (1999). Equity and excellence in public schools: The role of the alternative school. *The Clearing House, 73*(2), 72–75.

Slavin, R. (1996). Reforming state and federal policies to support adoption of proven practices. *Educational Researcher, 25*(9), 4–5.

Sprague, J. R. & Walker, H. M. (2000). Early identification and intervention for youth with anti-social and violent behavior. *Exceptional Children, 66*(3), 367–370.

Vann, M., Schubert, S. R. & Rogers, D. (2000). The Big Bayou Association: An alternative education program for middle-school, at-risk juveniles. *Preventing School Failure, 45*(1), 31–36.

Walker, J. & Hackman, D. (1999). Full service schools: Forming alliances to meet the needs of students and families. *NASSP Bulletin, 83*(611), 28–37.

Wong, K. (1994). Linking governance reforms to schooling opportunities for the disadvantaged. *Educational Administration Quarterly, 30*(2), 153–177.

Programs for 12
Adjudicated Youth

Miguel de los Santos
Jerry M. Lowe

Juvenile justice programs are primarily developed to
meet the needs of students who exhibit chronic
misbehavior in school or who have committed a
crime that warrants expulsion from school
or leads, through adjudication, to juvenile probation.

—*Miguel de los Santos & Jerry M. Lowe*

Objectives

1. Overview of the need for Juvenile Justice Alternative Education
   Programs (JJAEP)
2. Describe the purpose, design, services and staffing of JJAEPs
3. Review the legislation establishing JJAEPs in one state, i.e., Texas

Introduction

In the 1980's public education experienced a significant rise in negative student activity. Youth gangs intensified, the use of drugs grew, and the influence of the family social agencies and churches declined. As society broke down and school reform took shape with higher standards and inflexibility in educational alternatives, demonstrations of unacceptable behavior by students seemed to soar. And, while statistics on adult crime declined, or leveled off, juvenile crime rates continued to grow (Hack, Candoli & Ray, 1995, p. 352).

According to a state level summary by the Hamilton Fish Institute (2000), a 1996 report on crime in the United States by the U.S. Department of Justice, Federal Bureau of Investigation, juvenile crime in Texas was quite alarming. Data reported showed that of the state's student population of 3,945,367, large numbers were charged with different crimes:

Violent Crime	7,196
Property Crime	5,050,382
Murder or Manslaughter	217
Forcible Rape	439
Robbery	2,291
Aggravated Assault	4,249
Burglary	9,649
Larceny or Theft	38,835
Motor Vehicle Theft	4,360
Arson	538

In view of these youth crime phenomena, in and out of school, school officials faced the critical dilemma of either keeping student wrong doers in school to create havoc, or expel them from school to, in reality, contribute to the juvenile crime rates out of the school setting. In the Texas example later in the chapter, principals and superintendents opted to remove the small "2 to 5 percent of the student population that creates fear, harasses, intimidates, extorts, assaults other students or uses or distributes drugs on campus" (Hill & Hill, 1994, p. 45).

Expulsion was administratively efficient and expedient, and the removal of unruly students created safer schools. That the expelled students would become social ills outside of the school setting was not the schools' problem. Many would argue, as did a group of California parents, that administrators abuse their authority by using suspensions "opportunity transfers," and expulsions as control mechanisms (Ednews.org, 2002 p.1). Others, including many Texas school officials, would counter that in order to provide safe and orderly school settings for the greater majority of students, the 2% to 5% should be "written off."

Until recently, there were few, if any, school district educational programs to work with accused criminal youth offenders. These young people would sit in juvenile jail cells for short periods and then be released to the streets. In the mid-1990s a few for-profit and non-profit alternative programs emerged. Students who were ruled as incorrigible or charged with criminal activity by the school district were sent to these facilities. Services were contracted through the school districts and this allowed the students to remain in some form of a school setting rather than being pushed out "on the street."

Purpose of the Program

Juvenile justice programs are primarily developed to meet the needs of students who exhibit chronic misbehavior in school or who have committed a crime that warrants expulsion from school or leads, through adjudication, to juvenile probation. In order to effectively serve young people who fit this profile, juvenile justice facilities maintain a program of strong academic and disciplinary expectations. Many of these programs are structured after the "boot camp" model where students live each day within a "no tolerance zone" under the very strict supervision of a cadre of drill instructors or behavior modification staff members. Along with the academic work they complete, students find themselves in an environment where they must learn to manage conflict and anger. While many facilities are organized as day schools where students are transported from home each day, others house all students for a specific period of time under very strict supervision. The major focus of most juvenile justice programs is to have students perform academically at grade level, while achieving self-discipline and learning to have respect for themselves and others (Colorado Three Year Plan (2003).

Student Services Provided

Although the organizational structure of juvenile facilities maintained throughout the various states differs in a variety of ways, program offerings to students appear fairly consistent. Generally considered an alternative placement of last resort for adjudicated youth, most juvenile facilities provide the necessary preparation for students to obtain a high school diploma (issued through the local school district), a GED or specialized technical training that will allow them to enter society with a salable skill. This is the case whether the facility is operated by local or state government agencies or as private contracted services. Some students, after spending a designated amount of time at a juvenile facility, are able to return to their public schools where, in many cases, they graduate and continue on to colleges and universities. It is not uncommon for students to complete a vocational program in auto mechanics, plumbing, carpentry, electronics and a variety of construction trade skills. Business and industrial organizations in many communities offer cooperative, work-study opportunities to adjudicated students. These programs allow students to acquire the knowledge and skills that will increase their marketability in the work force. It is also not unusual for some of the cooperating businesses to employ these work-study students on a full-time basis once they have spent their required time in the juvenile justice system.

A variety of counseling programs are typically offered to each student depending on their individual needs as determined by some form of individual growth plan developed when students first enter the program. These counseling services may vary among daily group process sessions, positive behavior interventions, specific topic groups that focus on issues such as drug abuse and prevention, conflict resolution training, anger management, parenting and other topics that impact student progress. Individual counseling sessions are usually available to each student in response to their specific needs. Additional social services are provided such as alcohol and drug abuse prevention programs and a variety of youth opportunity services designed to enhance student career readiness and job placement (Southwest Key Program, Inc., Jan, 2004). Special education services, as required by law, usually remain the responsibility of the school district from which the student was expelled; however, some juvenile facilities provide these services as part of their regular programs.

Mentoring programs for students are also important components of most juvenile justice facilities and usually involve peer, community, and school based mentoring models. Peer mentoring allows positive relationships to develop between adjudicated youth and individuals their own age. Peers are selected from local schools, junior colleges, and universities as well as other civic organizations such as Boys and Girls Club, YMCA/YWCA and others. Community-based mentoring encourages students to become involved in civic activities designed to promote pride and a sense of belonging. School-based mentoring appears to be very effective in improving academic performance and student behavior.

Supervised physical activities are an important part of the educational programs offered at the majority of juvenile justice facilities. Teachers and administrators may learn much about students by observing them as they interact during team play. These activities are usually designed to provide students with a means of releasing energy, developing team skills and promoting healthy life styles. Other forms of recreational activities may include field trips to museums, plays and zoos as well as club activities such as board games, drama and choir.

Staff Qualifications

Operating under a state or county juvenile board of directors, most juvenile justice facilities employ certified teachers and administrators to develop and deliver the educational component of the program. In some programs, for example, principals of the juvenile justice facility are trained in the Urban Teacher Perceiver which is a constructed interview technique developed by The Gallup Organization, encompassing the following eleven themes: Commitment, dedication, individualized perception, caring, involver, empathy, positivity initiator, stimulator, input and concept. This perception instrument is used by the principal in carefully selecting all teaching, counseling and behavior management personnel. It is considered effective in acquiring employees who will be able to form positive relationships with students and their families. A number of certified bilingual teachers and counselors are generally included as well. Once employed, all personnel are given intensive training that will allow them to be effective in a very unique situation involving very unique students.

Staff Training

The majority of juvenile justice facilities provide annual training programs for all administrators, faculty and staff members. While the majority of training programs vary among facilities, most are designed to enhance employee knowledge and skills in their particular area of expertise. In some cases, cross training is provided for persons involved in multi-disciplinary activities.

Southwest Key Program, Inc. is a private, non-profit organization that operates over 30 community treatment facilities for delinquent youth in several states and Puerto Rico. As members of this organization, all staff are required to develop a yearly professional growth plan that includes training needs and expectations. In addition, all professional personnel are required to participate in forty hours of in-service at the beginning of each academic year. Teachers and counselors are required to complete an additional 18 hours of in-service activities during each academic year. Common in-service training topics for teachers may include modifications for special needs students, math across the curriculum, Lexia 180 Software-Reading Curriculum, Integrating technology into the classroom, and reading strategies. The counseling staff may receive training in peer culture, crisis management and intervention, group facilitation and strength-based staffing. Most juvenile justice facilities, whether public or private, include the intensive training of personnel as a major component of their program effectiveness.

JJAEP: A Texas Plan

Texas provides an example of a massive reform effort. In the spirit of modern school reform in Texas, Senate Bill I, Chapter 37 was enacted in 1995 to officially address the need of educating student offenders and expelled youth. Chapter 37 included the provision for Disciplinary Alternative Education Programs (DAEP) and Juvenile Justice Alternative Education Programs (JJAEP). The rationale for the new law was simply that adjudicated and expelled youth would be better served in formal educational settings than at home or on the streets.

Under Subtitle G: Safe Schools, Chapter 37; Discipline Law and Order of Senate Bill I as adopted by the Texas Legislature in May 1995, specific legal language is decreed relative to Disciplinary Alternative Education Programs (37.008) and Juvenile Justice Alternative Education Programs (37.012). Specifically the code directs the board of trustees of an independent school district "to adopt a student code of conduct for the district". In addition to establishing standards for student conduct, the student code must:

1. Specify the circumstances, in accordance with this subchapter, under which a student may be removed from a classroom, campus, or disciplinary alternative education program;
2. Specify conditions that authorize or require a principal or other appropriate administrator to transfer a student to a disciplinary alternative education program;
3. Outline conditions under which a student may be suspended as provided by Section 37.005 or expelled as provided by Section 37.007;
4. Specify whether consideration is given to self-defense as a factor in a decision to order suspension, removal to a disciplinary alternative education program, or expulsion;
5. Provide guidelines for setting the length of a term of:
   (A) a removal under Section 37.006; and
   (B) an expulsion under Section 37.007; and
6. Address through notification of a student's parent or guardian of a violation of the student code of conduct committed by the student that results in suspension, removal to a disciplinary alternative education program, or expulsion.

Further, Chapter 37.006, directly addresses the removal of students from classes for certain conduct. This includes but is not limited to conduct:

1. involving a public school that contains the elements of the offense of false alarm or report under Section 42.06, Penal Code, or terroristic threat under Section 22.07, Penal Code; or
2. in which the youth commits the following on or within 300 feet of school property, as measured from any point on the school's real property boundary line, or while attending a school-sponsored or school-related activity on or off school property:
   (A) engages in conduct punishable as a felony;
   (B) engages in conduct that contains the elements of the offense of assault under Section 22.01 (a) (1) Penal code;

(C) sells, gives, or delivers to another person or possesses or uses or is under the influence of:

 (i) marijuana or a controlled substance, as a defined by Chapter 481, Health and Safety Code, or by 21 U.S.C. Section 801 et seq.; or

 (ii) a dangerous drug, as defined by Chapter 483, Health and Safety Code;

(D) sells, gives, or delivers to another person an alcoholic beverage, as defined by Section 1.04, Alcoholic beverage;

(E) engages in conduct that contains the elements of an offense relating to an abusable volatile chemical under Sections 485.031 through 485.034, Health and Safety Code; or

(F) engages in conduct that contains the elements of the offense of public lewdness under Section 21.07, Penal code, or indecent exposure under Section 21.08, Penal Code.

The law references offenses on and off campus and is specific to offenses in Title 5 of the Texas Penal Code (offenses against the person). This briefing is found as Legal Exhibit FOC in the Edinburg Consolidated Independent School District policies regarding the placement of students in alternative education programs. The legal exhibit which references the Penal Code from Chapters 10 through 22 includes the most serious of offenses such as murder, capital murder, manslaughter, criminal negligence homicide, kidnapping, indecency with a child, sexual assault, injury to a child, terrorist threats among numerous other crimes.

Chapter 37 of the Texas Education Code clearly established in statute that certain offenses by students warranted serious disciplinary action. The law also focused on alternatives to the regular school in which students could continue to be educated even after having committed a serious offense and prior to having been formally sentenced by a court. Chapter 37, sections .008 and .0081 very directly address the assignment of student offenders into Disciplinary Alternative Education Programs specifying that:

(a) Each school district shall provide a disciplinary alternative education program that:

1. is provided in a setting other than a student's regular classroom;
2. is located on or off of a regular school campus;
3. provides for the students who are assigned to the disciplinary alternative education program to be separated from students who are not assigned to the program;
4. focuses on English language arts, mathematics, science, history, and self-discipline;
5. provides for student's educational and behavioral needs;
6. provides supervision and counseling;
7. requires that to teach in an off-campus disciplinary alternative education program, each teacher meet all certification requirements established under Subchapter B, Chapter 21; and
8. notwithstanding Subdivision (7), requires that to teach in a disciplinary alternative education program of any kind, each teacher employed by a school district during the 2003-2004 school year or an earlier school year meet, not later than the beginning of the 2005-2006 school year, all certification requirements established under Subchapter B, Chapter 21.

Also, the Code in Chapter 37 Section .011 deals with the most serious of "incorrigible" youth by establishing the Juvenile Justice Alternative Education Program (JJAEP). The code states that the juvenile board of a County with a population greater than 125,000 shall develop a JJAEP subject to the approval of the Texas Juvenile Probation

Commission. In counties with less than 125,000 in population it is not required to have approval by the Texas Juvenile Probation Commission for JJAEP programs. In addition to adopting a student code of conduct, JJAEPs must focus their academic programs on English language arts, mathematics, science, social studies and self discipline. Also each sending school district shall consider course credit earned by a student while in a JJAEP as credit earned in a district home school. Testing is a requisite, a high school equivalency program must also be offered, and parents are to be involved with district officials in assessing the students' progress on graduation plans (Texas Education Code, 2003). In contrast with juvenile boards, school districts may provide personnel as well as other services to a JJAEP and like school districts, JJAEPs must provide 7 hours of instruction daily for 180 school calendar days, unless waived by The Texas Juvenile Probation Commission.

The academic mission of JJAEP programs is to help students perform at grade level; and for pupil accountability purposes JJAEP students are considered to be enrolled at their regular campus. This includes students who participate in special education programs. Other considerations include timely placement for specified periods of time, transitioning of expelled students back to their regular campuses, student transportation and services for special education students. Funding for JJAEP is provided by the sending schools to the County Juvenile Boards in accordance with a memorandum of understanding between the districts and the Juvenile Boards.

ASSIGNMENT OF STUDENTS TO ALTERNATIVE EDUCATIONAL PLACEMENTS

A student may be removed from class and placed in an Alternative Educational Placement (AEP) if he or she violates sections 42.06 or 22.07 of the Penal Code. Also, a student who commits any or a combination of the offenses in Chapter 37.0036 of the Education Code, within 300 feet of school property or while attending a school sponsored or school-related activity on or off school property may be removed from class and/or assigned to an AEP.

Conduct containing the elements of retaliation against any school employee, deferred prosecution for a felony offense delinquent conduct as determined by a court or jury or reasonable belief by the superintendent or his/her designee that the student engaged in felonious conduct are additional reasons for assigning a student to AEP (Edinburg Consolidate Independent School District, Policy FOAB Legal 2001). In a county that operates a JJAEP, upon expulsion by a school district a student must immediately attend the JJAEP program from the date of expulsion, and these expelled students, unless detained or receiving treatment under an order of a juvenile court, must be enrolled in an educational program (Edinburg Consolidated Independent School District, Policy FOD Legal, 2001).

One non-profit organization which contracts with several large county juvenile boards across Texas to serve JJAEP students is the Southwest Key Program, Inc. in Austin, Texas. Southwest Key has operated JJAEP programs in several Texas counties, serving education needs, changing student behavior, offering therapeutic treatment, developing social skills and involving family in the educational lives of youth offenders. A major purpose for the above services has been to reintegrate students into their home schools (Southwest Key Proposal, p. 5).

The belief of this non-profit provider is that average students have made poor choices in their actions while at school or school functions, but they can learn from their mistakes and can thrive with consistently good teaching, positive reinforcement and experiences with success.

Summary

While the effectiveness of juvenile justice programs generally remains questionable due to inadequate funding and other management and local operational problems (National Conference of State Legislatures, 2004), some facilities located around the country appear to be successful in their approach to helping delinquent youths. As placements of "last resort" for young people who have been expelled from school and placed under the supervision of the juvenile courts, these facilities are providing opportunities for students to get their lives in order and become good citizens and productive members of society. Many are able to return to their home schools and graduate, and some even go on to major colleges and universities. Others are able to obtain a GED while some learn important career skills and become valued members of the work force. While not all states yet have legislation addressing the issue of alternative educational placement for expelled students, there appears to be a growing trend to develop relevant policies and procedures.

Successful programs utilize certified, carefully selected administrators and instructional staff who are intensely and frequently trained for their particular and unique positions. A highly trained team of certified counselors appears to be employed by most juvenile justice facilities and serves to help students develop self esteem, control their behavior, and learn to respect themselves as well as others.

As increased attention by state law-makers and school leaders continues to focus on the aspirations and special needs of at-risk youth, educational programs for adjudicated youth will not only become more prevalent, but will become an important component in state and local public education policy.

Applying Your Knowledge

The newly created Cactus County Consolidated School District (CCCSD) is located along the Rio Grande River in extreme western Texas. It is bound on the south by Mexico and to the north and west lies New Mexico. Until recently, students living in Cactus County attended school in an adjacent urban school system; however, due to re-districting efforts by the Texas Legislature, CCCSD was created to serve inclusively all PK–12 students residing in the county. While attending the neighboring urban schools, students residing in Cactus County were exposed to a variety of innovative programs and other offerings indicative of a major metropolitan area. When district lines were re-determined, however, school leaders in the new CCCSD found themselves immersed in the monumental task of planning operational programs and academic delivery systems to meet the needs of all their students. While many objectives have been met and the system continues to evolve into an outstanding school district, a major component of the long-range plan remains to be developed. The CCCSD board of education has charged the superintendent with the responsibility of investigating and initiating procedures involved in developing a facility for providing educational offerings, as required by law, for incorrigible or adjudicated youth in the district. Sending students to the facility previously utilized in the local urban school system is not an option due to overcrowding. Cactus County, Texas has a population of 132,000.

QUESTIONS

1. As the superintendent of CCCSD, what will be your first step in carrying out the request of the board?
2. What legal reference will determine the minimum program offerings available to students attending the juvenile facility? What are the eight minimum program offerings as required by law?
3. What governance options are available to the CCCSD school district in regards to the juvenile facility?

QUESTIONS FOR THOUGHT

1. In the public schools prior to the early 1990s, what procedures were generally in place to accommodate incorrigible youth?
2. What is the primary focus of most juvenile justice facilities?
3. What are the most common academic program offerings to students attending a juvenile justice facility?
4. Describe a typical mentoring program for students housed in a juvenile justice facility.
5. Some juvenile facilities utilize the Urban Teacher Perceiver in training their principals. What are the components of this instrument and why is it used?
6. Describe in general the training programs provided to staff members of a typical juvenile justice facility.
7. Describe the type of counseling programs offered to students housed in a juvenile justice facility.

References

Chapter 37. Texas Education Code, 2003 Colorado Juvenile Justice System (2003) *Three year plan*. Retrieved from: *http://dcj.state.w.us/ojj/default.htm*.

Educationnews.org (2002 November) The Sheffield Report—Part 2.

Hack, W. G., Candoli, I. C. & Ray, J. R. (1995). *School business administration: A planning approach*. Boston, Massachusetts: Allyn and Bacon.

Hamilton Fish Institute (2000). School level data and trends. Retrieved April 27, 2004 from *HFI@HAMFISH.ORG/data/state/*.

Hill, M. & Hill, F. W. (1994). *Creating safe schools: What principals can do*. Thousand Oaks, CA.: Corwin Press, Inc.

National Conference of State Legislatures. (2004). *Alternative strategies for troubled youth*. Retrieved on July 17, 2004 from: *http://www.ncsl.org/programs/asi/youth.htm*.

Policy FOAB Legal. Edinburg Consolidated Independent School District. Policy Manual, Section F. 2002.

Southwest Key Inc. (2000). Proposal to the Cameron County, Texas Juvenile Board of Judges. Juvenile Justice Alternative Education Programs.

Teacher Leaders 13

Gayle Moller

Teacher leaders " . . . lead within and beyond the classroom, identify with and contribute to a community of teacher learners and leaders, and influence others toward improved educational practice"

—*Katzenmeyer & Moller, 2001, p. 4.*

Objectives

1. Define share leadership and teacher leadership
2. Describe the principal's role in supporting teacher collaboration
3. Identify barriers and supports to teachers leading in collaboration

Introduction

Successful principals in this complex profession of education acknowledge the need to share leadership roles and take actions to do it. Sometimes, principals do not take into account the potential for leadership within the teaching staff, including teachers in special instructional programs. In addition, general education teachers, in collaboration with teachers in special instructional programs, can form leadership teams that effectively deal with significant issues directly related to their collective responsibilities for students. This commitment to action is even more important when considering the special instructional programs where teachers face significant challenges not only in teaching their students, but also in building relationships with other adults in the school. Often isolated more than those teachers in the mainstream of the school's activities, these teachers flourish in a school culture where the principal promotes teacher leadership within an inclusive faculty and staff.

Teacher leadership exists in schools whether or not the principal supports its development. To be effective, principals must be intentional in developing positive teacher leadership that results in improved student learning.

These teachers are viewed by peers as competent, credible and approachable. Effective teacher leaders not only influence others, but they are accountable for the results of their efforts (Moller & Pankake, forthcoming).

Teacher leaders assume both formal and informal roles. Traditionally, people think of teacher leaders as department chairpersons or team leaders, but, actually, there are a variety of teacher leadership roles. Teachers take on formal roles, such as lead teacher, literacy coach, or staff developer. The formal roles hold certain expectations established by the school or the school system. Perhaps the more powerful roles are informal. A teacher sees a need, feels passionately about the issue, and takes action. This informal leadership may result in new initiatives such as increased student activities, more parent involvement, or increased collaboration with the community. Regardless of the type of leadership, these teachers are proactive in finding ways to help the school and, most importantly, the students.

Building leadership capacity (Lambert, 2003) is the principal's primary responsibility. Capacity building is a task that cannot be fully delegated, even though other administrators and teacher leaders can promote this mission. Until there is a different structure in schools, teachers look to the principal for authentic support of their leadership efforts. Occasionally, there will be groups of teachers who subversively provide this type of leadership, in spite of the principal, but normally teachers will resist taking on additional responsibility if the principal gives only token attention to the process.

Before making a commitment to promote teacher leadership, the principal should examine the benefits to the students, the school's community, and to the leadership within the school. For some principals this is a transformation in their understanding of who is the leader. Regardless of the principal's perspective, the decision to support this model requires more than adopting a "program." This is a way of doing business in schools and requires the principal's ongoing support and dedication of energy and attention.

Benefits of Teacher Leadership

Faced with demands from a multitude of sources, the principal must make choices. One option is for principals to pretend that they have the answers to everyone's concerns. Another alternative is for principals to ignore the important issues and focus on procedural infractions. Hopefully, principals can see beyond these options and seek help from teachers in addressing the upsurge in problems facing schools. The emerging multifaceted nature of schools, the public's higher-level expectations for results, and the increasingly diverse student population force principals to abandon the "hero" stance and to build the capacity of teachers to take on leadership roles in order to address substantive challenges.

Teachers in special instructional programs may arrive at the school with skills that are different than the general education teachers. Many of these skills are leadership skills. Here are examples of the leadership skills many teachers in special instructional programs acquire:

- supervising paraprofessionals in their work with special needs students,
- developing action plans that require accountability,
- assuming consultative role with general education teachers,
- managing cases,
- brokering resources,
- serving as liaison with parents and community leaders.

Another reason for promoting teacher leadership is to retain quality teachers. The current shortage of teachers, especially in special program areas, reflects alarming statistics describing why teachers leave the profession. A primary reason for the lack of teacher retention is attributed to poor working conditions. A report prepared for the Center on Personnel Studies in Special Education states: ". . . it is estimated that as many as half of all new special educators leave the field within the first three years as a result of poor administrative support, poor preparation, complex job responsibilities, and overwhelming paperwork requirements" (DiPaola & Walther-Thomas, 2003, p. 13). In a series of research projects, Ingersoll and Smith (2003) reported that although salary is cited as behind a decision to quit, even more teachers shared that working conditions influenced them to leave the profession. Four specific areas of concern were: ". . . student discipline problems; lack of support from the school administration; poor student motivation; and lack of teacher influence over schoolwide and classroom decision making" (Ingersoll & Smith, 2003, p. 14). Recently, beginning special education teachers were asked what their greatest challenges were during the first year of teaching and their responses included:

- administration won't give you the time of day,
- after the first two weeks, I was emotionally drained,
- no clear information on how to do things.

Talented teachers with specialized training are walking out of the schools to find jobs in which they are treated as adults and given benefits beyond just an increase in salary. Principals do not have much control over salaries for teachers, but they can influence the working conditions in the school.

The increasing student diversity demands multiple perspectives from teacher leaders and others to meet their needs. This diversity is espoused to be a value, whereas, in reality, people may view this as a problem. As principals face the demand to meet higher standards for all students, principals must take advantage of the different talents teachers can bring in order to build an inclusive professional community. If principals claim to support inclusion and differentiated instruction in classrooms, then how can they deny that this is how the adults should function in the school? No matter how successful a school is perceived, there are always more concerns, issues and problems than there are leaders.

Teacher leadership can result in expanded collaboration and professional learning among the professional staff. Presently, there is significant support for the building of professional learning communities in schools (Hord, 2004; Huffman & Hipp, 2004; Louis, Kruse, & Marks, 1996). Although there are many instances of teachers achieving individual accomplishments, a significant benefit of teacher leadership is how these teachers can influence others toward improved teaching and learning. Every teacher has the potential for leadership. In professional learning communities, this potential may emerge based on the expertise of a teacher or the teachers may collectively learn to improve their practice.

Beyond the practicality, there is a basic ideological reason to put efforts into building teacher leadership. Schools, at times, do not reflect the model of democracy for which they were originally designed. If the students see that teachers are without voice in the decision making, they will believe that they, too, lack influence. The educators' efforts to build an inclusive professional community provide the students with an understanding of how their classrooms are microcosms of the larger school where every person can contribute. In addition, as adults, students may honor diverse opinions and encourage everyone to participate in the leadership of organizations in which they are members.

As principals take on the challenge of building leadership, it is wise to be cognizant of how teachers in special instructional programs must navigate the school culture and what ingrained barriers exist in schools that keep teacher leadership in an inclusive professional community from becoming a reality.

Marginalized in the School Culture

Teachers in special instructional programs often face exclusion from the mainstream of school life. University undergraduate and graduate programs design course requirements keep students in separate tracks. Students in general education and special instructional programs do not have an opportunity to learn about each other's roles and responsibilities or to examine their opinions on how students learn (Shoffner & Briggs, 2001). The itinerant nature of a number of special instructional programs and the lack of time for collaboration contribute even more to these feelings of separateness. If there is not a concerted effort by the school leadership to build an inclusive professional community, then this sense of isolation will almost certainly exist.

The principal's role is to build an inclusive school culture so that all teachers can contribute to the leadership in the ways that match their talents and interests. Tapping into both the general education and special program teachers' gifts can result in a school culture that promotes positive teacher leadership. Within this isolation dilemma rest two tracks of separateness. One is between the general education teachers and those other educators in the school who share instructional responsibilities for the same students. The other track includes those teachers whose work parallels the general education teachers' work, but who seldom share instructional responsibilities.

SHARED INSTRUCTIONAL RESPONSIBILITIES

There are teachers who share instructional responsibilities and are most likely the people who must work together for these students. The counselors, special education teachers, teachers of the gifted and talented, and teachers of ESL students work with the same students as the general education teachers regarding overlapping instructional responsibilities. Strategies are evolving to bring these special program teachers together with the general education teachers to collaborate rather than working separately. An example of this relationship is a teacher leader, who worked with students exhibiting behavior/emotional disorders, and her attempt to build relationships with her counterparts in general education. Dismayed by the expectations the general education teachers had for the students she taught, this teacher collaborated with one general education teacher who, she believed, would be open to a new discipline approach. As a result, this teacher expanded her influence beyond her classroom to resolve an issue that concerned her.

The adult-to-adult relationships are especially relevant in attempts to build inclusive classrooms for special needs students. Ferguson, Ralph, & Sampson (2002) suggest that current roles for special education teachers reflect ". . . less about working with students and more about working with grownups" (p. 145). These teachers are advocates for the students they serve, but they must develop relationships with other teachers in order to execute the students' educational plans.

PARALLEL INSTRUCTIONAL RESPONSIBILITIES

In contrast, other teachers in special programs work with the same students as general education teachers, but there are few opportunities for these teachers to come together. For example, vocational education, art, music and physical education teachers work with the same students as general education teachers, but unless there is an effort to integrate curriculum, the teachers work separately. These teachers are especially isolated from the professional conversations in this era of academic testing. So much of teachers' and principals' attention is focused on high stakes testing that any subject not tested tends to fade to the background of conversation and activity in the school.

Even further removed from collaboration with general education teachers are the special programs teachers who are located outside the physical school plant, for example, alternative education teachers and those who teach in criminal justice facilities. Articulation between the faculties of "regular" schools and teachers in programs for disenfranchised youth is virtually non-existent. One principal of an alternative school program set as a goal to communicate with leaders in the schools where the students were originally assigned to attend. He hoped to influence the teachers' perspectives regarding the students in the alternative program. If the principals of these schools do not share, there will not be sharing between faculty members.

Teachers in special instructional programs are parallel to the general education teachers. They are often left to their own devices to develop collaborative relationships among themselves. One vocational education teacher leader designed an open house for general education teachers to visit the special program classrooms. Another art teacher developed relationships with the fifth grade teachers so that she could integrate what they were teaching into her classes. In these examples of teacher leadership, the principals approved the teachers' plans, but had little involvement in advocating or even attending the events. An opportunity to promote teacher leadership was lost.

The complexity of teacher relationships cannot be ignored by the principal. After understanding the different types of isolation those teachers in special instructional programs face, the principal needs to examine the barriers to building teacher leadership.

Barriers to Teacher Leadership

There are many reasons why teachers find it difficult to lead and to collaborate together. Principals' reluctance to share leadership, too little scheduled time, lack of quality professional development, and physical isolation are challenging barriers, but they can be overcome. The more difficult barriers involve relationships. Teachers resistant to changes, sub-groups of teachers who can sabotage change, and educators' reluctance to value conflict are barriers that demand skillful leadership.

THE NEED FOR PRINCIPAL LEADERSHIP

Regardless of the relationships between general education and teachers in special instructional programs, the potential for tapping into these teachers' talents are often overlooked. Many principals may be unaware of this talent pool due to their distraction by the multitude of responsibilities or they may be unwilling to acknowledge that all teachers, even these teachers in special instructional programs who travel on the periphery of school life, can contribute to the school's leadership.

TIME

There is never enough time in schools to meet the needs of all the students or for teachers to discuss how to work together to determine how to address these needs. When asked about the greatest obstacle to working with other teachers, inevitably teachers report the lack of time (Akins, Parkinson, & Reeder, 2002). The structure of American schools offers teachers minimal time for the deep conversation that is necessary to build relationships for collaboration. Snippets of time are grabbed in hallways and parking lots, but the luxury of meeting in a comfortable setting for an extended period of time is rare. What many organizations in the private sector take for granted, teachers rarely experience.

THE NEED FOR PROFESSIONAL LEARNING

Teacher leadership and professional learning are tightly linked. In many school districts, professional learning still consists of fragmented workshops unrelated to a focus on a school's students and their learning. As teachers collaborate, attention must be paid to the professional learning. Attempts at collective learning are minimal and there is even less sharing of personal practices. In many schools professional development continues to be a mandated performance issue, rather than a tool to generate substantive adult learning. Both the content and the models of staff development in the school are pre-selected for teachers. Little, if any, interest in individual faculty needs is present; the traditional training model is the only model used.

PHYSICAL LOCATION

Teachers in special instructional programs are often placed in classrooms that are far removed from the main classrooms. With minimal time away from student responsibilities, there are few opportunities for teachers to interact in a meaningful way and still be present when the students return to the classroom. Teachers in vocational education programs may be placed in facilities that house unique equipment and it is not possible for their classrooms to be near the general education classrooms. Similar situations often occur for music/band teachers, art specialists, physical education teachers and others.

RESISTANCE TO COLLABORATION

Teacher leadership and, in turn, teacher collaboration are alien in the majority of schools or only found in pockets of teachers within a department or a grade level. Educators are socialized to be isolated even during their student teaching (De Lima, 2003). In addition, teachers value autonomy in their work with students and collaboration threatens this (Little & Bartlett, 2002). America's society values individual accomplishments. The resistance to an inclusive professional community reflects these values. Educators experience minimal contact with other adults except during lunch or at the mailboxes. In addition, the current structure of schooling presents barriers to efforts at collaboration.

SCHOOL CULTURES

A fully developed inclusive professional community is rare in schools. Even if there were plenty of time and physical facilities that promoted communication, collaboration focused on student learning is "counter cultural" in teaching. School cultures can be dangerous territories. Walk into a teachers' lounge in such a school and a person immediately feels excluded. Even in schools that are viewed as high performing, there may exist sub-cultures of teachers who can cause concern for even the most experienced principal. Reminiscent of the high school cliques that keep certain people on the fringe of the action, this teacher leadership can take on a negative quality.

CONFLICT AVOIDANCE

Educators enter the profession with a desire to help others. They strive to build harmony so that they can survive in the classroom while caring for their students. Conflict is discouraged and avoided by most educators. Many teachers do not like to be called "teacher leaders," because they believe that it will harm their relationships with their colleagues.

Conflict is healthy in professional communities (Achinstein, 2002). If educators truly value the diversity of their students, then the challenge is to accept and honor the differences in their colleagues. The prevalent focus on consensus building may be a detriment to community building. The familiar "parking lot" conversations often reflect a lack of agreement and the lost voices in attempts to gain consensus.

Fortunately, there are efforts to build support systems for teacher leaders and to encourage teachers to collaborate and overcome these barriers. There are schools across the country where principals and teachers are learning together to improve student achievement.

Principals' Roles in Building Teaching Leadership

Once principals decide they will be purposeful in the promotion of teacher leadership, there are beliefs, skills and leadership strategies that are essential (Moller & Pankake, forthcoming). Foremost is the principal's belief regarding teacher leadership and how all teachers must contribute within an inclusive professional community. Then there is the need for principals to provide supportive conditions to build and sustain teacher leadership. Finally, teacher leadership does not grow in a vacuum and the principal must facilitate collaboration.

BELIEFS

Few people are fooled when a principal states a personal belief, but acts in ways that do not support that belief. The principal must be clear about his or her beliefs about teacher leadership in an inclusive professional community and how this is vital to the success of the school. This demands more than a printed vision statement in the office. Effective principals facilitate the development of a shared vision, articulate the vision, make decisions based on the vision, and help others to support the vision. If the principal does not believe in promoting teacher leadership within a professional community, it will not happen.

A good strategy for principals in their exploration of their beliefs about teacher leadership is to examine their personal experiences as a teacher. Most principals were teacher leaders and can remember which administrators truly supported their growth and development. In contrast, there will be memories of principals who did not value teacher leadership and established obstacles to what teachers hoped to accomplish.

A principal's belief system is the key to promoting teacher leadership and building an inclusive professional community. As the person with the formal power over resources, the principal must believe it is possible and beneficial to work collaboratively with teachers in shared leadership roles. Even if teacher leadership is possible, unless the principal wants it, it is unlikely to be pursued. There are principals who do not desire, or perhaps even fear, sharing school leadership with others.

Not only must the principal believe teacher leadership is possible, the teachers must be included in developing a shared vision of how the adults will work together. Changed relationships are some of the most difficult challenges, and resistance should be expected. Not everyone will adopt the shared vision, but principals can move forward with the people who are ready and willing with the expectation that others will "get on board" as things develop.

The use of time provides an example of how a shared vision is a pre-requisite to teacher leadership and collaboration. Before the issue of time can be addressed, the faculty, staff, and, especially, the principal must believe that collaboration is essential to the school's improvement. With the physical structure of schools contributing to the isolation of teachers and the socialization of teachers to work alone, collaboration is not the norm. Many faculty members will claim that their school is "like a family," but few school faculties move beyond this collegiality. Once the faculty and staff members believe that collaboration is beneficial, then the time structures will be used for the purpose of professional conversations toward the improvement of teaching.

With all the attention on the value of professional learning communities, many principals jump on the bandwagon so that they can claim that their school reflects this model. With good intentions, these principals work with the teachers' schedules to build time for teachers to "dialogue." The teachers are told to meet and talk with each other about their profession. After initial confusion about these assignments, teachers soon find ways to subvert these efforts. Meanwhile, many principals are distracted with other duties or new projects and the time for professional collaboration becomes imperceptible as teachers take the lead to use this precious time for their individual responsibilities to the school and their students.

An alternative approach is for the principal to personally engage teachers in discussion regarding collaboration and the use of time. Arrangements for visits to other schools where mature professional learning communities exist can help teachers understand the value of working together and see how it can be accomplished. Principals can invite teachers to work on creative schedules to build time into the school day. (See Schroth, Beaty, & Dunbar, 2003 for scheduling options.)

Once the school leaders are committed to teacher leadership and collaboration, then the focus must be placed on how to support the teachers. Only when people, especially the principal, believe in this structure will the supportive conditions that are put into place serve a purpose.

SUPPORTIVE CONDITIONS

If the principal and the faculty members are clear about their beliefs about teacher leadership, the school's resources can be aligned to these beliefs. Fiscal resources, human resources, and structures to support teacher leaders are critical to the school's success. Underlying each decision regarding resources should be these two questions:

1. How does this decision promote improved teaching and learning for students in our school?
2. How will this decision support teacher development that serves to improve teaching and learning for students in our school?

After personnel costs are removed from a school's budget, there are relatively few discretionary dollars to use within a school. Yet the decisions regarding the use of these diminishing funds can reflect how the principal views professional collaboration. Too often these decisions are made easy by allocating the same amount of money to each teacher regardless of the need. As teacher leaders take the risk to assume additional responsibilities, decisions about funds may be distributed differently. The students' needs and the school's attempts to meet those needs must determine where the money is spent.

In addition, personnel decisions should be based on these same two questions. As principals conduct the most important task of their role—the selection of teaching staff—they must consider these consequences. Here is where the principal can exhibit a belief in teacher leadership. If the selection of faculty and staff are crucial to all programs, teachers should be involved in this process. Teachers are in a position to know what the students' needs are. Before inviting teachers to participate in the selection process, the principal must make it clear what their roles will be. If the principal is not ready to turn the hiring of teachers over to a consensus decision-making method, the teachers must know that they will advise the principal, but the final decision will be made by the principal. On the other hand, if the teachers are going to be equal members in an interview team and the decision will be made by the team, the teachers should know that as well (Bateman & Bateman, 2001).

Once quality teachers are selected, the hard work begins. The strategies that the school uses to orient new teachers, whether experienced or beginning teachers, can make a difference in the retention of these teachers. Practices such as assigning mentors, buddy-teachers, and other induction approaches are essential to help new teachers understand the school's culture and to adopt the belief that teacher leadership in inclusive professional communities is the norm. Leaving induction to chance can result in "war stories" that quickly tell the new faculty member that it is best to stay isolated within the classroom.

Also, new teachers need mentors with similar content knowledge to help them. This may require creative ways to link with teachers from other schools who teach in the same areas. Many beginning teachers lament the lack of contact with other teachers in their fields. Although a teacher in another field can help a new teacher learn the school's culture, they are unable to help the new teacher with content pedagogy. The following quote was shared by a beginning special education teacher:

> Even when you have one (a mentor), [he/she] had no idea of what my job description was.
> It would be nice to have a mentor in the county with your same degree.

Learning to work together demands professional development. Understanding the value of quality, results-driven professional development is a knowledge base that every principal and teacher leader must acquire. Developing a substantive plan for professional learning is critical to building teacher leadership and encouraging collaboration. There are leadership skills, as well as instructional skills, that every teacher needs to learn in order to be an effective member of the school community. The principal's role is to be a co-learner with the teachers and then reinforce the use of the skills.

Professional learning requires that time be set aside within the school day. Creative strategies must be built to find time for teachers to work together. Relying on teachers to use their personal time will result in teacher burnout. The principal's role is to build schedules and find supportive structures, such as coverage for classes, to give teachers time during the contract day to work together.

Providing supportive conditions relies on building positive relationships with the teachers. Littrell & Billingsley (1994) examined general and special education teachers and the relationships between their job satisfaction and principal support. Both groups of teachers reported that emotional support was the most important type of support that administrators can provide. Principals' actions that build a climate of collaboration, rather than competition, influence a higher level of commitment from teachers. Walking around the school and finding opportunities to positively interact with teachers can help provide them the social support they need.

FACILITATING COLLABORATION

Principals have a responsibility to teachers of special instructional programs to facilitate their collaboration with each other and with the general education teachers. Hiring a teacher and then leaving that person alone to build relationships is risky. Even though teachers like to claim that there is an egalitarian ethic in their profession, there is a social structure in teaching roles. There often is no logic to this structure because it depends on the unique power bases of teachers. In some schools, the teachers with power are the teachers of those subjects or grade levels where there is accountability testing. In another school, it will be the teachers of advanced placement courses. Other examples of sources of power are the teachers who go fishing or attend some outside organization, such as church, together. The reason for the power is not as important as how to encourage teachers to work together.

Teachers with Shared Instructional Responsibilities

With the busyness of school life, teachers find it difficult to collaborate even with people who are closest to them. The quick planning over a short lunch or an infrequent conversation in the hallway are usually the only times available for people with common schedules to see each other. Often these are teachers whose classrooms are in proximity to each other. Teachers in special instructional programs may be near each other for collaboration; however, special instructional programs are often housed in areas of the school building, away from the general classroom teachers with whom they are to collaborate.

For teachers who must share instructional responsibilities, the decisions about who will work together are crucial. Taking time to assess the faculty members' relationships to each other can help develop teams that are compatible. Placing a new special education teacher with a teacher who does not value the inclusion of special needs students can place the new teacher at risk. Instead, principals can draw on the positive teacher leaders when selecting the best team configurations.

A "... web of relationship spanning the school (that) must be created and nurtured" (York-Barr & Vandercook, 2003). Finding ways to facilitate these interactions is a challenge for any leader, but may be an opportunity to tap into teacher leadership talent. If the faculty has a shared vision for an inclusive community, the first step is to have conversations with teachers about the difficulty of collaboration among general education teachers and teachers of special instructional programs. Teacher leaders might facilitate these conversations. At first, the reasons for collaborating or not that will emerge will be superficial, such as the physical proximity and conflicting schedules. As conversations get to the root causes, the reasons that emerge may be represented by statements such as the ones below:

General Education Teacher	*Special Programs Teacher*
I feel uncomfortable with her in the classroom and don't know how to assign her tasks.	I feel like a helper in her classroom, rather than a professional.
He promises to come to my classroom every day at 2 o'clock, and there are too many times that he doesn't show up. I can't depend on him.	The principal told me to be accessible for parents and sometimes they come into the school when I am supposed to be in her classroom.
She acts like she knows everything about Susan (the student). I've taught her for three months and I have some ideas about her needs.	I have a master's degree and expertise to share about Susan (the student) and she won't listen.

These are the deep-rooted reasons that block effective communication between the general education teachers and teachers in special instructional programs. To move beyond reasons revealed on the surface demands leadership beyond the principal. Teachers, who are credible with others, can help other teachers get to these issues. The principal's role is to be an advocate for teacher leaders who are willing to build an inclusive professional community based on an understanding of the real obstacles to collaboration. The principal's involvement does not stop with encouraging these conversations. At times, the principal should be a contributor to the conversation. On the other hand, the principal must be attuned to know when the conversation should be among only the teachers.

Teachers with Parallel Instructional Responsibilities

Teachers who work in special instructional programs that do not intersect with the general education teachers provide another type of challenge in achieving collaboration. Although many of the students may be shared between these teachers and the general education teachers, both groups of teachers may believe there are few areas in which they have to collaborate for instruction. For example, vocational education teachers teach students who are also in general education classes, but the goals of both programs may not be viewed as integrated. In addition, there may be teachers of special programs for which none of the students interact with general education teachers. Examples of this type of fragmentation are widespread at all levels of schooling. Even at faculty meetings, teachers tend to sit together with friends and rarely are their conversations across the teaching areas. The few attempts at integrating curriculum are often abandoned due to the energy it takes to do this effectively.

Principals can approach this problem with their own solutions or they can bring the problem to the teachers to see who would be willing to find solutions. Often just bringing problems out in the open for discussion can reveal how it violates the school's shared vision of an inclusive professional community. The initial plans may be small, but any attempt to bring all faculty members together for collaboration to solve the school's universal problems can result in significant changes.

At first, strategies may be contrived. For example, seating at the faculty meetings could be pre-arranged. Once the initial resistance to not being able to sit with friends subsides, the teachers will find that they have common instructional concerns if they are led through a process to explore their similarities. Then teachers will find ways to build more communication across the grade levels, special instructional programs, and content areas.

Principals face the responsibility of supporting these decisions. This may involve physical relocation of classrooms, blocks of quality time for collaboration, or additional adult coverage in the classroom to allow teachers time to share. Teachers watch to see if principals will follow through on their commitments. Fiscal resources, human resources, and other supportive conditions should be allocated to support the teachers' decisions that focus on the improvement of student learning. Not every decision can be supported, but the decisions that are feasible must move forward. This support is another measure of the principal's belief in teacher leadership in an inclusive professional community. In addition, the teacher's commitment to leadership responsibility needs to be monitored. This does not mean that teachers will be placed in a threatening position, but the principal can help teachers establish benchmarks for accountability. These benchmarks are assessed as teacher leaders move toward their goals.

Finally, no other person sends as strong a message as the principal about what is important and what is not of value. Co-learning with teachers, turning faculty meetings over to teacher leaders for professional development, and frequent conversations in the hallways about teaching and learning are ways that a principal can let the staff know that their work is vital. To do this demands finding ways to deal with other administrative responsibilities. There is a temptation to focus on paperwork, parent complaints, and discipline issues, rather than moving into the teachers' world.

Summary

Working conditions make a difference in teacher job satisfaction and, therefore, the retention of teachers. Teachers in special instructional programs are, by the nature of their work, isolated from the general education teachers. To improve working conditions, the principal is the leader of promoting teacher leadership within an inclusive professional community. Teachers are adults and they want to work in a school where they are respected and supported. The lack of attention to these factors will result in unhealthy attrition and possible emergence of negative teacher leadership.

Beyond retention of teachers, the principal and school will benefit from positive teacher leadership, possibly even reducing personal stress. Teachers in special instructional programs bring leadership skills that can contribute to building an inclusive professional community. With the increased student diversity, schools must capitalize on diverse teacher perspectives to address the students' needs. Through teacher leadership and teacher collaboration, the professional community will move toward collective learning. Finally, an inclusive professional community models for students how adults should work together in a democracy.

Barriers prevent the development of teacher leadership. If the principal does not believe in sharing leadership, he/she will be unwilling to provide time, physical proximity, or quality professional development to achieve this goal. Also, the teaching culture often works against teacher leadership by causing staff members to resist change, form negative sub-groups, and avoid productive conflict.

If there is a shared vision for teacher leadership within an inclusive professional community, supportive conditions must be in place to realize this goal. Supportive conditions include fiscal resources, human resources, and structural systems. In addition, the principal must facilitate teacher collaboration.

Until there is a different leadership structure in schools, the principal is the person who must take responsibility for building healthy workplaces. With all the other demands on administrators, personal survival may depend on developing teacher leaders. Teachers will take on the roles if there is authentic support from the principal. Principals sometimes assume that teachers want only to teach and not accept other forms of leadership responsibilities in the school. Generally, this is not the case; in fact, many teachers are looking for opportunities to exercise more influence in the school. Schools need many people leading; no one person or small group of people can solve all the school's problems. The goal is to build a critical mass of teacher leaders so that leadership is viewed as an assumed part of the culture of the teaching staff.

Applying Your Knowledge

Leticia Patterson returned to Washington Middle School following a national conference. Several of the sessions that Mrs. Patterson attended focused on shared leadership in the school. While Mrs. Patterson had always thought of herself as a democratic leader, after attending these sessions she was not so sure any more. She was interested in exploring with the faculty some ways in which she could share leadership with them and in which they could become more collaborative with each other. Mrs. Patterson decided she needed to consider how to begin the exploration. The school's faculty has a mix of new and veteran teachers; however, there was not a strong culture of trust in the school.

QUESTIONS

1. What recommendations would you make to Mrs. Patterson as first steps in pursuing her idea of collaboration?
2. Does the mix of new and veteran teachers in the school facilitate or create barriers to collaboration? Explain.
3. How will the current culture of the school affect the collaborative initiative? How will the efforts to become more collaborative affect the current culture?

QUESTIONS FOR THOUGHT

1. What are some ways that barriers to collaboration in schools could be reduced?
2. What characteristics do teacher leaders have? Do these characteristics differ between special programs and general education teachers?
3. How would a principal's job change if shared leadership was the norm in the school? Would teachers' jobs change also? How?
4. If money was not an issue, what actions would you take to create a collaborative culture in a school?
5. Have you had a positive or negative experience with collaboration? What made it positive or negative?
6. What should be done if some teachers in a school are not interested in or willing to collaborate?

For Additional Information Online

Association for Supervision and Curriculum Development *http://www.ascd.org*

National Staff Development Council *http://www.nsdc.org*

Teacher Leaders Network *http://www.teacherleaders.org/about.html*

References

Achinstein, B. (2002). Conflict amid community: The micropolitics of teacher [Electronic version]. *Teachers College Record, 104*(3), 421–455.

Akins, K. P., Parkinson, K. M., & Reeder, P. H. (2002). The perceptions of third through fifth grade classroom teachers and special service teachers toward their involvement in collaborative instruction. Retrieved July 8, 2004, from *http://0-www.edrs.com*.

Bateman, D. & Bateman, F. B. (2001). *A principal's guide to special education.* Arlington, VA: Council for Exceptional Children.

De Lima, J. A. (2003). Trained for isolation: The impact of departmental cultures on student teachers' views and practices of collaboration [Electronic version]. *Journal of Education for Teaching, 29*(3), 197–219.

DiPaola, M. F. & Walther-Thomas, C. (2003). *Principals and Special Education: The Critical Role of School Leaders.* Retrieved July 8, 2004, from *http://www.coe.ufl.edu/copsse/pubfiles/IB-7.pdf*.

Ferguson, D. L., Ralph, G., & Sampson, N. K. (2002). From "special" educators to educators: The case for mixed-ability group of teachers in restructured schools. In W. Sailor (Ed.), *Whole school success and inclusive education: Building partnerships for learning, achievement, and accountability* (pp. 142–162). New York: Teachers College Press.

Hord, S. M. (2004). Introduction. In S. Hord (Ed.) *Learning together, leading together* (pp. 1–14). New York: Teachers College Press.

Huffman, J. B. & Hipp, K. K. (2004). *Reculturing schools as professional learning communities.* Lanham, Maryland: Scarecrow Press.

Ingersoll, R. M. & Smith, T. M. (2003). The wrong solution to the teacher shortage [Electronic version]. *Educational Leadership, 60*(8), 30–34.

Katzenmeyer, M. & Moller, G. (2001). *Awakening the sleeping giant: Leadership development for teachers,* (2nd Edition). Thousand Oaks, CA: Corwin.

Lambert, L. (2003). *Leadership capacity for lasting school improvement.* Alexandria, VA:Association for Supervision and Curriculum Development.

Little, J. W. & Bartlett, L. (2002). Career and commitment in the context of comprehensive school reform. *Teachers & Teaching, 8*(3/4), 345–356.

Littrell, P. C. & Billingsley, B. S. (1994). The effects of principal support on special and general educators' stress, job satisfaction, school commitment, health, and intent to stay in teaching [Electronic version]. *Remedial & Special Education, 15*(5), 297–312.

Louis, K. S., Kruse, S. D., & Marks, H. M. (1996). Schoolwide professional community. In F. M. Newmann & Associates (Eds.), *Authentic achievement* (pp. 179–204). San Francisco: Jossey-Bass.

Moller, G. & Pankake, A. (forthcoming). *Principals and teachers: Partners in sustaining leadership.* Larchmont, NY: Eye on Education.

Sergiovanni, T. J. (1995). *The principalship: A reflective practice perspective,* 3rd ed., Boston, MA: Allyn & Bacon.

Shoffner, M. F. & Briggs, M. K. (2001). An interactive approach for developing interprofessional collaboration: Preparing school counselors [Electronic version]. *Counselor Education & Supervision, 40*(3), 193–198. York-Barr, J. & Vandercook, T. (2003). Lessons learned on the way toward inclusion. *Impact, 16*(1), 4–5. Retrieved July 8, 2004, from *http://ici.umn.edu/products/impact/161*.

Staff Development for Special Programs

14

Jody Westbrook-Youngblood

> . . . the focus of all professional learning should be on the students,
> what they need to know and be able to do,
> and what the teachers need to know to accomplish that.
>
> —*Jody Westbrook-Youngblood*

Objectives

1. Describe the NSDC standards for professional learning
2. Explain a planning cycle for professional growth of teachers in special instructional programs
3. Describe successful initiatives in a variety of settings.

Introduction

Virtually every district in the nation participates in staff development for its teachers, administrators and other school employees. In some cases, it is a state law, while in other cases, it is an identified need of a campus, district, department, or division. What is meant by the term "staff development?" According to the National Staff Development Council (NSDC) website, "Staff Development is the term that educators use to describe the continuing education of teachers, administrators, and other school employees" (National Staff Development Council, 2004). Additionally, NSDC asserts that successful staff development focuses on the "knowledge, skills and attitudes" of the adults in schools "so all students can learn and perform at high levels."

The term staff development is used interchangeably in this chapter with similar terms such as in-service education, professional development, continuing education and professional learning. Each of these terms is used, albeit differently by different groups, to refer to the continuing education of adults in schools.

Guskey (2000) asserts that in the history of education, we have never before seen the emphasis currently being placed on professional learning of educators. He adds that virtually every reform, every innovation, and every plan for improving schools includes the need and support for professional development and that our knowledge base in education is rapidly expanding. Indeed, educators are obligated to know what techniques and strategies will best serve their students. This is true of all educators, but perhaps more critical for the teachers of special populations, whose needs include staying abreast of current research and best practices of general education classrooms as well as for their specific assignment. Special Education is not in lieu of general education, but rather an additional service; therefore, special education personnel must stay current with general education requirements. One of the major provisions of the Individuals with Disabilities Act (IDEA) is labeled "Personnel Department, In-service." This provision is described by Hallahan and Kauffman (2003) as training for teachers and other professional personnel, including training for regular teachers to meet the needs of students with disabilities. Labeled as the Comprehensive System of Personnel Development (CSPD), §300.380 of the Code of Federal Regulations (CFR) requires that each State shall develop and implement a comprehensive system of personnel development that "ensures an adequate supply of qualified special education . . . personnel." CFR section 300.382—Improvement Strategies , requires states to prepare general and special education personnel with the necessary knowledge and "collaborative skills" to be successful with special needs students. Additionally, it requires each state to work with institutions of higher education to prepare personnel for working with children with disabilities.

Interviews with a dozen educators in K–12 schools and 10 university professors from across the nation revealed that teachers in special education classrooms, resource rooms, and other pull-out programs participate in continuing education gatherings related to their specific assignment more frequently than in regular education sessions. Generally, these gatherings focus on laws, regulations and requirements with some attention given to pedagogical matters. While learning about, and following, compliance issues is necessary and expected, the delivery of good instruction to special needs students is just as necessary and expected.

Proper planning and recognition of the differing needs of the teachers of special populations can ensure appropriate, continuous, student-focused professional learning, resulting in the continuing growth of their students. Structured and collaborative interaction with regular education teachers can provide opportunities for the special educator to focus on student growth while working in a collegial and collaborative manner. To be successful at collaborative goal setting, Elmore (2000) reminds us that improvement is . . . a function of learning to do the right thing in the setting where you work.

This chapter will describe the standards for professional learning which have been developed and endorsed by the National Staff Development Council and explain a cycle for planning appropriate professional growth for Special Programs teachers. Additionally, successful initiatives in a variety of settings will be described.

Standards for Staff Development

The National Staff Development Council has adopted standards for staff development. Planned around a framework called the Nested Process, each standard further details the critical components that will lead to student-focused, professional learning. The context/process/content framework was originated by Sparks (1983) as a method for organizing the research about successful professional development. Over the last 20 years, the model has emerged as an organizer for assessing and planning for effective staff development.

Figure 14.1 depicts the nested process, also called the CPC Model, referring to these components: Context, Process and Content.

The Context/Process/Content components are described in the *Standards for Staff Development:*

Context (Figure 14.2) standards address the organization, system, and culture in which the new learning will be implemented. They describe the structures that must be in place for successful learning to occur (NSDC, 2001).

Important considerations in the context include:

- the degree to which *learning communities exist.* Key components of this indicator include the formation of small learning teams which meet frequently, work with each other to improve student learning, and whose focus is on school and district goals,
- the degree to which *leadership* is skillful and supportive of staff development. Key components of this indicator include attention to schedules and incentive

---

Figure 14.1   **CPC Model**

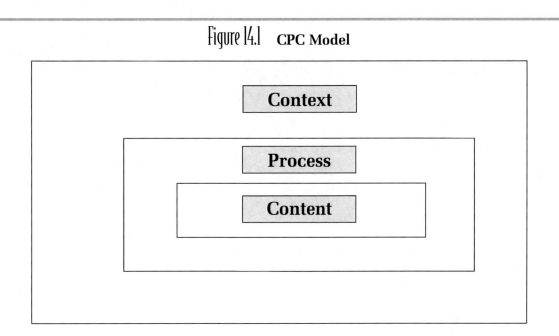

Figure 14.2   Context of the CPC Model

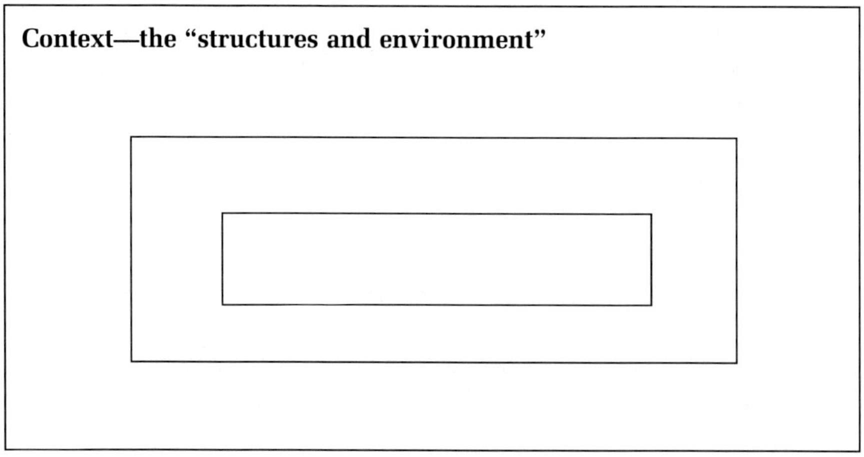

Context—the "structures and environment"

systems which support staff development, a recognition that staff development is a critical strategy for supporting improvements, and leaders being involved in their own continuing education,

● the degree to which *resources* are committed to staff development. Key components of this indicator include issues related to the timing of staff development (should be a part of the everyday work), a dedicated portion (10%) of the school or district budget and a dedicated portion of each workday (25%) to staff development. This does not necessarily imply removing teachers from instructional time, but refers to situations in which professional learning occurs in a job-embedded manner.

Process (Figure 14.3) refers to the "how" of staff development. It describes the learning processes used in the acquisition of new knowledge and skills. Process standards address the use of data, evaluation, and research (NSDC, 2001).

Important considerations in process standards include:

● the use of *data* to make decisions. Key components of this indicator include the disaggregation of student learning data to determine what the students need to know and be able to do. From that, identification of what the adults need to know and be able to do to facilitate the students' learning and continuous monitoring of progress towards students' achievement,

● the use of *evaluation* to verify effectiveness of staff development efforts. This would include multiple sources and extend on a continuum from satisfaction of the participants with the delivery of the program to the increase in achievement of students,

● the use of *research-based models* and *decision-making.* Key components of this indicator include the practice of relying on education research, studying research before adopting approaches or programs of improvement and using pilot studies when research is not available or inconsistent in findings,

● the use of an effective *design.* Major components of this indicator include the use of a variety of models and strategies, technology support and consistent follow-up for each and every change implementation,

● the identification of *learning.* Important pieces of this indicator include the acknowledgement that what is expected of teachers in their teaching repertoire is

Figure 14.3   **Process of the CPC Model**

Process—the "how"

Figure 14.4   **Content of the CPC Model**

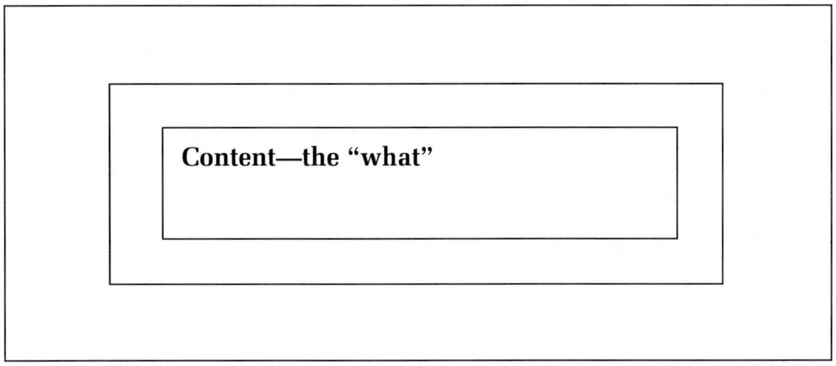

Content—the "what"

extended to them as learners, that coaching supports their efforts to use new skills and that the change process and its concomitant concerns are addressed with appropriate interventions,

- the skills and opportunity to *collaborate.* Key components of this indicator include the development of skills required to be effective group members, the productive resolution of conflict and the effective use of technology for collaboration. This component is especially important as educators of special needs students and general educators work together.

Content (Figure 14.4) refers to the "what" of staff development. Content decisions begin with an examination of what students must know and be able to do. Staff development content addresses the knowledge and skills that ensure all students are successful.

Important considerations in content standards include:

- the recognition that *equity* issues must be addressed. Key components of this indicator include respect for differing cultural backgrounds, the communication of high expectations, and the modifications needed for individual students,

- the expectation that *quality teaching* is offered to all students. Important points in this indicator include the development of teachers' profound knowledge of what they teach, the growth of instructional techniques, and the understanding and appropriate use of assessment skills to monitor student progress,
- the acknowledgement that *family involvement* is of paramount importance. Key points of this indicator include skills to be developed to build consensus between the community and the educators, productive relationships with parents, and the use of technology to communicate with all stakeholders.

These standards apply to all educators, but can clarify even more clearly the needs of those who work with special needs students. By using the Self-Assessment included in the publication *Standards for Staff Development,* a campus can plan their professional growth experiences. Special program departments, staff, grade levels or teams can use it as well to discuss and set goals and plan their professional learning experiences.

Professional Development Planning Model

Selection of professional development goes beyond choosing a workshop, or an engaging guest speaker to fill requirements. An appropriate planning cycle is shown in Figure 14.5, followed by a brief descriptor of each step. Each step is then described in more detail in subsequent paragraphs.

Step One: Use of Data refers to making decisions for professional learning based on a variety of data sources.

Step Two: Creation of a Professional Learning Plan requires that decisions are made which reflect appropriate content which the adults should learn, what the new strategies look like when implemented with fidelity, and how this plan will be communicated.

Figure 14.5   **Professional Development Planning Model**

Step One:
Use of data

Step Four:
Monitoring and
Evaluation

Step Two:
Creation of a Professional
Learning Plan

Step Three:
Selection of one or more staff
development models

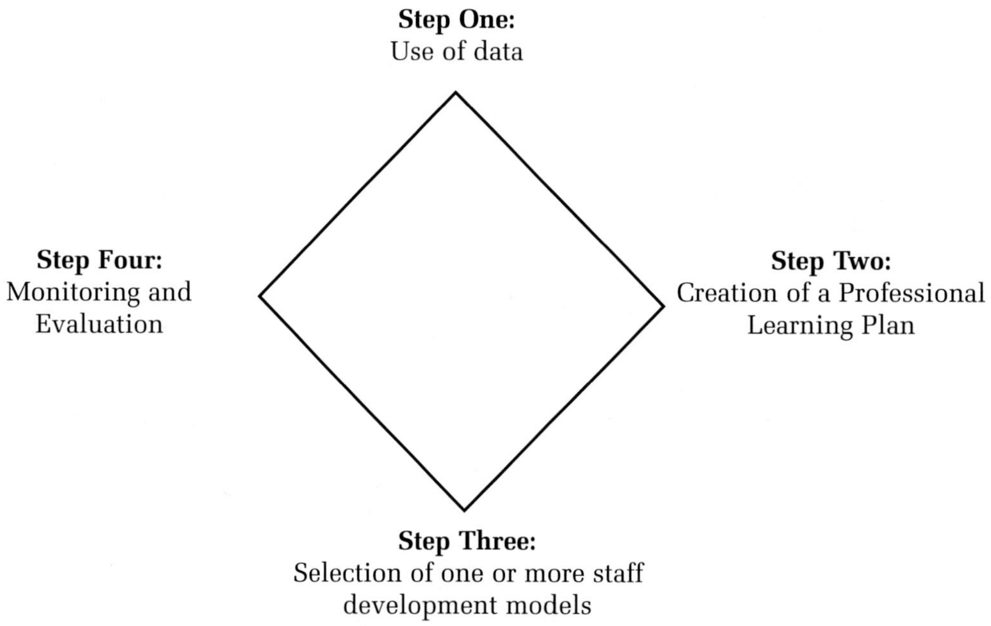

Step Three: Selection of One or More Staff Development Models: The image many individuals have of staff development is a traditional workshop model. However, there are a number of recognized models.

Step Four: Monitoring and Evaluation: It is no longer sufficient to evaluate professional development in terms of number of attendees and how satisfied they were with the refreshments, the engagement of the speaker and the comfort offered by the setting. The impact on students' learning is the reason professional learning should occur and the measure by which it should be judged successful.

STEP ONE: USE OF DATA

As described in the **Process** section of the standards, the use of data (Figure 14.6) to influence decisions is of paramount importance. Frequently, the term "data" invokes a visual of standardized or criterion test data. Certainly, in this day and age of accountability testing, reporting, and comparisons, this type of data is critical. For example, if in the process of disaggregating data, a campus notices that one math objective was consistently missed by almost all the 5th and 6th grade girls, questions need to be asked to determine why this occurred. Is it because the girls aren't listening and the boys are? Is it because the teacher calls on boys and not on the girls? Or, perhaps, it is because the math manipulatives are being used more by the boys than girls. Perhaps no manipulatives are being used at all, and should be. Discussion should focus on whether this instance is an instructional issue, or a curricular issue and whether it is campus specific or a district-wide issue. Once a determination is made as to the source of this phenomenon, appropriate interventions and/or updated training can be offered to the teachers.

Other types of data can also help influence decisions about what educators need as a focus for professional learning. The correct development and implementation of Individualized Educational Plans is an issue of concern for special programs teachers. Hallahan and Kauffman (2003) maintain that the IEP is the most important component of the focus on the needs of individual students with disabilities in that it outlines what teachers plan to do to meet an exceptional student's needs. Data about the student is the foundation of a special needs child's IEP.

Figure 14.6   **Step One: Use of Data**

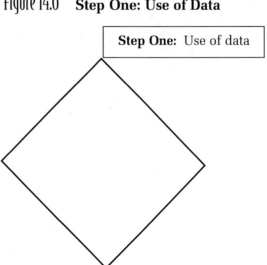

Teacher attendance and retention rates are a source of data, as are discipline records, use of library and media, and student attendance. Parent surveys, student surveys, and teacher input can be valuable sources of data to influence what the educators need to be learning. Parents and educators met recently in a district in the North Texas area to discuss the excessive use of restraint of learners with emotional or behavior disorders. Their identification of the source of this issue enabled them to develop a plan for better interventions into the behaviors that caused the excessive use.

STEP TWO: CREATION OF A PROFESSIONAL LEARNING PLAN

First, election of appropriate content for the educators must be determined. Returning to the example in Step One, let's assume that the campus discovers that no math manipulatives are being used after Grade Four, and that this situation exists district-wide. A determination that the teachers need to learn to use math manipulatives is made and written into the Professional Learning Plan (Figure 14.7). The district can assist with identifying strategies and commercially-produced programs that include math manipulatives. A team of stellar educators can be brought together to create a plan for the use of math manipulatives, a professional learning plan and how to follow up on the implementation of the use of manipulatives. For the special needs teachers, the plan would include how to adapt the use of manipulatives for those students who have difficulty in using manipulatives.

An additional requirement in this step is to have a crystal-clear plan of what the new behaviors or strategies would look like when successfully implemented. A tool from the Concerns-Based Adoption Model (CBAM) can assist in this effort. The Innovation Configuration, sometimes referred to as an Implementation Matrix, is like a road map in that it gives direction. Hall and Hord (2001) maintain that widespread change in most schools often occurs in very small amounts and that this situation is due to a lack of clarity about what the change is and what it will look like when fully implemented. By determining at this step what the new content (program, adoption, innovation) will look like when successfully implemented, and communicating that expectation, the chances are greater that changes can be made.

Finally, a communication component must be designed and fully implemented. Kotter (1996) states that in a three month period, an employee will hear 2,300,000 words,

---

Figure 14.7   **Step Two: Creation of a Professional Learning Plan**

Step Two:
Creation of a
Professional
Learning Plan

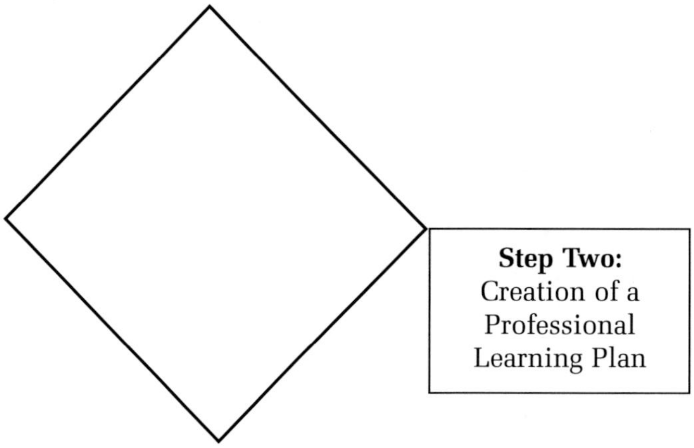

of which 13,400 words will be about a major change effort. That consumes only .0052 of the total communication pie—only a small sliver of what needs to happen. Kotter wryly observes that it is no wonder that very little implementation occurs with new change efforts. The implementers simply don't have enough information about the change!

STEP THREE: SELECTION OF ONE OR MORE STAFF DEVELOPMENT MODEL(S)

In the professional learning plan, a determination of what type of staff development model(s) will be used is needed (Figure 14.8). Sparks and Loucks-Horsley (1989) identified five major professional development models: training, observation/assessment, involvement in a development/improvement process, individually guided activities, and inquiry/ action research. Guskey (2003) extended this list, quoting Drago-Severson (1994) as including study groups and mentoring. A brief description of each model follows:

- Training—This is typically described as a workshop. It includes an instructor, face-to-face or on-line, with objectives and specific outcomes.
- Observation/Assessment—this model is typically described as a coaching model and includes collegial observation and feedback. This does not imply evaluation as it is strictly for analysis and reflection of one's teaching.
- Involvement in a Development/Improvement Process—An example of this model would be curriculum development committees, strategic planning committees, or committees charged with designing new programs.
- Individually Guided Activities—In this model, an individual educator would select their own goals and the activities that would reach those goals.
- Inquiry/Action Research—In this model, educators follow five steps as described by Calhoun (1994). These steps are:
  1. Determine a problem that all stakeholders have an interest in solving.
  2. Collect, organize and interpret information.
  3. Scrutinize the related research and literature.
  4. Prioritize possible solutions.

Figure 14.8   **Step Three: Selection of One or More Staff Development Models**

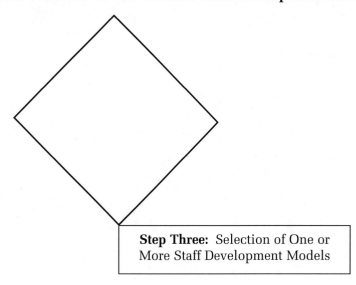

Step Three: Selection of One or More Staff Development Models

5. Try out the new solutions; determine their effectiveness.

- Study Groups—In this model, an entire campus staff would come together to read a common book, study a common problem or scrutinize student work. To be successful, study groups have to have structured meetings and a razor-sharp focus on their goal.
- Mentoring—This model would usually involve pairing a successful and experienced educator with a less experienced, new to the ranks educator. Some states require this for new teachers, but even teachers or principals who are experienced, but new to a district, could benefit from this type of relationship.

Each of these models has strengths and limitations, and each can stand alone. However, it is likely that a combination of models would benefit the learning of all educators. In some cases, a campus has started with a study group to examine the literature and processes which address their students' needs, followed by participation in another model, Inquiry/Action Research. After examination of the information gained from their research, they participated in yet another staff development model, Training. To sustain their learning, they then could use the model called Observation/Assessment to support each other in implementation of skills and strategies learned in the Training model.

STEP FOUR: MONITORING AND EVALUATING

Monitoring and evaluating new learnings are two critical pieces in this planning model (Figure 14.9). Fullan (2001) reminds us that there must be both pressure and support for educators, general and special, to change. The use of another tool from the Concerns-Based Adoption Model (CBAM) can assist in offering support for those trying out their new learnings from their professional development model. Stages of Concern, shown in Figure 14.10, offers diagnostic information, as well as appropriate interventions. A person who is concerned about keeping up with the materials of a new innovation or strategy does not need to go to another workshop on how to extend the innovation. He or she needs to receive an intervention that shows how to organize the materials.

Figure 14.9   **Step Four: Monitoring and Evaluating**

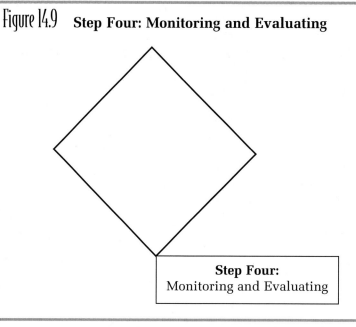

Step Four:
Monitoring and Evaluating

Figure 14.10   Stages of Concern (CBAM)

Stages of Concern: Typical Expression of Concern about the Innovation

Stages of Concern		Expression of Concern
6	Refocusing	I have some ideas about something that would work even better.
5	Collaboration	I am concerned about relating what I am doing with what other instructors are doing.
4	Consequence	How is my use affecting kids?
3	Management	I seem to be spending all my time getting material ready.
2	Personal	How will using it affect me?
1	Information	I would like to know more about it.
0	Awareness	I am not concerned about it (innovation).

Evaluation of staff development is most commonly practiced at the end of a workshop by the distribution of a survey which queries the participants about their comfort, how interesting they found the session, how organized the presenter and materials were, and similar details. These are important issues, but Guskey (2003) offers five levels of evaluating professional development. These are described below.

LEVEL ONE: PARTICIPANTS' REACTIONS

As noted above, this is typically a survey or questionnaire, and reveals more about the participants' interest and comfort than substantive information. It does help with improving design and delivery of professional development. At a recent bilingual symposium held on a Saturday in a large urban district, the participants rated the speaker as very interesting and very prepared. They rated the materials as "average" and the room comfort as "too cold" and "too loud."

LEVEL TWO: PARTICIPANTS' LEARNING

This level determines the participants' knowledge or skills as a result of their participation in a staff development session. Assume that a group of teachers of the deaf or hard of hearing attend a session on how to incorporate American Sign Language with a Total Communication philosophy. At the end of the session, they could record their personal plans on how to achieve this new technique, and develop a time line for this achievement. After a period of time, the group could reconvene or communicate by email to convey their success at that point.

LEVEL THREE: ORGANIZATION SUPPORT AND CHANGE

At this level of evaluation for professional development, the measures include the provision of time to attend professional learning opportunities, the alteration of the school day to accommodate conversations about their learning, and administration and organizational support for the implementation of an innovation. This can be determined by analysis of committee meetings, questionnaires, structured interviews and participant portfolios. The information is used to document organizational support. If the educators of students with learning disabilities are attempting to try new formative assessments to guide their teaching, and no resources, time, or support is given by the district (organization), the likelihood of a successful change is minimal.

LEVEL FOUR: PARTICIPANTS' USE OF NEW KNOWLEDGE AND SKILL

Educators of multicultural and bilingual learners should, according to Banks (1994) address the transformation approach so that a variety of perspectives about any given situation can be experienced from a variety of groups. To determine the success of the participants in a professional development event related to this aspect, one would determine their use in a variety of ways. Participant interviews, supervisor interviews, and student interviews could all reveal the successful use. Additionally, questionnaires could be distributed to each of the groups and any others in attendance. Focus groups would allow discussion of individual views on the success at any given point in time. Implementation logs and reflections kept by participants could provide rich information on specific processes.

LEVEL FIVE: STUDENT LEARNING OUTCOMES

As noted earlier, the IEP is the main avenue by which special educators focus on the students' success. Imagine that the educators of learners with physical disabilities attend a staff development event and return to their classrooms with cognitive, affective and psychomotor outcomes for their students. This can be measured by student behavior, group tasks, and portfolios of students' work and questionnaires. Teacher-designed assessment can reveal student achievement with great accuracy and are yet another source of information.

Summary

Student learning is the reason for continuing education for educators. Yes, in some cases it has become the fulfillment of a time requirement, or a mandate. But the focus of all professional learning should be on the students, what they need to know and be able to do, and what the teachers need to know to accomplish that.

A newly anointed physician, out of medical school for only three months, registered for a continuing education course and called her parents to ask about restaurants in the city where the course was being held. Her parents, surprised that she was already attending continuing education, queried her, "Why are you attending continuing education courses? You just finished medical school!" Her reply has a lesson for all of us. She said, "While some techniques and practices will always be appropriate and provide continuity, the knowledge base is growing so rapidly that we must constantly be updating our information. After all, it's a matter of life or death. We are responsible to our patients."

And so it is with our students. It is a matter of life and death of the intellect and achievement of our students. They deserve the best we can offer.

Applying Your Knowledge

Cynthia was just appointed principal of a large urban high school. A major reason for her appointment is her strong background in curriculum and instruction. The high school as a whole demonstrates average performance on the state achievement tests. The problems, however, are revealed with data disaggregated into subpopulations. African-American males and Hispanic males are doing very poorly on all subtests (English, Mathematics, Science, and Social Studies). Hispanics, both males and females, have the highest drop-out rates with 30% of Hispanics in the entering freshman year leaving before graduation.

An even more startling revelation to Cynthia is that the proportion of minority students placed in special education programs is almost twice that of majority students. Cynthia and her department chairs have examined this data. Cynthia now believes that it is time to have the faculty examine the information and begin planning for what changes to make and how those changes will happen. Cynthia has set aside about 10% of this year's budget for professional learning opportunities for the staff.

QUESTIONS

1. How could the information in this chapter assist Cynthia and the department chairs in their change efforts?
2. What are some ways that the money set aside for professional learning be spent that would impact classroom level change in the school? Explain.
3. Develop a draft agenda for the meeting with the faculty. What topics will you cover, what processes will you use?

QUESTIONS FOR THOUGHT

1. How could the NSDC Staff Development Standards be used in school improvement planning?
2. Should professional learning for teachers in special instructional programs differ from professional learning for teachers in regular education? Why or why not?
3. How does your school or district evaluate staff development? Which of Guskey's five levels are in use?
4. Given the staff development models described in the chapter, what percent of staff development in your district or school is allocated to each model? Is this a good distribution? Why or why not?

References

Banks, J. A. (1994). Transforming the mainstream curriculum. *Educational Leadership,* *51*(8), 4–8.

Calhoun, E. F. (1994). *How to use action research in the self- renewing school.* Alexandria, VA: Association for Supervision and Curriculum Development.

Drago-Severson, E. E. (1994). *What does staff development develop? How the staff development literature conceives adult growth.* Unpublished qualifying paper, Harvard University.

Elmore, R. F. (2002). *Bridging the gap between standards and achievement.* Washington, D.C.: Albert Shanker Institute.

Fullan, M. (2001). *Leading in a culture of change.* San Francisco: Jossey-Bass.

Guskey, T. R. (2000). *Evaluating professional development.* Thousand Oaks, CA: Corwin Press, Inc.

Hall, G. E. & Hord, S. M. (2001) *Implementing change: Patterns, principles and potholes.* Boston: Allyn and Bacon.

Hallahan, D. P. & Kaufmann, J. M. (2003) *Exceptional learners: Introduction to special education with casebook,* (9th ed). Boston: Allyn & Bacon.

Kotter, J. P. (1996). *Leading change.* Boston: Harvard Business School Press.

National Staff Development Council. (2001). *Standards for staff development: Revised.* Oxford, OH: National Staff Development Council.

National Staff Development Council. (2004). Retrieved June 6, 2004 from *http://www.nsdc.org.*

Sparks, D., & Loucks-Horsley, S. (1989). Five models of staff development for teachers. *Journal of Staff Development. 10*(4), 40–57.

Sparks, G. M. (1983). Synthesis of research on staff development for effective teaching. *Educational leadership. 41*(3), 65–72.

Accessing Central Office Resources

Anita Pankake

Noe Sauceda

Administering special programs in a school is one among
many areas for which principals and teachers need the help
and support of central administration. Taking full advantage
of the resources (human and non-human) that exist at
district's central office is a responsibility as well
as an opportunity for school leaders.

—*Anita Pankake & Noe Sauceda*

Objectives

1. Provide an understanding of the role of central office staff in
   regard to schools
2. Present a model that promotes collaboration and cooperation
   between the school and central office staff members
3. Demonstrate how school leaders can best access the persons and
   resources available in central administration

Introduction

Almost every special program in a school district is accompanied by one or more specialists, consultants, directors, coordinators, or assistant superintendents who function externally to the classroom delivery of that program. Often, though not always, the individuals who occupy these positions are located at the school district's central office. According to the National Center for Educational Statistics (May 1995), over 31,000 positions comprise some aspect of central office operations other than the superintendent. More recent statistics from the U.S. Department of Education (February 2000) identified more than 40,000 positions under the category of "Instruction Coordinators." Robinson (1992) estimated that approximately 4.3% of an average school district's budget is allocated to support these central office positions.

Traditionally, the purposes of such positions have been to monitor and control decisions and resources related to specific programs and administrative functions. Additionally, responsibility for support, assistance and coordination of program efforts for the district as a whole often appear in the formal job descriptions for such positions. Unfortunately, these central office positions have not always been viewed as particularly helpful by the intended audience, i.e., individuals at the school. The perspective of principals and teachers regarding the responsibilities and practices of these various administrators is often less than positive. Rather than seeing the superintendent and the central office administrators as individuals whose roles are to serve and support, the individuals operating at the delivery points of these programs (principals and teachers) see people in these positions as creators of complications, confusion, and massive paperwork. A particularly poignant description of such perceptions is offered by Sarason (1996):

> The dominant impression one gains is that school personnel believe that there is a system, that it is run by somebody or bodies in some central place, that it tends to operate as a never ending source of obstacles to those within the system, that a major goal of the individual is to protect against the baleful influences of the system, and that any one individual has and can have no effect on the system qua system . . ." (p. 163).

Whitaker & Moses (1994) point out that within the TQM philosophy proffered by W. Edwards Deming the most important job of leaders is to find and remove barriers in the organization that might be preventing people from being successful. Whitaker & Moses, then, transfer this perspective to the school superintendent by stating that, "It is up to the superintendent to remove the hurdles faced by principals and teachers as they initiate change. Central office personnel must begin to view themselves not as regulators, but as leaders who help initiate improvement efforts and involve others in those efforts" (p. 166). They go on to assert that, "One thing is certain, school level changes are near impossible without the help and support of central administration" (Whitaker & Moses, 1994, p. 166).

The structure of the school organization has recently been modified by the concept of site-based management (SBM). SBM was introduced as a means of refocusing management back to student, teaching and learning outcomes. It has now been widely recognized that special program decisions as a category of decisions are better made or influenced in part by professionals at the school site, especially teachers and principals.

Teacher empowerment is considered one of the most significant reforms within the education profession and as a concept for facilitating effective school leadership has become synonymous with site-based decision management. Advocates of this leadership concept agree that site-based decision making is a potentially powerful mechanism for achieving teacher empowerment resulting in a campus leadership team that is better able to respond to the unique needs of the individual school. The central office administrator-principal relationship has become a key point of review and importance in an educational environment of high stakes accountability. Principals are now held accountable for program and educational outcomes and so it follows that authority for some measure of program and educational program decision making must be delegated to the campus.

Consistent with this power of view, Ray, Hack and Candoli (2001) suggest that effective organizations should create planning cadres that address the planning function. This team would undertake all planning activities for the campus, including the establishment of educational goals, the development of educational programs reflecting the goals, the identification of resources needed to implement programs, the allocation of physical and human resources for implementation and an evaluation process which supports a continued plan development.

Since program implementation responsibility has not yet become completely the role of the principal, it makes sense that the principals and staff must maintain an effective relationship and lines of communication with central office program administrators. A close relationship between campus staff and central office special program staff is essential in facilitating the achievement of student performance goals of a campus. Central office special program staff will continue to exercise the monitoring and control functions under site-based management. This function becomes even more critical to the overall organization since many new centers of activity are created at each campus and so must be controlled and monitored.

Administering special programs in a school is one among many areas for which principals and teachers need the help and support of central administration. Taking full advantage of the resources (human and non-human) that exist as district's central office is a responsibility as well as an opportunity for school leaders. Central office, no matter how large and complex or small and overworked, can provide information, technical assistance, legal advice, networking with programs in other districts and regions, clerical support, and myriad other essentials for the quality operations of special programs at the building level. This chapter will give an overview of central office in terms of definition and design and some information regarding significant changes that are being initiated and/or being thrust upon central office administrative operations because of efforts to decentralize and increase site-based decision-making for school improvement efforts. The last section offers some specific ways in which school leaders can access and utilized central office services and support. A tone of advocacy is evident throughout the chapter. Neglect of or inappropriate use of the resources available to school leaders—in this case, those at central office—result in missed opportunities to do our best for the children to be served.

A Brief Overview Central Office

Today, the fact that there is a central office staff in a school district is taken for granted. Now and then there may be some grinching about the organization being "top heavy" or "having too many people 'over there'", but, according to English (1992), administrative roles other than the principal and superintendent have become a fixed part of our thinking regarding school district administration. The general development of central office is described by Knezevich (1984). He marks the beginning of central office administration with what he refers to as the "one-person-office-of-the superintendent." During this time an individual in the position of superintendent often taught one or two classes, coached, and/or did the district's clerical work. Other duties at the central office were formed as assists to the initial administrative position of school superintendent. Knezevich (1984) divides the development of central office into three phases:

1. Phase one began when superintendents were relieved of non-administrative functions such as teaching and coaching.
2. Phase two occurred when personnel were hired to assume the clerical and non-professional administrative responsibilities of the school district.
3. Phase three was initiated when enrollments in elementary and secondary units became large enough to merit their own full-time administrators.

As might be expected, large districts were the first to move through these phases and actually develop a central office team. As various federal and state initiatives have been implemented, new and different needs for specialized administrative positions have developed. Many larger districts have one or more central office administrative or supervisory positions devoted each to special education, guidance and counseling program, migrant education, bilingual and ESL programs, programs for the gifted and talents, career and technology education, and myriad others. The number and focus of specialized management positions at the district level varies between and among school districts and can change with any federal or state legislation or state department initiative.

Orlosky, McCleary, Shapiro, & Webb (1984) claim that "To understand the configuration of administrative and supervisory positions of a district central office, one can subdivide the responsibilities of the superintendent as required by the number, complexity and size of tasks into a range of positions occupied by specialists. This configuration is referred to as the superintendency" (p. 50). Central office management for the district is created when a function or set of functions is divided into specific tasks and delegated to a specialist. Depending on the nature of the tasks delegated, the administration will be structured into levels with assistant superintendents in charge of one or more functions. Major tasks under the responsibility of an assistant superintendent may be assigned to directors. Although titles may differ, two- and three-level hierarchies of administrative specialists are not uncommon.

Little uniformity exists in titles and the commensurate responsibilities of central office positions from one district to another. Such variation in these positions exist to the extent that a study by Association for Supervision and Curriculum Development completed in the 1980's concluded that the roles of central office supervisors were so unique from one district to another that they were "non-comparable" (Snyder, Giella, & Fitzgerald, 1994). Knezevich (1984) demonstrates this vividly in the following statements, "Members of the administrative team include personnel with such diverse titles as deputy, associate or assistant superintendent; director; supervisor; administrative assistant; coordinator; and consultant, all of whom are attached to the office of the superintendent of schools." However, the distinguishing characteristic of central office administrators is that they "... are charged with responsibilities that are system-wide in scope but limited in range within the institutions. Thus, the supervisor of music's functions are system-wide in scope but confined to music; the assistant superintendent in charge of elementary education is responsible for elementary education only, but in all parts of the system" (p. 312).

An important distinction to be made between and among central office administrators is related to knowing the hierarchical power and authority of their roles. English (1992) differentiates the two types of positions, "line" and "staff." He defines line positions as those "directly concerned with implementation" and staff positions as "those who support, but do not directly deliver instructional programs" (p. 147). Perhaps even more important for our purposes in this chapter is the contrast between the two types of positions offered by Wiles and Bondi (1983). They describe line personnel as the "formal leadership" in the schools and school districts and staff personnel as those "who advise and consult others of the organization, formally and informally, but have no authority" (pp. 113–114). Position titles sometimes help in revealing the line or staff authority of central office administrative positions, but they are no guarantee.

Central office administrators working with special programs or in other areas may also differ in the focus of their positions responsibilities, i.e., "generalists" or "specialists" (Campbell, Cunningham, Nystrand, & Usdan, 1985, p. 226). Generalists, such as superintendents and principals, have a wide range of responsibilities encompassed in their positions. Individuals in positions that have a focus on one area or single group of functions are specialists. Some of these positions are advisory (i.e., staff) positions, others have line authority. School districts need both kinds of positions to operate; generalists need advice and information from a variety of specialists to make good decisions and someone needs to see the "big picture" of the school system operation which goes beyond any one specialty area.

An understanding of the traditional perspectives helps one to appreciate the monumental changes being proposed (and in some places implemented) regarding the purpose and practice of central office administration (Pankake & Boyter, 1998). According to Whitaker & Moses (1994), "Historically, the superintendent and central administration have assumed the roles of primary decision makers and enforcers of school board policies. Although the roles of central administration still include being accountable for decisions, they are gradually changing from enforcing ones to supporting ones" (p. 166). These changes provide important opportunities for school leaders to use and even help develop central office resources as supports for, rather than barriers, in the administration and delivery of special programs.

Major reform and restructuring efforts have influenced the roles and responsibilities of central office personnel as well as the individuals in the school sites. A shift from the traditional control and monitoring roles toward roles more focused on services and supports that assist with improved student performance generally in the school is occurring in varying degrees in districts across the nation (Hord & Smith, 1993). Thus, "Central staff are no longer the sole authority figures, distributing directives and monitoring compliance" (Hord & Smith, 1993, p. 23). Rather, in the "new central office staff members must learn to operate without the crutch of hierarchy and have only themselves to rely on" (Hanna, 1988, cited in Tewel, 1995, p. 66). Accordingly, Tewel (1995) admonished that ". . . success [in central office positions] now depends on figuring out whose collaboration is needed to act on good ideas. In short, the new work implies very different ways of obtaining and using power and influence" (p. 66). School systems, like businesses and government agencies, are trying to create flatter organizations, or as Tewel (1995) described it—a need to "become leaner, less bureaucratic, and more entrepreneurial" (p. 65). Certainly some school districts' central office administration would fit perfectly in one or more of the traditional schemes described earlier. Others, however, are in the midst of trying to implement the new roles, relationships, and responsibilities that accompany the system restructuring. As with any system, making a change in one area of the system results in associated changes in other areas of the system. Consequently, as changes occur in the structure and operations at central office, changes will be enabled and required in response at the school level.

Proposed changes in central office administrative operations are numerous. They include: more channels for action created, especially, cross-department projects, interagency ventures, and collaboration with various professional associations; the creation of "more potential centers of power" to provide "the opportunity for greater flexibility" (Tewel, 1995, p. 66). To accomplish these changes, central office administrators and supervisors must (a) shift to being facilitators and sources of technical expertise to help the school in their efforts to change (Hord & Smith, 1993), (b) begin sharing and in some instances relinquishing decision-making authority in many areas of school operations (Hord & Smith, 1993), and (c) start thinking cross-functional and building multiple networks (Tewel, 1995, p. 67). According to Tewel (1995), survival and thriving for central office administrators will depend on finding knowledge and services of value to individuals at the building sites. This will happen only if these individuals spend more time working across boundaries with peers and other staff members over whom they have no direct control but need to use their interpersonal and negotiating skills. Power will evolve from personal strengths of the individuals, not from organizational structure (Tewel, 1995).

An important point made by Tewel (1995), and one to be kept in mind as these various concepts of the traditional and contemporary operations regarding central office administration are linked, is that, "While the old organization no longer exists on paper, . . . it continues to haunt the minds, habits, and performance of staff." (p. 76). School leaders need to assess the situation in their district and take advantage of both the old and/or the new in terms of leadership opportunities. Obviously not all districts will have made the transition from the traditional, more centralized structure to the more decentralized, autonomous site operations. Being able to analyze how a district actually is operating (whether or not that is what's described in the organizational chart and/or the operational philosophy) will be important in taking advantages of the resources available.

Accessing and Using What's Available

As the new ways of operating become embedded in the central office, school leaders will need to respond appropriately. In order to take full advantage of the collaborative, facilitative, shared decision making, support, and assistance perspective developing at the central office, similar perspectives need to be developed at the school site. Sarason (1996) point out, "More than any other single position in the American School hierarchy, the principalship represents the pivotal exchange point, the most important point of connection between teachers, students, and parents on the one hand and the educational policy-making structure—superintendent, school board, and taxpayer—on the other. Through the principal's office pass both the needs, problems, and issues of the local community and the problems and issues that accompany the implementation of policies flowing downward from the top of the school bureaucracy" (p. 180). This statement emphasizes the importance of the school leadership in making use of all resources that may improve the quality of programs. Following are some ideas on how school leaders can take advantage of the new opportunities developing as the restructuring at central office occurs or how to take better advantage of the existing opportunities if restructuring of central office is yet to be initiated in the current situation.

One of a number of consequences from reform efforts at central office is that personnel and other program resources are being decentralized and located at the school rather than at central office. The relocation of specialized positions from central office to schools is among the recent changes being observed across the country. An attempt to move the resources as close to the point of instructional impact for students as possible is an assumption driving decisions regarding central office restructuring. According to Delehant (1990), "The traditional, centralized district organization is being replaced with a structure that directs all resources that bear upon student performance to be the work of the schools. The responsibility and accountability for decisions that affect student performance are shifting from central management to the schools" (p. 17). This reallocation is an effort to assist improved student performance in the school generally not just in the specific special programs. Locating human and non-human resources where the programs are happening allows some authentic on-site technical assistance to be afforded to students, teachers, and building administrators alike.

Delehant (1990) notes that as the restructuring occurs in Rochester, NY, "Central office staff are being asked to review services and methods of delivery to ensure they are compatible with and support the schools' new roles" (p. 17). Conversely, such changes require that school leadership become good customers. What can this mean for schools leaders?

Knowing your priorities. As central office administrators offer support and assistance, they will need to know what your priorities are in order to make the best use of their time, knowledge, and skills in addressing the needs at the various school sites. Central office resources will be limited. To get the best service and assistance school leaders need to be clear about what they need, when, and how they perceived it might best be delivered.

Offering feedback on the quality of services and assistance. As Hunter (1982) noted, everybody likes to have an answer to the question, "How am I doing?" In fact, it is necessary to have some sense of this in order to know how to adjust to improve the quality of services. The only ones who have the information on how well those at central office are meeting needs will be individuals at each building site. Therefore it is incumbent on the building leadership to set up various means of collecting feedback on the services and assistance provided and convey this information to those at central office. Without such information, whether or not activities are truly resulting in quality services will be a best guess on the part of the central office personnel (Pankake, 1998).

Getting information about who can do what for whom. Depending on the size and complexity of the central office staff, there may be several sources of information available. Knowing who has the information and services that you need will increase the efficiency and accuracy with which central office can respond to any request. Representatives from the school site may find it helpful to both themselves and their central office administrators and supervisors to spend some time learning about who knows what and who can do what regarding the various special programs operating in the building. This may well be a point at which knowing who are the generalists and who are the specialists in the central office will become quite useful. It will also be helpful for the school leadership to understand the line and staff divisions at central office. This will prevent them from asking for a decision from someone who does not have the authority to make it, and will lead to asking for advice from those who truly have the expertise in that particular area.

Some of the resources available at central office may not be encompassed in personnel specifically allocated to the administration of special programs. For example, the central office unit dealing with staff development may be of great assist in a variety of areas. While they may not have specific information about a particular program they may well be able to locate who does. If there is a particular knowledge base needed by the school staff to implement new strategies, the staff development personnel can find, organize its presentation, and maybe even fund it.

Another central office unit that may be helpful to school leaders as they look to make quality improvements are the administrators in the central office who work with personnel matters. Generally these people are experts in certification requirements and can be most helpful in identifying applicants that meet the paper requirements as well as the practice requirements. Personnel office administrators and staff may also be involved in the allocation of time for individuals who serve more than one school, i.e., the "traveling teachers" or "shared personnel." Staying informed about who makes these assignments and, in turn, keeping those individuals informed about the school's needs for the services of these staff members will make it more likely that staff allocations are based on needs, not just numbers.

Another opportunity for building level access to central office resources that is presenting itself more frequently is participation in district level planning. Many districts are implementing vertical teams in their planning processes to ensure that a variety of perspectives are being considered at the planning stages of all operations and of any new initiatives. School leaders need to have personnel ready and willing to take part in these activities as the opportunities arise. Full participation in these opportunities requires that school leaders know the interests, skills, and talents of their staff members. School leaders would do well to get acquainted with everyone in their organization to discover what talents and areas of expertise exist (Pankake, 1998). Knowing who has had special training in a particular area, who may be bilingual but not working in the bilingual program, who has some community connections and involvement that might assist on a school or district project, who is looking to pursue a school administration career, and who is looking to accept some leadership responsibilities but does not wish to leave their classroom assignment can help assure that when central office extends an invitation to participate, your school is ready to respond.

"Specialists" at central office can be a wealth of information regarding the rules, regulations, and reports that seem to be part and parcel of every special program. The role of school leader is much more of a generalist than a specialist. "Generalists" have a wide range of responsibilities included in their jobs, while "specialists" usually have their responsibilities focused on one area or group of functions operationally or programmatically (Campbell, et al, 1985). Individuals with specialized information related to various school and district programs are often located at the district level. However, their specialized knowledge is only a phone call, e-mail or office visit away. They know the latest in their area. School leaders who access this specialized knowledge can help ensure quality programming for students and help avoid complaints and litigation situations for everyone.

Specialists may also have established contacts and working relationships with individuals in external agencies that provide needed services and support to students and/or their families. School leaders can work through the central office specialists to move more quickly and effectively in accessing personnel and information located in these external agencies. Taking advantage of the bridges and communication networks already in place through central office specialists can facilitate interagency cooperation in providing services for students and reduce bureaucratic frustrations for everyone.

Closing Comments

"With a decades-long drive to push reform to the school level, central office has too frequently become the bad guy in these efforts. The accusations of central office 'interference' in reform are many . . . " (Richardson, 2000, p. 1). It is time to end the traditional blame game of "them" and "us" when considering school reform with a focus on quality programming for all students. Schools and school systems won't improve with leaders spending their time waiting for each other to change. If the oft used term "systemic change" has any real meaning for quality education, surely it is that all levels and all individuals working at those levels in the educational system have some responsibilities for making changes. Leaders at both central office and school sites have important roles to play in the school improvement process and the implementation of special programs. Central office efforts to become less bureaucratic and dominating and more service and support oriented are taking hold in many systems throughout the country; other systems are likely to follow. However, when the efforts to change toward this decentralized service and support structure are initiated, school leaders must simultaneously reciprocate by recognizing this and taking action to access the information and services offered. This can be done in myriad ways, only a few of which have been offered here.

Applying Your Knowledge

The new superintendent has expressed a desire for some major changes in the roles, relationships, and responsibilities for all leadership personnel throughout the district. She has asked that you and three of your colleagues from other schools serve as members of a restructuring task force (RTF). Other members of the task force are: the Director of Staff Development, the Assistant Superintendent for Non-Instructional Support Services, one of the Bilingual Instructional Facilitators, the Early Childhood Education Services Coordinator, the Director of Social, Psychological, and Psychometric Services, the Administrative Assistant for Business and Purchasing, two parents, and a Program Administrator for the Educational Service Center for the region.

To get things underway, the superintendent has hosted a continental breakfast and now everyone is seated at the conference table. The superintendent calls the meeting to order and repeats her desire for the RTF to explore some of the major issues that may be preventing quality delivery of instructional and support services to the children enrolled in the district. She reinforces that it is her intent to determine ways in which positions, procedures, and resources can be reallocated and restructured to increase the quantity and quality of services for all children. She has provided two individuals from her office to serve as scribes for the meeting. Her goal for this session is to have everyone offer ideas on what they perceive to be problems or issues that should be explored by the RTF.

You are feeling optimistic about this effort and the leadership of the superintendent. In a variety of informal meetings with your school leadership colleagues, you have been openly critical of operations at central office, especially as they related to services for special needs students and the quality and relevance of teacher inservice offerings. Suddenly you are jogged from your satisfied reflection when you realize that the superintendent has just spoken your name. All eyes at the conference table are on you and the scribes have their markers in hand as the superintendent says to you, " . . . let's have you start us out. Have you experienced any difficulties in securing the assistance you need from those of us at central office?"

QUESTIONS

1. How will you respond to the superintendent's questions with honesty, but in such a way that it keep the discussion positive and open?
2. What do you think about the make-up of the task force membership? Is there anyone you believe should be added to the group? Anyone currently on the group that you believe probably shouldn't be? Explain.
3. Will you share information about the work of the RTF with others in your school? Will you seek their input? Why? How?

QUESTIONS FOR THOUGHT

1. How might knowing which central office administrators are in "line" positions and which are in "staff" positions impact building leaders in their work with special programs?
2. Give a brief history of the development of the central office. Discuss what you believe will be the future of the central office given the current climate.
3. What are some professional development issues related to the delivery of quality special programming that the central office might support? What forms would this support take?
4. If a decision were made to reallocate the resouces and responsibilities of one central office position to your building, what position would you request? Why? How would you put the resources to work? What responsibilities would you give the person in this position?

For Additional Information Online

American Association of School Administrators (AASA) *www.aasa.org*

National Staff Development Council (NSDC) *www.nsdc.org*

Association for Supervision and Curriculum Development (ASCD) *www.ascd.org*

Education Week *www.edweek.or/ewhome.ht.*

Also, many universities and private agencies have policy analysis units that could be helpful.

Each of these organizations has affiliate organizations in most states. State affiliates could be sources of information more specific to the unique information requirements of a particular area.

References

Campbell, R. F., Cunningham, L. L., Nystrand, R. O., & Usdan, M. D. (1985). *The organization and control of American schools* (5th edition). Columbus, OH: Charles E. Merrill.

Delehant, A. M. (1990). A central office view: Charting a course when pulled in all directions. *The School Administrator, 47*(8), 14, 17–19.

English, F. W. (1992). *Educational administration: The human science.* New York: HarperCollins.

Hord, S. and Smith, A. (1993). Will the phones go dead? *Insight,* (Winter), 23–26.

Hunter, M. (1982). *Mastery teaching.* El Segundo, CA: TIP Publications.

Knezevich, S. J. (1984). *Administration of public education: A sourcebook for the leadership and management of educational institutions* (4th edition). New York: Harper & Row.

National Center for Educational Statistics (May, 1995). *Statistics in brief.* Washington, DC: U.S. Department of Education OERI, NCES–95–213.

National Center for Educational Statistics (February, 2000). *Institute of Education Sciences.* U.S. Department of Education, Washington, DC.

Orlosky, D. E., McCleary, L. E., Shapiro, A. & Webb, L. D. (1984). *Educational administration today.* Columbus, OH: Charles E. Merrill.

Pankake, A. M., & Boyter, G. A. (1998). Central office career choices for women. In B.J. Irby & G. Brown (Eds.), *Women Leaders: Structuring Success,* (pp. 168–179). Dubuque, IA: Kendall/Hunt Publishing Co.

Pankake, A. M. (1998). *Implementation: Making things happen.* Larchmont, NY: Eye on Education.

Pankake, A. M. & Fullwood, H. L. (1999). "Principals of inclusion": Things they need to know and do. *Catalyst for Change, 28*(2), 25–26.

Parsley, J. F. (1991). Reshaping student learning. *The School Administrator, 48*(7), 9, 11,13, &14.

Ray, J., Hack, W. G., & Candoli, L. C. (2001). *School Business Administration: A planning approach.* Needham Heights, MA: Allyn & Bacon.

Richardson, J. (2000, October). Central office guidance strengthens the whole district. *NSDC Results,* (October), 1 & 6.

Robinson, G. (1992). *School administration under attack: What are the facts?* Arlington,VA: Educational Research Service.

Sarason, S. B. (1996). *Revisiting "The culture of the school and the problem of change."* New York: Teachers College Press.

Scambio, E. J., & Graber, J. (1991). Reform through state intervention. *The School Administrator, 48*(7), 8, 10, 12, & 14.

Snyder, K. J., Giella, M., & Fitzgerald, J. H. (1994). The changing role of central office supervisors in district restructuring. *The Journal of Staff Development, 15*(2), 30–34.

Tewel, K. J. (1995). Despair at the central office. *Educational Leadership, 52*(7), 65–68.

Whitaker, K. S. & Moses, M. C. (1994). *The restructuring handbook: A guide to school revitalization.* Boston, MA: Allyn and Bacon.

Wiles, J. & Bondi, J. (1983). *Principles of school administration: The real world of leadership in schools.* Columbus, OH: Charles E. Merrill.

Parental Involvement and Engagement

16

History and Examples from Two Schools

Miguel Guajardo
Danna Beaty
Francisco Guajardo

> Reaching out to families that have historically
> not been connected in family inovlement
> programs can have lasting effects
> on student and teacher success.

—*Miguel Guajardo, Danna Beaty & Francisco Guajardo*

Objectives

1. To inform the reader of public policy initiatives that encourage and sustain parental participation in the education of their children
2. To introduce the reader to traditional and nontraditional methods for parental engagement in the education of their children
3. To discuss conditions that nurture parental engagement
4. To present urban and rural school strategies to engage parents in building the school culture
5. To introduce to campus leaders specific strategies proven to be effective in involving parents in the educational processes of their children

Introduction

The idea of partnership programs is not new to education. For centuries, communities have had an instrumental role in the development of future generations. However, recent history has seen a decline in this communal interest as society has moved toward a more self-centered view of the professional, political and personal life. Schools have also been the training ground for America's communities and democratic system. The value that a community places on its schools is often reflected in the pride it takes in its neighborhoods, parks and storefronts. Schools can support the social and economic welfare of the community by joining hands with local businesses and organizations to promote a more promising tomorrow by producing a better educated citizen. This chapter describes a historical overview of parental involvement programs. It articulates rationales for the need to create effective partnerships and uses alternative parental involvement programs from an urban school and from a rural school to illustrate how leaders can engage parents and the community beyond the traditional Parent Teacher Association model.

Why Parent Partnerships?

Micheal Fullan (2001) writes that sustained school change will not originate from the top down[4] conventional approach characterized by authoritative decision making exercised by top administrators. On the other hand, an approach driven by bottom up impulses may also not yield optimal conditions. Rather, a combination of top down and bottom up modes creates the most profound and sustained change in schools. In that context, schools include community members as partners to build schools that work well for a greater number of students. Ample evidence exists suggesting that schools in our society mirror communities where they reside (Mickelson, 2003; Oakes, 2003; Guajardo, 2002; Anyon, 1997; Giroux, 1989). In inner cities we see the housing patterns dictating the schools children will attend, in the Southwest we see the multi-language issues that children and families bring with them, and Oakes (1985) makes the case that tracking practices channel privileged into professional training routes, while these same practices direct poor and minority children toward a working class oriented curriculum. The latter curriculum exposes children to more rote experiences and learning. Ample historical and academic documents tell us that while some of these practices are deliberate (Varenne & McDermott, 1999), others have become woven into the subconscious of schools and their personnel (Spindler, 2000). These traditional socio-historical practices that marginalize children support the argument for including parents and child advocates in the educational process. This has proven to be an effective method for keeping schools accountable and focused on child-centered instruction and decision-making in the best interest of children.

Historically these practices of marginalizing children from low SES and communities of color have prompted public officials to adopt public policy intended to remedy these unjust practices. As public policy proposed parental involvement programs during the War on Poverty, so did academics who were committed to helping build strong schools that in turn prepare healthy children and citizens. One of the first broad-based school reform initiatives that advocated for parents to play an important role in building strong schools was James Comer's School Development Process, also known as the Comer Process (Joyner, 2004). The Comer Process holds parental involvement as one of

[4]This language is employed for the purpose of articulating the prevailing mental models.

its major tenets. It espouses that parents participate in substantive ways in creating a positive school climate and even in being an integral part of the decision-making process in schools. Parents should not be on the periphery. On the contrary, the Comer model suggests the necessity of having parents as central players in the governance and school management process.

Historical Background and Public Policy

Until the late 1960s, parental involvement usually took the form of reinforcing discipline at home, helping with the occasional homework assignment and baking goods for class parties and bake sales. Most families were dual parent households with mothers who did not work outside the home. The 1960s brought about change in the family structure. More and more mothers went to work outside the home and single parent households became more commonplace. Consequently, the challenge of raising and educating children grew increasing complicated. Furthermore, as schools integrated, disparities between the educational preparation programs of white and minority children as well as that of children from middle and working class families began to surface as an ugly blemish on the face of the American educational system.

President Lyndon B. Johnson declared a "War on Poverty" in an effort to equalize opportunities for success among the American social classes. Two acts passed during his presidency have had lasting effects for children of poverty: the Economic Opportunity Act of 1964, responsible for the establishment of the Head Start program in 1965, and the Elementary and Secondary Education Act (ESEA) of 1965; Title I of ESEA would emerge as a profound instrument of change as it evolved over the next 40 years.

The Economic Opportunity Act of 1964 was responsible for the establishment of the Head Start program in 1965. Head Start centers promote "comprehensive child development programs and have the overall goal of increasing the school readiness of young children in low-income families" (Head Start, 2000, p. 1), focusing on the entire family, making education and support available to parents. Head Start offers parents the opportunities and support for growth so that they can identify their own strengths, needs and interests, and find their own solutions" (45 CFR 304.40). Believing that lasting change can only occur if there is change in the family, parents are expected to undergo appropriate training and then to serve as volunteers at their child's center. If educational aides are needed at the center, parents of children enrolled in the program are to be recruited first.

Title I was designed to assist educationally and economically deprived children. It was not until the passage of the Hawkins-Stafford Consolidation amendment in 1988 that parental involvement was formally introduced to Title programs. In 1994, Title I was reauthorized under the Improving America's Schools Act (IASA) and parental/community involvement was recognized as a valuable tool for promoting student achievement. According to the Center for Law and Education, the strengthened parental involvement component called for:

1. Policy development at the district and school levels, including parental involvement in the development of school improvement initiatives;
2. The development of "compacts" between teachers/parents/students/administrators which committed involved parties to major responsibilities held by each in order to provide for a quality educational experience; and
3. Building capacity for parent involvement through such means as increased training and enhanced partnerships with community organizations and businesses.

Additionally, schools that received Title I funds were required to: 1) hold a parent meeting to explain Title I; 2) meet with parents so that they might participate in decisions about their child; and 3) give parents information about the program.

The most recent reauthorization of Title I occurred with the passing of the No Child Left Behind Act of 2001 (NCLB). This controversial piece of legislation called for increased performance of schools and students with an emphasis on highly qualified teachers and paraprofessionals. When a school fails to provide the student with the quality of education mandated by NCLB, the child's parents have a right to request and receive a transfer to a school that can meet the standards.

The late 1980s saw an increased interest in the term parent involvement and researchers began to explore the possibility of a stronger force—that of school, family, and community partnerships. Growth in this field of study was assisted by the federal government's creation in 1990 of the National Center on Families, Communities, Schools and Children's Learning. The Center's purpose is to conduct an active research and development program on school and family partnerships from birth through high school (Epstein, 2001). In addition to its research agenda, the Center created an International Network of over 300 researchers in the United States and more than 40 nations "to encourage and to share work on many topics related to school, family, and community partnerships" (p. 40).

Why Community Partnerships?

According to the Census Bureau, the percentage of homes operating below the poverty level in 1999 was 11.9% for families from all races, 7.7% for whites, 23.6% for blacks, and 26.5% for Hispanics. America is becoming more culturally diverse, with a decline in the white non-Hispanic population from 75.6% to 71.9% during the period 1990 to 2000, a slight increase in the black population from 12.3% to 12.9%, and a marked increase in the Hispanic population from 9.0% to 12.6% during the same period. At the same time, levels of poverty have risen within these population groups that have experienced the most growth. As society grapples with poverty and changing demographics, barriers informed by cultural characteristics, family structure, socioeconomic status, and time increasingly limit a school's ability to establish successful family partnerships.

Though parental involvement programs since the inception of Title programming have focused on low income, immigrant, and other disadvantaged families, those programs have generally not fared well. The values and approaches to these programs often marginalize the exact people those same programs are meant to target. Meetings between school officials and parents are often conducted in English, which is largely incomprehensible to many of the targeted parents, and presentations are often delivered in large group settings in places such as school cafeterias and gymnasiums. Smaller settings tend to be more effective with most people, but especially with poor, immigrant, and other marginalized parents who feel distanced from school culture and environment.

In addition, with demands for more "output" with less "input," schools must focus on inclusion of *all* parent groups in the policy development pertaining to family involvement programs. Epstein cites some important patterns relating to partnerships that have emerged from studies conducted at the elementary, middle and high school levels.

- partnerships tend to decline across the grades, *unless* schools and teachers work to develop and implement appropriate practices of partnership at each grade level,
- affluent communities currently have more positive family involvement, on average, *unless* schools and teachers in economically distressed communities work to build positive partnerships with their students' families,
- schools in more economically depressed communities make more contacts with families about the problems and difficulties their children are having, *unless* they work at developing balanced partnership programs that also include contacts about the positive accomplishments of students,

● single parents, parents who are employed outside the home, parents who live far from the school, and fathers are less involved, on average, at the school building, *unless* the school organizes opportunities for families to volunteer at various times and in various places to support the school and their children (p. 11).

Reaching out to families that have historically not been connected in family involvement programs can have lasting effects on student and teacher success. Often a lack of trust exists on the part of the parent. It could be that the parent had a negative experience in school as a child or has had a previous experience with the school concerning another child in the family. Once the sense of trust is violated, the parent will view future encounters with school personnel as suspect. This further complicates the school's ability to successfully provide a quality educational experience for the child. A much greater effort on the part of the school will now be required to reestablish a positive relationship between the family and school. Proactive steps to engage families initially would be less time consuming, on average, and would provide a more desirable end result. Studies have established that students of parents who are actively involved in their child's education are more likely to graduate high school and pursue higher education (Chavkin & Williams, 1993; Delgado-Gaitan, 1992; Epstein, 2001).

Parental Involvement vs. Parental Engagement

Scribner, et al. (1999) found that in many schools largely populated by Hispanic students, parental involvement is often measured by the frequency with which parents visit the school and participate in school events by physically being there. Being absent or present defines whether the program is successful or failing. On the other hand, high-performing Hispanic schools tend to transcend that model. Actual engagement occurs in those schools where parents feel as if they are a part of the school culture, and when they do, they participate in a wide range of school functions. Lopez (2001) expands the definition of parental involvement when he discusses immigrant and migrant families' concept of parental involvement, which is defined and practiced by the work these parents do with their children at home. This work includes teaching children the "value of work ethic, the value of hard work, work as a lesson of life, the value of school, and using work to learn skills" (pp 423–433).

One successful parental involvement initiative is the Alliance Schools movement. Alliance schools refuse to accept the traditional constructs that have historically defined parental involvement and they prefer to call their process "parental engagement." An inherent assumption in this process is that parents do what they can to contribute to the education of their children at home. This type of participation differs radically from traditional parental involvement narratives. The Alliance model views social systems as entities that must be reconfigured in order to respond to a rapidly changing world. Inherent in this reframing is the fact that parents must build power to be effective agents of change within the school culture (Shirley, 1997; 2002). To this end, parents and organizational leaders engage in conversations, action research, and formulating actions to proactively respond to the needs of children's families and the communities in which they reside. The organizing that takes place is broad-based and the issues are identified by the people that are most immediately impacted by them, namely the family and members of the network. At the core of this type of engagement is the process of understanding and building power that through participation and design will reconfigure the school culture.

The academic and public policy literature is comprehensive and worth reviewing, but the focus of this chapter shifts in an attempt to respond to the role of parental involvement and the role of educational leaders in understanding, creating, and nurturing the role of parents on their campuses. This interest originates as a mandate by public policy and as a necessary action that will help create the condition for schools and families to be successful. This knowledge base is also important for schools to continue to be institutions where democratic processes can prevail and the democratic spirit be taught as well as practiced.

Programs Designed for Parental Engagement: A Look at an Urban School and a Rural Border School

CITY ELEMENTARY

The program and experience described here are derived from personal experiences and participation of one of this chapter's authors in an urban school. Shared here is an experience that is based on observations and participation in the development and maintenance of a healthy school environment. At the core is the role of parents in helping the school identify its guiding values, its expectations, and ensuring success for all students. A reflection of the process and a representation of the events will be synthesize and reported.

City Elementary is situated in a middle class neighborhood; it has a strong history of school and community partnerships, but more recently, the school has shifted in its demographics and the student population is now 19% Anglo, 32% African American and 45% Latino. The school has a strong relationship with the community and its history is well preserved by teachers and parents. The recent history of principals in this school, on the other hand, has been less than steady. In a span of six years, the school has had four principals. While principals come and go, parents have maintained a strong presence at the school. At City Elementary parents routinely tutor students, assist with administrative duties in the school office, and help teachers prepare for class. Bilingual (English-Spanish) parents also utilize their language skills to translate lessons and other important information to Spanish-speaking parents, and volunteers also participate in the grant-writing strategies as the campus searches for the additional resources.

The coordination of these efforts was born from ideas of organizing, advocacy training, and power-sharing philosophies learned by parents through the Industrial Areas Foundation (IAF). IAF workshops include training parents and other community members on the art of conversation, small group facilitation, identification of issues that impact schools, and in the development and implementation of action plans in response to issues impacting schools and communities. A number of these parents have participated in this skill building and leadership development process. They subsequently return to their home campus and apply the skills as part of their parental involvement work. Specifically, these strategies and ideas of engagement gave birth to the room-parent model. Under this framework there is one coordinator that is the contact between a group of room parents and the PTA board members.[5] The room parent network consists of a parent from each classroom in the school. Each of the parents in the network has a child in the room and they serve as the source of information to all the parents and families in their classroom. The dissemination of information is the most common duty, but other responsiblities are to facilitate the discussion of issues, the development of skills, and the organizing of events, field trips, fundraisers, and other school-wide events as

---

[5]Traditionally this duty has been shared by co-coordinators.

they arise. This model has remained effective and successful because of the constant conversation that takes place between the coordinators and room parents on a weekly basis.

The room parent network has been successful in organizing around a number of important issues. Some examples of the pressing issues include identification and selection of a new school principal, facilitating the arrival of new families into the school, and fundraising activities to secure resources for priority projects for the campus.

The network has also exercised its organizational power on occasions when parents have sensed injustices at the school. When the larger City Independent School District attempted to eliminate teaching positions in physical education, music, and art, the parent network organized a school walkout and found widespread support from other parents, the school staff, faculty, and even school administrators. This action helped the school keep two of the three teacher positions slated for elimination.

The role of parents in this school is of great consequence; it is not simply about parents making Xeroxed copies for teachers or organizing minor school events. On the contrary, parental engagement included the creation of spaces for parents to be involved in teaching children, providing teachers with time for reflection, setting the agenda to educate their children, policy issues, staffing, and budgeting decisions.

This process has proven effective in organizing, recruiting parents, sharing information, developing skills, and maintaining the institutional memory. One of the authors of this article even served as a substitute teacher/volunteer when he was in the building. However, the success of this program and practice is contingent on the support and philosophy of the school administrator. The program functioned most effectively when campus administrators shared the philosophical belief that parents and families have an important role in helping shape, nurture, and sustain the school culture.

LLANO GRANDE HIGH SCHOOL

Llano Grande High School is located 15 miles north of the Texas Mexican border in the Rio Grande Valley. Its student population is comprised of 98% Hispanic students, and the town has historically been defined by a fluctuating agricultural economy. According to the 2000 Census, approximately 40% of the student body participated in migrant field work, and 35% of the students come from immigrant homes. By most indicators, Llano Grande, Texas is considered one of the most impoverished communities in the state.

For many years Hispanic parents were reluctant to participate in parental involvement programs at this school because activities were conducted in English. During the 1990s, however, the high school began convening its meetings in Spanish and English, and it also initiated innovative strategies to reach out to parents. Specifically, the school integrated into its social studies and language arts classes a research project through which students, teachers, and parents explored their own stories for the purpose of getting to know one another. Teachers and students received training sessions on how to build their own story through reflective practices and community based research. In essence, the exploration of autobiography and family histories became a lynchpin around which teachers and students gained a greater sense of themselves—and subsequently their own story. Teachers and students also received training on how to conduct interviews with parents and with other community members, and on how to utilize this process for the purpose of engaging parents on issues of teaching, learning, and the broader process of public education. After several years of practicing this pedagogy through cultivating one's story and collecting oral histories, many of these parents who once were students and teachers became involved in a community leadership initiative that has been sustained for three years (Guajardo & Guajardo, 2002, 2004).

Youths and parents participating in the leadership program have organized school board candidate debates, a public seminar series, and have founded a nonprofit organization dedicated to building the capacity of youths and parents for the purpose of community improvement. In addition, parents and teachers have created a global educational infrastructure that has allowed more than two dozens youths from this rural community to travel and study in places such Austria, Brazil, Peru, Italy, South Africa, Turkey, France, Mexico, and England. Indeed, this model is built on the concept of transformative education, and hundreds of student and parent participants built research, organizational, and teaching and learning skills as they have engaged in this process. In short, this parent engagement process has broken the isolation of school, culture, and geography, and everyone in the community is better for it.

School Leaders' Role in Partnership Programs[6]

In the City Elementary example, the most effective element from the campus administrators viewpoint is the respect that is provided for parents and families. This includes the respect for their identity, their beliefs, their voice, and their participation. When respect for parents exists in a school, the environment is ripe for parents and school personnel to create together a shared sense of a power relationship that facilitates dealing with school, community, and other issues that face both the school and the community.

Respect for families' identity is displayed and articulated by responding to the family and children's academic, social, and economic needs. Under this practice the school personnel is available for responding to issues of language for the delivery of bilingual education services and second language acquisition for parents and siblings. Other social needs the campus responds to include medical services, immigration support, driver's license acquisition, employment, and transportation to name a few. The campus administration understands that if these social issues are not addressed, the children cannot receive the needed support for learning from the parents. Indeed, this support is not sufficient, but it is a necessary condition for children to succeed.

Additionally, allowing parents to voice their opinions has been critical for relationship building on campus. Building positive relationships and dialogue between parents and the school administration is a necessary condition for establishing a strong school culture. The strong relationships have helped the campus community deal with difficult issues in a respectful and positive manner.

Another condition for building strong partnerships on campus was the ability and willingness for the school leader to listen. The listening skills are critical especially when parents and school administration do not agree with each other's position. Relationships based on open communication allow the school community to move forward when difficult situations arise or when dissenting opinions exist. The staff has learned that there are issues that the campus administrator cannot publicly challenge where the central administration is concerned. Rather, parents use their voice and become advocates for the school in these instances. This political practice and awareness from the campus protects the campus leader from potential political and institutional repercussions. The parents have thus created a buffer zone between the central administration and the campus administrator. This does not happen without anxiety, but the interdependence that develops between parents and the school leader facilitates overcoming other difficult situations.

---

[6] The attributes of the campus administrator are a culmination of the four administrators the campus saw during the past six years.

The combination and constant negotiation of these skills and conditions created the relational power that allows the school community to act when they face critical issues impacting their survival. These issues include staffing, budget, curriculum, and maintenance of teachers, and other staff.

As articulated above, when an administrator violates the respect and trust, and does not share pertinent information impacting the campus and their children, the trust necessary for building strong community is compromised and tensions escalate. The more successful conditions during the last six years are predicated on respect, conversations, and relationships based on trust. Clearly, as campus leaders there is much to consider, but the one issue that cannot be relegated to the margins is the role of parents and their participation in developing, nurturing and sustaining the campus culture.

Summary

The concept of parental partnerships was initially mandated by public policy to respond to social conditions and economic inequities that existed in neighborhoods and schools. The prevailing belief that if parents are involved in their children's education their children will succeed has been held and embraced by both political liberal and conservatives alike. The concept of parental involvement has been defined in numerous ways that range from parents as assistants and clerical help to parents as tutors, political actors, and even agents for school and community change. Parents are becoming more informed about the complexities of schools and are beginning to demand to be participants in the process of educating their children. These demands have evolved as parents have become more aware of their ability to organize and build power. However, this evolution of parental engagement can be problematic if educational leaders are not trained to deal with the political dynamics of parents who may be fully engaged. It is imperative that school leaders understand the potential for such training, and the unlimited potential that meaningful parental engagement can have on the education of children.

Applying Your Knowledge

SCENARIO I:

Think of specific situations when a school leader resisted parental involvement activity in a classroom or school.

What were the conditions that led to this resistance?

Who was involved?

What was the outcome?

What did the leadership and the school learn from this experience?

SCENARIO II:

A parent informs the school that her two children, one in the third grade and the other in the fifth grade, will not take the state mandated test because of the undue stress the children have experienced and because the parent believes that high stakes testing has engendered unfavorable learning conditions in the school. The parent informs the school her position is a moral one based on a set of values, and she will consequently not allow her children to be subjected to this oppressive schooling process. She and her spouse favor different forms of assessment, but they are vehemently opposed to high stakes testing and will not allow their children to participate. In addition, these parents have utilized the room parent network to inform other families of their position and have organized other parents who are contemplating a boycott on the day of the test. How does a school leader respond to these issues, as she considers the needs of the children, parents, and as she deliberates upon the policy mandates, political issues, and the community building process?

What are the first steps a school leader should take?

How will the school leader respond to this family?

How will the central administration be informed?

What are the political ramifications for the school and district?

How should the media be handled in this situation?

Reflect on the differences between the school leader's emotions and the professional/organizational responsibilities and duties.

For Further Information Online

National Parent Teacher Association *http://www.pta.org/*

Parental Involvement In Education *http://www.cppp.org/kidscount/education/parental_involvement.html#top*

References

Anyon, J. (1997). Ghetto schooling: a political economy of urban educational reform. New York: Teachers College Press.

Chavkin, N., & Williams, D. (1993). Minority parents and the elementary school: Attitudes and practices. In N. Chavkin (Ed.), *Families and schools in a pluralistic society* (pp. 73–83). Albany, NY: State University of New York Press.

Delgado-Gaitan, C. (2002). School Matters in the Mexican American Home: Socializing Children to Education. *American Educational Research Journal. 29*(3), 495.

Epstein, J., Sanders, M., Simon, B., Clark-Salinas, K., Jansom, N., Van Voorhis, F. (2001). School, Family, and Community Partnerships: Preparing Educators and Improving Schools. Boulder, Colorado: Westview Press.

Fullan, M. 2001. The new meaning of educational change. New York: Teachers College Press.

Giroux, H. A. (1989). Schooling for democracy: critical pedagogy in the modern age. London, Routledge.

Guajardo, M. & Guajardo, F. (2002). "Critical Ethnography and Community Change." In *Ethnography and Schools: Qualitative Approaches to the Study of Education.* Trueba, H. & Zou, Y., eds. Maryland: Rowman and Littlefield.

Guajardo, M. & Guajardo, F. (2004). "The Impact of Brown on the Brown of South Texas: a Micropolitical perspective on the education of Mexican Americans in a rural South Texas community." *American Educational Research Journal,* Fall 2004.

Joyner, E. T., M. Ben-Avie & Comer, J. (2004). *Transforming School Leadership and Management to Support Student Learning and Development.* Corwin Press. Thousand Oaks, California.

Lopez, G. R. (2001). The Value of Hard Work: Lessons on Parent Involvement from an (Im)migrant Household. *Harvard Educational Review* v71 n3 p. 416–37.

Varenne, H. & McDermott, R. (1999). Successful Failure: The School America Builds. Boulder, Colorado: Westview Press.

Murnane, R. J. & Levy, F. (1996). Teaching the new basic skills: principles for educating children to thrive in a changing economy. New York: Free Press.

Mickelson, R. A. (2003). Measuring Racial Disparities and Discrimination in Education. *Teachers College Record* Volume 105, Number 6, August 2003, pp. 1052–1086. Teachers College, Columbia University.

Oakes, J. (1985). Keeping track: how schools structure inequality. New Haven: Yale University Press.

Scribner, J. et al. (1999). "Building Collaborative Relationships with Parents. In Reyes, P., Scribner, J, & Paredes-Scribner, A., eds. (1999). *Lessons from High Performing Hispanic Schools: Creating Learning Communities.* New York: Teachers College Press.

Shirley, D. (1997). Community organizing for urban school reform. University of Texas Press. Austin: University of Texas Press.

Shirley, D. (2002). Valley Interfaith and school reform: organizing for power in South Texas. University of Texas Press. Austin: University of Texas Press.

Spindler, G. D. (Ed.) (2000). Fifty years of anthropology and education, 1950–2000: a Spindler anthology. Mahwah, N.J.: L. Erlbaum Associates.

Index